Relational Database and SQL
SQL
Third Edition

Lucy Scott

ISBN-13: **978-1-0878-9969-5**

DEDICATION

TO LISA.

CONTENTS

ACKNOWLEDGMENTS

We are grateful to Dr. Youlong Zhuang for reviewing this edition.

CHAPTER 1: INTRODUCTION TO DATABASE

Chapter Learning Objectives

1.1 Recognize the differences between data and information.

1.2 Recognize the different types of database.

1.3 Interpret database environment.

1.4 Compare database schema and database state.

1.5 Recall relational database history.

1.6 Execute SQL scripts.

1.7 Recall the major usage of DML and DDL commands.

1.1 Data and Information

Businesses need data for their day to day operations as well as for decision making. When you checkout at a local grocery store, the business stores your payment information unless you are paying with cash. Even if you are paying with cash, the business updates their inventory items so that they know when to reorder from their suppliers.

Data on what you buy can also be used for decision making. It shows what sells well and what does not sell, or which products contribute most to profits and which ones don't. This type of data is especially useful when accumulated at large, into what is called 'big data.' Companies can use big data to do analysis and discover trends and patterns for the business. Many business decisions are made based on big data.

At school, data about you is stored in a database. When you register for an online course, the record is kept and the number of available seats for the class is deducted by one. At the end of the semester, your instructor would enter your grade for that specific course into the database. Data on your grade could look something like this:

Student Name	Course Title	Final Grade
Lucy	Introduction to Database	

Figure 1.1: Enrollment data

At the end of the semester, after you receive a grade, the data will be updated:

Student Name	Course Title	Final Grade
Lucy	Introduction to Database	A

Figure 1.2: Grade data

Data is everywhere, and has all sorts of applications. For example, if you buy two gallon-size bottles of milk at three dollars each from a grocery store, what pieces of information count as data?

At its simplest, the data includes the products you buy (gallon-size bottles of milk,) the quantity of the product you buy (two,) and the unit price for the product ($3.00.) Data of the transaction will look like this (actual data will also usually include a timestamp, showing date and time of transaction):

Product	Quantity	Unit Price
Gallon milk	2	3.00

Figure 1.3: Sales data

If you pay with a credit card, the data will also include your name, card number, and card expiration date, among other pieces of data. However, regardless of payment form, the inventory of that specific product will be updated, as such:

Product	On Hand	Unit Cost	Supplier
Gallon milk	198	3.00	Diary Wholesaler

Figure 1.4: Inventory data

Thus, as demonstrated by the examples, data is defined as raw fact that has meaning and is measurable. Raw fact means that data is specific, stating "five bottles of milk" instead of "a few bottles of milk." By stating "five bottles of milk," one is giving meaningful data that is measurable. Not meaningful data could include age, which is calculated differently in certain parts of Asia, and thus loses meaning due to its variability. Data on date of birth would be more meaningful. For data to be measurable, it must have a specific quantity, such as "seven bottles of milk" instead of "five to ten bottles of milk."

Information is processed data that has value and meets the need of the user. The database should be designed to store all data that a business needs, meaning it should include unprocessed raw data, and be able to provide information that the user needs.

For example, as an employee in a company, you can store the date of birth into a database, because the data is raw fact and can be used to calculate the age.

As you can see in Figure 1.3, you recorded all the purchases, which is raw data. With raw data, you can get information for the user, including today's sale, this week's sale, this month's sale, etc.

	Today's sale	This week's sale	This month's sale
Gallon Milk	120	800	3120
Cheese (lb)	21	155	610

Figure 1.5: Sales information

As shown in Figure 1.1, you recorded data of all students' registration for courses which is raw fact. Even though a complete database would have an overwhelming amount of data, the database should be able to easily output information, such as a list of students who are enrolled in a particular course.

Course: Introduction to Database	
First Name	Last Name
John	White
Larry	Green

Figure 1.6: Course enrollment information

Information is the result from processing raw data to reveal meaning. Information can be used as the foundation for decision making. For example, based on the sales information, the manager can decide to reorder more or less of a certain product. Based on course enrollment information, a school administrator can decide whether to cancel a class or add more sections.

As a database developer, it is important for you to understand that data must be properly stored so that meaningful information can be created from the data. You may have noticed that, based on the sales data in

Figure 1.3, you cannot generate the sales information in Figure 1.5. You will need to add the date of transaction to Figure 1.3 so that each sale transaction can be correctly summed to each category (today, this week, this month).

In this book, you will learn how to develop a database to store raw data, and how to produce information by processing the data. In each chapter you will learn database development and SQL.

Review Question 1.1
The data can be defined as _____.
a. raw fact that has meaning and can be measured
b. information we use daily
c. numbers
d. numbers or strings

Review Question 1.2
Information is the result of _____.
a. hard work
b. processing raw data to reveal its meaning.
c. calculation
d. computer power

Review Question 1.3
The database should be designed to store all _____ that a business needs and be able to provide _____ that the user needs.
a. data, data
b. information, information
c. data, information
d. information, data

Review Question 1.4
In this book, you will learn how to develop a database to store raw data, and how to produce information by processing the data. In each chapter you will learn _____ and _____.
a. database design, SQL
b. database development, SQL
c. database design, information production
d. database development, information production

1.2 The need for organization of data: Database

As you can see, data is everywhere. A manager of a grocery store could use a notebook to keep inventory. An instructor could post student grades by classes and IDs on the office door.

A database is a collection of organized data. There are many ways to organize data. Database design determines the way you organize the data. For very simple data, you can use a flat-file database. Each line of the flat-file database holds one record. The sales data in Figure 1.3 is an example. Flat-file databases are not always convenient, for the database is not structured, and there are no apparent relationships between records. Thus, you will need to read the entire file to find a specific record.

Another way to organize data is in a hierarchical database, in which the data is organized into a tree-like structure. A hierarchical database begins with a flat-file parent table, and then branches out into children tables, due to the limitations one flat file database has. The relationship between parent tables and children tables allows a parent table to have multiple children but a child table to have only one parent.
For example, data on students can be stored in a parent table:

Student Id	First Name	Last Name
1001	John	White
1002	Larry	Green

The parent table can then be branched out into multiple children tables, including the two below:

Student Id	Course Number	Grade
1001	CS101	A
1001	CS102	C
1002	CS101	B

Student Id	Club Name	Date Joined
1001	Squall watch	3/12/2017
1002	Chess Master	4/23/2017

Figure 1.7 Hierarchical database

In the example, the parent table holds the student data. Each record provides a student's data, such as ID, first name, and last name. The first child table holds the student's course and grade data, and the student ID column links each child table record to the parent table. Note that a student may register for multiple courses. The second child table holds the data on student activities, which is connected to the parent table through the student ID column.

The most popular way of organizing data is through a relational database. The main focus of this book is on how to organize and use a relational database.

Review Question 1.5
A database is _____.
a. a collection of data

b. a collection of organized data
c. any computer file
d. a collection of numbers and text

Review Question 1.6
Which of the following databases is the most popular and the focus of this book?
a. flat-file
b. spreadsheet
c. hierarchical
d. relational

Review Question 1.7
What type of database is not structured, and has no apparent relationships between records, thus making it necessary to read the entire file in order to find a specific record?
a. flat-file
b. spreadsheet
c. hierarchical
d. relational

Review Question 1.8
Data is organized into a tree-like structure. The relationship allows a parent table to have multiple children tables but a child table can only have one parent table. This is describing which type of database?
a. flat-file
b. spreadsheet
c. hierarchical
d. relational

1.3 Mini-world

Databases contain data that is related to some part of the real world. The part of the real world the data is related to is known as the mini-world. For example, if you build a database about a library, then the mini-world is the library. Another example, if the database is for a tutoring center of a university, then the mini-world is the tutoring center.

The database should be an abstract of the mini-world. Take for example building of a database for a library. When a borrower checks out a book, the inventory for that specific book should be one less in the database. The copies available recorded in the database should reflect the physical number of copies in the library (mini-world.)

The first step for a database designer is to understand the mini-world. A database that doesn't relate to a mini-world has no purpose. The process of understanding the mini-world is a part of database requirements determination, a topic often covered in system analysis and design books. We will continue talking about this process in the next chapter.

Review Question 1.9
If a database is for a tutoring center of a university, then the mini-world is the _____.
a. tutoring center
b. university
c. database
d. tutors

Review Question 1.10
A database should be a(n) _____ of the mini-world.
a. data center
b. abstract
c. storage
d. organizer

Review Question 1.11
The first step for a database designer is to understand the _____.
a. users
b. designers
c. mini-world
d. whole world

Review Question 1.12
The part of the real world the database is related to is known as the _____.
a. partial database
b. partial world
c. mini-world
d. mini-database

1.4 Database Management System (DBMS)

We learned that data is ubiquitous and is organized into databases. The next natural question would be what tools are available for creating, maintaining, and using the databases.

Like how you use a word processor to write your term paper, you use DBMS to create a database and access the data. A Database Management System is a computer system that allows the user to develop, maintain, and use the database. This book will cover both how to develop and use the database. Instead of following the sequence of how to develop the database first and then how to use it later, this book will cover aspects of both in each chapter. This way, readers will have more exposure to the use of databases.

Examples of DBMSs include: Oracle, SQL Server, MySQL, DB2, and SQLite, among others. In this book, you will learn how to use SQL Server, but the knowledge can be easily applied to other DBMSs.

Review Question 1.13
Word processor software to your term paper is like _____ to databases.
a. table
b. data
c. DBMS
d. spreadsheet

Review Question 1.14
Which of the following is NOT a DBMS?
a. Oracle
b. MySQL
c. SQL server
d. IBM

1.5 User data and Metadata

The DBMS will need two types of data: user data and Metadata. The user data includes data that users are interested in. For example, customer data (customer name, address, and contact information) is of interest to business users.

Metadata includes data that describes the user data. Metadata makes it easier for a DBMS to search and work on the user data. For example, CustomerName is a column name that describes the data in that column, such as *Skyler Johnson,* which is the user data. So CustomerName is considered metadata and *Skyler Johnson* is user data. CustomerName has to be alphanumeric. It cannot be integers. Therefore, the data type of the column describes what user data is acceptable for the column. Data type is another example of metadata.

The DBMS uses metadata for the structure of the user data. The metadata is data about data.

Review Question 1.15
The _____ is the data that users are interested in.
a. user data
b. interest data
c. metadata
d. database

Review Question 1.16
The DBMS uses _____ for the structure of the user data. It is data about data.
a. user data
b. interest data
c. metadata
d. database

1.6 The Relational DBMS (RDBMS)

The word "relational" in relational databases refers to a table. So, the RDBMS organizes user data into tables. A table contains one or more records and each record contains one or more fields. For example, a student table may have thousands of individual student records and each student has a first name, last name, and date of birth field. The most popular way of organizing data is through the relational database. We will use the terms DBMS and RDBMS interchangeably.

StudentId	First Name	Last Name	Date of Birth
1234567	Skyler	Johnson	2001-03-21
2234567	Lucy	Scott	2002-11-25
3234567	Linda	Smith	2001-09-22

Review Question 1.17
The word "relational" in relational databases refers to a _____.
a. relationship
b. link
c. table
d. record

Review Question 1.18
In relational databases, a table contains one or more _____.
a. records
b. tables
c. fields
d. relations

Review Question 1.19
In relational databases, a record contains one or more _____.
a. records
b. tables
c. fields
d. relations

1.7 Database system

The database system includes the DBMS software together with the data itself. Sometimes, the applications are also included. It defines the structure and the relationship between the database and the DBMS. It aims at the synchronization of the two for the purpose of better user experience.

It is important to differentiate the database system from a DBMS. A DBMS is the tool that is required for working with a database. But it is the database system that the business uses for day to day operations or decision making.

Review Question 1.20
A _____ is the tool that is required for working with a database.
a. DBMS
b. MBA
c. DBA
d. programming language

Review Question 1.21
The _____ includes the DBMS software together with the data itself. Sometimes, the applications are also included.
a. database system
b. database
c. system
d. RDBMS

1.8 Database environment

Let's have a high-level view of what a database environment looks like

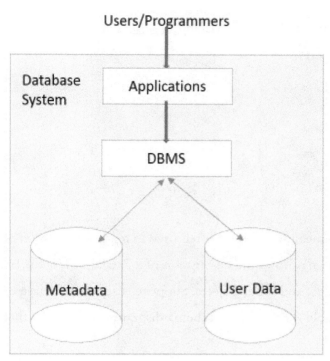

Figure 1.8 Database Environment

Think of the database as the stuffed animals in a claw machine. The player has no interaction with these stuffed animals unless if the claw, analogous to the application, selects a stuffed animal, analogous to a specific piece of data, for the user.

The user works on the application program written in a programming language such as C# or Java. The application program, in turn, works with the DBMS, which can include SQL Server, or Oracle, by issuing SQL statements. And, the DBMS manipulates the database via metadata.

For example, a business user opens the application program (e.g. a web browser) and enters a customer name, then clicks on a button to display the orders by this customer. The application program will communicate with the DBMS to find all orders of this customer by issuing SQL statements and send the data back to the application to be displayed. In this process, the DBMS depends on the metadata (e.g. table and field names) to find the user data.

Review Question 1.22
Which of the following is a typical sequence when a user works with a database?
a. user -> applications -> DBMS -> metadata (via user data)
b. user -> applications -> DBMS ->user data (via metadata)
c. user -> DBMS -> applications -> metadata (via user data)
d. user -> DBMS -> applications -> user data (via metadata)

Review Question 1.23
The _____ usually works with DBMS directly by issuing _____ statements.
a. users, SQL
b. users, NOSQL
c. programmers, SQL
d. programmers, NOSQL

1.9 Schema

The term schema usually has two meanings. One is often used in textbooks to refer to the entire structure of the database. The database schema shows the description of a database. It is the blueprint of a database. It defines tables, fields, relationships, and other objects. Suppose, a simple database contains only two tables, a course table and an instructor table. The database schema diagram will look like this:

COURSE

CourseID	CourseTitle	Location	InstructorID

INSTRUCTOR

InstructorID	FirstName	LastName	Office

Figure 1.9 Database schema diagram

The database schema is different from the database state. The database state is a snapshot of all the data in the database at a particular moment in time.

CourseID	CourseTitle	Location	InstructorID
1001	Introduction to Database	Classroom Building 201	101
1002	Introduction to SQL	Classroom Building 202	101

InstructorID	FirstName	LastName	Office
101	Lucy	Scott	CB401
102	Linda	Smith	CB405

Figure 1.10 Database state

The schema is relatively stable while the state is constantly changing. When the database state changes, the schema must be respected.

The second meaning of schema is a container that holds one or more database objects, such as tables and views. Along this line of thinking, the smallest unit of meaningful data is a field. One or more fields are grouped into a record. One or more records are grouped into a table (specific pieces of data from the table can be pulled to be placed in a view, which censors the other information.) One or more tables are grouped into a schema. And one or more schemas are grouped into a database. In the SQL sections of the book, you will see how schema is used under this meaning.

Review Question 1.24
What are the two meanings of schema in database concepts?
a. structure and command
b. structure and container
c. command and container
d. command and SQL

Review Question 1.25
When a database state changes, the database _____ must be respected.
a. designers
b. developers
c. containers
d. schemas

Review Question 1.26
A database schema is the _____ of the relational database.
a. art
b. blueprint
c. requirement
d. end result

Review Question 1.27
One meaning of schema is a container that holds one or more _____.
a. databases
b. fields
c. relationships
d. database objects, such as tables and views

1.10 A brief history of relational database

Before the RDBMS era, the use of databases was too costly due to the complexity of database management, which in turn required a high level of training for programmers. Plus, a single program could only be tied to a single database, which made it difficult to have another program use the same data.

Dr. E. F. Codd of IBM set out to solve this problem by providing data abstraction, which allows application flexibility with data. The application simply tells the computer what data it needs and lets the DBMS figure out how to retrieve them.

The relational database era began with the publication of a paper by Codd in 1970 on *Communications of the ACM*, titled "A Relational Model of Data for Large Shared Data Banks." In the paper, he proposed to build databases with tables of rows and columns.

The next major event came when D. D. Chamberlin and R. F. Boyce published in 1974 a paper called "SEQUEL: A Structured English Query Language" from *Proceedings of the 1974 ACM SIGFIDET Workshop on Data Description, Access and Control.*

The first commercial RDBMS was introduced by Oracle (then called Relational Software Inc.) in 1979, followed by many so-called RDBMS that were not really "relational". In 1985, Codd developed twelve rules (actually thirteen counting from 0 to 12) as a campaign to prevent the original relational database ideas from being diluted.

Today, relational databases are popular, although they are challenged all the time. The first major challenge was Object-Oriented Database Management Systems (OODBMS) in the 1980s, followed by Object-Relational Database Management Systems (ORDBMS) in the early 1990s. Next, the XML database came into existence in the year 2000. Currently, a new technique called NoSQL is becoming popular, although none of the challenges have taken the place of relational databases.

Review Question 1.28
Before the RDBMS era, the use of databases was very _____.
a. easy
b. simple
c. costly
d. convenient

Review Question 1.29
Which of the following was a problem for using databases before the RDBMS era?
a. businesses were not interested in using databases
b. there was no data in business
c. it required highly trained programmers
d. not many businesses could afford the hardware

Review Question 1.30
Which of the following was a problem for using databases before the RDBMS era?

a. a single program could only be tied to a single database, which made it difficult to have another program use the same data
b. there was not much data in business
c. a database could not be connected to the internet
d. not many businesses could afford the hardware

Review Question 1.31
Who is usually considered the founder of the relational database?
a. the president of IBM
b. the president of Oracle
c. the president of Microsoft
d. Dr. E.F. Codd of IBM

Review Question 1.32
The first commercial RDBMS was introduced by _____.
a. IBM
b. Microsoft
c. Oracle
d. Google

Review Question 1.33
Which of the following is not a modern, popular challenger of the relational database?
a. Object-Oriented Database Management System
b. Object-Relational Database Management System
c. XML database
d. hierarchical database

1.11 Install Microsoft Visual Studio Community 2022

Before you can practice the SQL sections of this book, you will need Microsoft SQL Server (DBMS) installed in your local computer. You probably already have Visual Studio installed in your computer for learning a programming language such as Visual Basic, C#, or C++. In that case, you just need to install the database part. Figure 1.11 shows the user interface of Visual Studio installer. Make sure you checked "Data storage and processing" during installation. If you are using an earlier version of Visual Studio, the installation is very similar.

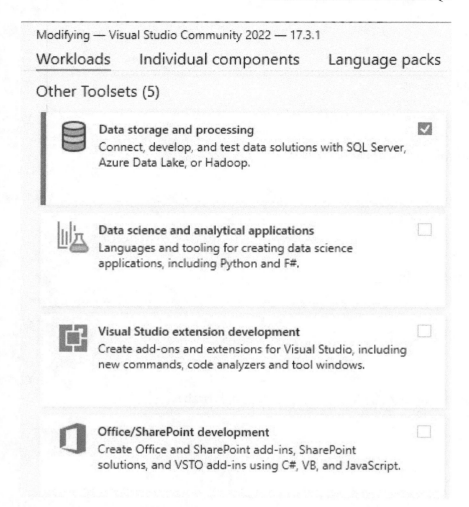

Figure 1.11 Install SQL Server Express (DBMS) on your local computer

1.12 Install database for practice:

After you install the DBMS, you will need a database, which you can download the script from goo.gl/ftzOxl

Follow the steps below to install the database:

Open Visual Studio. On the Visual Studio start window, click on "continue without code ->" (Figure 1.12)

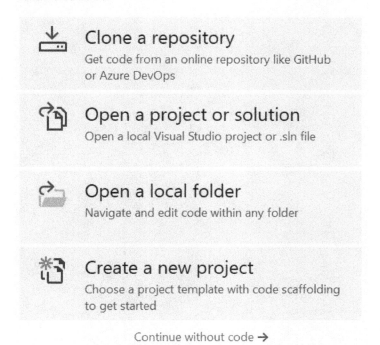

Figure 1.12 Visual Studio start window.

On the new window, click Tools on the menu, then SQL Server, then New Query as shown in Figure 1.13

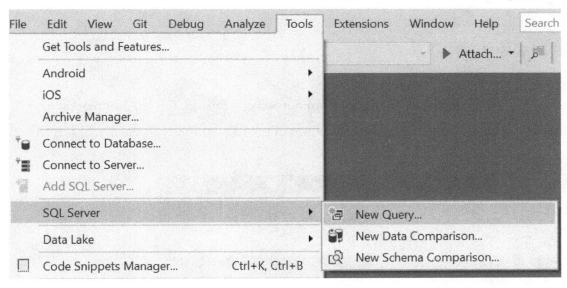

Figure 1.13 Start a new SQL script window on Visual Studio

A connect window will pop up as shown in Figure 1.14. Type "(LocalDB)\MSSQLLocalDB" into the Server Name field and click on the "connect" button.

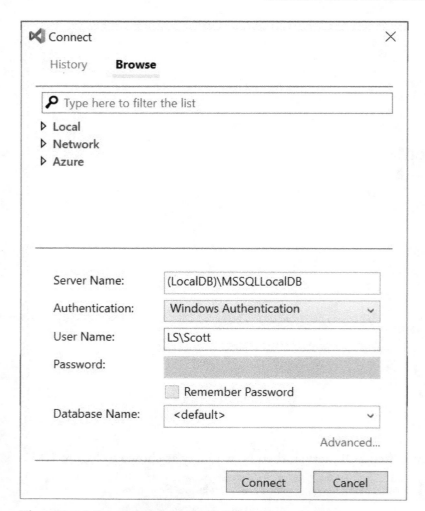

Figure 1.14 Connect to the SQL Server

An SQL Editor will be displayed. Download the script from our website (goo.gl/ftzOxl) and paste it into the SQL editor. Click on the "Execute (Ctrl+Shift+E)" button in the top left to install the database into your local DBMS. Refer to Figure 1.15 for an example.

```
WholesalerSQLQuery.sql    ⇥ ×
▷ ▾ ■ ✓ 圆 ⬜ ⬛ ⬛  LifeStyleDB                          ▾ 窗 圍 ▾ ⬚ 圓
     1 ⊟USE master;
  Execute (Ctrl+Shift+E)
     3   IF DB_ID(N'LifeStyleDB') IS NOT NULL DROP DATABASE LifeStyleDB;
     4
     5   CREATE DATABASE LifeStyleDB;
     6   GO
     7
     8   USE LifeStyleDB;
     9   GO
    10
    11   CREATE SCHEMA HR AUTHORIZATION dbo;
    12   GO
```

Figure 1.15 Partial display of the code for creating the database for practice

Next you will learn how to issue a simple SQL statement. You will follow these same steps when you practice SQL for the rest of the book.

Close the SQL editor. Do not close the Visual Studio. Then start a new SQL editor by following the steps listed below:

Click on "Tools" => "SQL Server" => "New Query" again to open a new SQL Editor. Enter (LocalDB)\MSSQLLocalDB again as shown in Figure 1.14. Type in the following line of SQL into the SQL editor:

```
SELECT * FROM Sales.Customers;
```

Change "Available Database" dropdown from the default "master" to "LifeStyleDB" and click on the "Execute" button to run the SQL statement. The result should look like Figure 1.16:

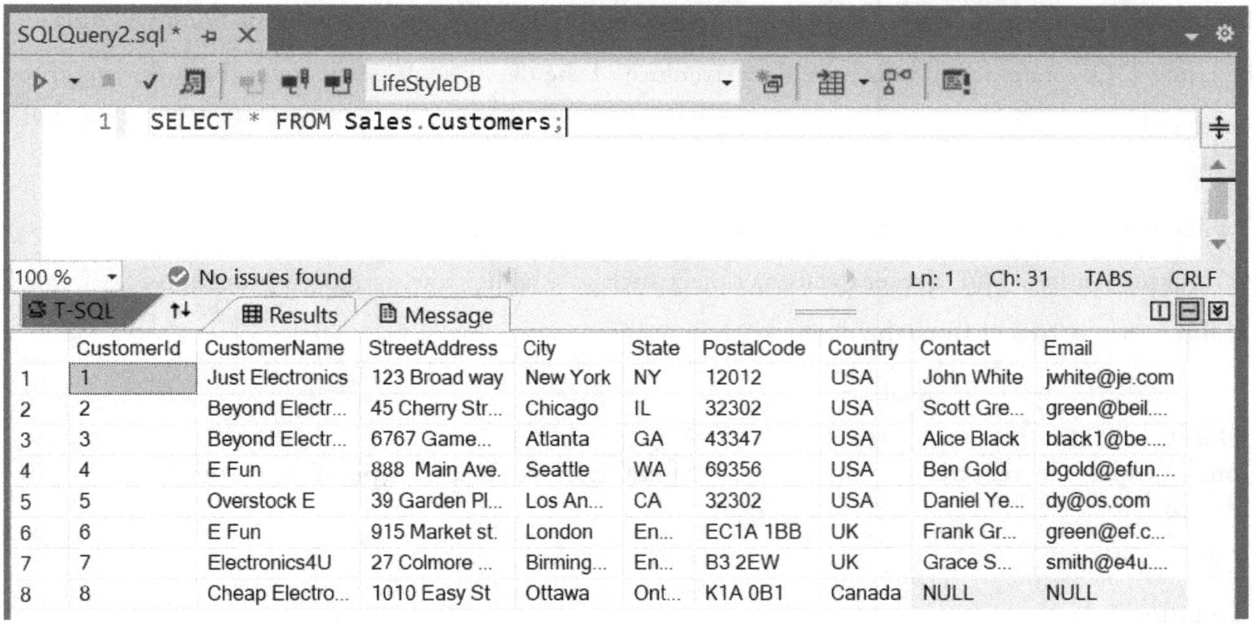

	CustomerId	CustomerName	StreetAddress	City	State	PostalCode	Country	Contact	Email
1	1	Just Electronics	123 Broad way	New York	NY	12012	USA	John White	jwhite@je.com
2	2	Beyond Electr...	45 Cherry Str...	Chicago	IL	32302	USA	Scott Gre...	green@beil....
3	3	Beyond Electr...	6767 Game...	Atlanta	GA	43347	USA	Alice Black	black1@be....
4	4	E Fun	888 Main Ave.	Seattle	WA	69356	USA	Ben Gold	bgold@efun....
5	5	Overstock E	39 Garden Pl...	Los An...	CA	32302	USA	Daniel Ye...	dy@os.com
6	6	E Fun	915 Market st.	London	En...	EC1A 1BB	UK	Frank Gr...	green@ef.c...
7	7	Electronics4U	27 Colmore ...	Birming...	En...	B3 2EW	UK	Grace S...	smith@e4u....
8	8	Cheap Electro...	1010 Easy St	Ottawa	Ont...	K1A 0B1	Canada	NULL	NULL

Figure 1.16 Windows for SQL statements and output

1.13 Types of SQL Statement

In this book, you will learn two types of SQL statements. The first one is Data Manipulation Language (DML). It will allow you to use the statements SELECT (strictly speaking, this is not a DML, we include it here for convenience,) INSERT, UPDATE, DELETE, and MERGE to manipulate data. These statements affect the data stored in the database.

SELECT will retrieve zero or many rows or columns from one or more tables in SQL Server. You will spend most of your time on this command in this book.

INSERT will add one or more new records to a table or a view in SQL Server.

UPDATE will change existing data in one or more columns in a table or a view.

DELETE will remove zero or many rows from a table or a view.

MERGE will perform insert, update, or delete operations on a target table based on the results of a source table.

The second type of SQL statement is Data Definition Language (DDL). It enables a database administrator to create database objects like schemas, tables, constraints, and stored procedures. You can either create these objects through a graphical user interface or by issuing DDL script statements. This book will only cover the latter. DDL statements define the data structure of the database. We will cover the following three DDL commands:

ALTER will change an existing object, such as by adding a field to a table.

CREATE will form a new SQL Server database object such as a table, view, or stored procedure.

DROP will remove an object from the database.

Review Question 1.34
Adding one or more new records to a table or a view in SQL Server is what type of SQL command?
a. DML
b. DDL

Review Question 1.35
Creating a new SQL Server database object such as a table, view, or stored procedure is related to what type of SQL command?
a. DML
b. DDL

1.14 Chapter Summary

In this chapter, you learned the basic concepts that are necessary to understand the database environment. The major concepts include, data, field, record, table, schema, and database. You also learned how to run SQL statements on SQL Server Express through Visual Studio 2019 Community Edition. This chapter ends with an introduction of different types of SQL commands that you will learn the details of in the rest of the book.

1.15 Discussion Questions

Discussion 1.1

Many people agree that the concepts of data and information are different, but use the terms interchangeably anyway. What is your opinion?

Discussion 1.2

Database focuses on the user data. Why does it also include the metadata?

Discussion 1.3

What's the difference between DBMS and database systems?

1.16 Solutions to the Review Questions

1.1 A; 1.2 B; 1.3 C; 1.4 B; 1.5 B; 1.6 D; 1.7 A; 1.8 C; 1.9 A; 1.10 B; 1.11 C; 1.12 C; 1.13 C; 1.14 D; 1.15 A; 1.16 C; 1.17 C; 1.18 A; 1.19 C; 1.20 A; 1.21 A; 1.22 B; 1.23 B; 1.24 B; 1.25 D; 1.26 B; 1.27 D; 1.28 C; 1.29 C; 1.30 A; 1.31 D; 1.32 C; 1.33 D; 1.34 A; 1.35 B;

CHAPTER 2: DATA MODEL AND SQL SELECT STATEMENT

Chapter Learning Objectives

2.1 Recognize the characteristics of a good model.

2.2 Extract business rules from business descriptions.

2.3 Identify entities from business rules.

2.4 Identify relationships from business rules.

2.5 Compare levels of data abstract.

2.6 Execute SQL SELECT ... FROM statement.

2.7 Implement ORDER BY clause.

2.8 Implement DISTINCT and TOP keywords.

2.1 Data Model

We build models to better understand more complex real-world objects or events. A model is an abstraction of a mini-world. There are three characteristics of a good model: first, the model must map the mini-world object. For example, a 3D model for a ten-story building that has yet to be built must resemble a ten-story building, and not something irrelevant. Secondly, the model should be an abstract, meaning smaller details are forgone so the focus can be centered on the more important base details. For example, the 3D model may lack color in order to focus on structure. The purpose of the model is to function as a communication tool for stakeholders, and so some minor details may be dropped. The third characteristic is that the model must fit its purpose and intended audience. For example, the 3D model of the building would be intended for potential investors rather than engineers, who would need a blueprint for a model instead.

Figure 2.1 Different models are built for different purposes.

A data model is a specific form of a model, so all three characteristics of a model apply. However, a data model also has its own characteristics. A data model has to include constructs, which is the structure of the database, operations that work on these constructs, and constraints for the data.

Constructs are entities and the relationships among the entities. You will learn more about entities and relationships later in this chapter. Operations are specifications for how to insert or update a construct. You will learn the SQL statements concerning that throughout the book. Constraints are restrictions on data that allow the data to reflect the mini-world more accurately.

For example, suppose we are interested in a mini-world about teacher assignments (who teaches what course) in a small school. The constructs or the entities would be INSTRUCTOR and COURSE. The relationship would be "an instructor teaches multiple courses and each course is taught by exactly one instructor." The operations would be how to add a new course or update a course. A constraint can be that an instructor must teach at least three courses per semester.

In this book, we focus on one particular relational data model, called the Entity-Relationship (ER) model. An ER model contains three major concepts: entity, relationship, and attribute. These concepts will be introduced in this chapter and further explained throughout the rest of the book.

Review Question 2.1
According to the author of the book, why do we build models?
a. to better understand more complex real-world objects or events.
b. to have a hobby for students.
c. because model building is a required skill for college students.
d. because model building is a good way to learn the concepts of databases.

Review Question 2.2
A model is _____ a mini-world.
a. similar to
b. an abstraction of
c. a detailed reflection of
d. an entity of

Review Question 2.3
Which of the following is a characteristic of a good model?
a. The model must map the mini-world objects.
b. The model should provide all the details of the mini-world.
c. The model should always be smaller than the real object.
d. The model should be fun to build.

Review Question 2.4
Which of the following is a characteristic of a good model?
a. The model is just a map for directions.
b. The model is just an abstract; certain details are purposely ignored.
c. The model should always be smaller than the real object.
d. The model should provide learning purposes.

Review Question 2.5
Which of the following is a characteristic of a good model?
a. The model is just a map for directions.
b. The model is just a detailed mini-world.
c. The model should always be smaller than the real object.
d. The model should fit its purpose.

Review Question 2.6
A data model has to include _____, which is the structure of the database, _____ that work on these
constructs, and _____ for the data.
a. constructs, operations, constraints
b. structure, operations, constructs
c. operations, constraints, constructs
d. modules, packages, sources

Review Question 2.7
In a data model, the _____ are entities and the relationships among the entities.
a. constructs
b. operations

c. constraints

d. modules

Review Question 2.8

In a data model, the _____ are specifications for how to insert or update a construct.

a. constructs

b. operations

c. constraints

d. modules

Review Question 2.9

In a data model, the _____ are restrictions on data that allow the data to reflect the mini-world more accurately.

a. constructs

b. operations

c. constraints

d. modules

Review Question 2.10

Which of the following is NOT a characteristic of a good model?

a. The model must map the mini-world objects.

b. The model is just an abstract; certain details are purposely ignored.

c. The model should always be smaller than the real object.

d. The model should fit its purpose.

Review Question 2.11

Which of the following is NOT a component of a data model?

a. Engines

b. Constructs

c. Operations

d. Constraints

Review Question 2.12

Which of the following is NOT a concept of ER model?

a. entity

b. relationship

c. attribute

d. blueprint

2.2 Business Description

Before modeling for a mini-world, you will receive a document known as a business description from the user you are modeling for. The business description contains information on what the user wants of the database, including expectations and specific criteria that must be met in order to receive the user's approval. The expectations serve as a roadmap for the endeavor of database development. The criteria serve as a user acceptance checklist.

In other textbooks, the process of documenting business description is often called systems analysis or gathering requirements. An important aspect of the business description is that it strictly contains what the business wants, not how to develop it. In other words, it is not a technology document. For example, a business document can say that they want to display an employee's age when the employee's data is displayed on a form, but the document should not say the age must be stored in a database table, because that's a technical decision for the database designer.

The business description is a communication tool, not a contract. So, if the database designers do not understand an object or event, they should ask. The designers should never tell the business manager how to run the business. The purpose of the document is that both sides, the business manager and the database designer, understand the requirements in the way they are intended to. It is a good idea that both sides learn the language used by the other. For example, the meaning of 'customer' may be pretty obvious to many people, but in a company that serves truck drivers for shipping, the term can be confusing. It can mean the truck drivers who use the company's service, or the customers who want the goods to be shipped. If the database designers are unsure what group in that scenario counts as the 'customer,' they need to ask.

A business description is mainly based on an interview with the business users. However, do not forget to collect supporting documents, such as forms, reports, notes, and screenshots that may contain sample data. These documents are important because not many people can remember all items on a form or a report. By looking at the forms and reports, you can see what sort of data the user plans on keeping. Figure 2.2 shows a sample invoice from our fictitious company, LifeStyle LLC. From the invoice, you can see that customer name and address are musts for an invoice, so your database needs to be able to store those data.

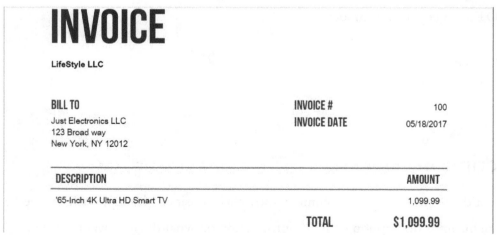

Figure 2.2 Sample invoice from the customer

Here are two examples of business description:

Case Example 1

ContinueEducation is a small online school. It offers courses that reflect current job market demands. It has small class sizes which allow good interaction between the students and the instructors.

A course is taught by just one instructor while an instructor can teach multiple courses. A student can register for zero or many courses. A course must have at least 5 students and at most 20 students. At the end of the semester, the student will receive a letter grade for the course he or she registered for. Students are allowed to register for the same course in different semesters.

Case Example 2

LifeStyle LLC is a small electronic wholesaler. Even though the company has a small number of employees, it has suppliers and customers all over the world, thanks to the internet.

The company needs an inventory management system which will help the managers determine the inventory at any time. For each product, the company wants to know the product name, supplier, and deliveries. Each product comes from just one supplier while one supplier can provide multiple products. A delivery should show the date, quantity, and unit price. A product can have zero or many deliveries while a delivery is about exactly one product.

The company wants to keep a sales record for each customer. The record includes the customer's name, the employee who served the customer for that order, the product, quantity, unit price, and the date the order was placed. An order may include more than one product.

Some employees supervise other employees. Each employee has just one boss. Certain employees have no boss (e.g. the CEO).

Review Question 2.13
The first step in data modeling is _____.
a. writing the business rules
b. documenting the business description
c. identifying constructs
d. determining operations on objects

Review Question 2.14
The business description document usually includes _____.
a. the detailed budget and the schedule for the new system
b. the list of tables in the new database

c. user expectations and criteria to measure success
d. the names of the tables in the new database

Review Question 2.15
The business description serves as a _____.
a. contract between the customers and the developers
b. communication tool between the customers and the developers
c. strategic plan for the development team
d. measure of how well the development team is doing

Review Question 2.16
A business description usually includes _____.
a. names from top management
b. no more than one page of paper
c. supporting documents
d. database name

2.3 Business Rules

Business rules are derived from the business description and focus on the policies and rules of the mini-world. Business rules should also serve as a communication tool. When writing these rules, you may ask the users for clarification or additional information on the business description.

For Case Example 1 (Section 2.2), sample business rules that focus on entities and their relationships are:

Each student can take up to six courses as a full-time student ("six courses" is not in the original description. It is added with the approval of the users).

Each course must have at least five students and no more than 20 students.

Each course is taught by exactly one instructor.

Each instructor can teach zero or several courses.

Each student will receive a letter grade for each course he or she took by the end of the semester.

For Case Example 2 (Section 2.2), sample business rules are:

A product is supplied by just one supplier.

Each supplier can provide several products.

A customer can place many orders.

Each order is from just one customer.

An order must be completed by an employee.

An employee can help complete multiple orders.

Each order must have at least one product.

Each product can appear in zero or many orders.

A manager can supervise multiple employees.

An employee can have only one manager.

You may notice that business rules begin with a singular noun such as "a product" or "each supplier". Can you identify the issues with the following business rules?

A customer can place many orders.

Many orders can be placed by a customer.

If you realize that these two rules are actually one, you get the correct answer.

You may also notice that most business rules are paired with two objects. Such as this:

A customer can place many orders.

Each order is from just one customer.

Here, the two objects are customer and order. The two rules show the relationship from each object to the other.

Review Question 2.17
The _____ is/are derived from the business description and focus on the policy and rules of the mini-world.
a. abstracts
b. business rules
c. business policies
d. mini-world

Review Question 2.18
Each business rule typically starts with _____.
a. singular verb
b. singular noun
c. plural verb
d. plural noun

Review Question 2.19
Most business rules are paired with _____.
a. one object
b. two objects
c. three objects
d. four objects

2.4 Entity

To develop a data model with Entity-Relationship Diagram (ERD), you need to identify the entities, relationships, and attributes from the business rules. In this section, you will learn how to identify the entities. An entity is a person, place, object, event, or concept in the mini-world about which you wish to develop the database. Read the business rules carefully. Focus on the nouns in the business rules that may be the entities.

For the Case Example 1 (Section 2.2), there are the following entities:

STUDENT *(persons who want to take courses)*

COURSE *(objects offered by ContinueEducation)*

INSTRUCTOR *(persons who teach courses)*

You may have a question. How about the staff? They are the employees who help the students register for courses. Shouldn't they be an entity? It all depends on if the customer (ContinueEducation) wants to keep records on assistant staff, such as whether a staff member helped a student. If yes, then include them.

What about the name of the school? Should we make it an entity? Usually no. We don't need to make a table (entity) just to store the school's name, which rarely changes and typically does not affect the areas of interest of the user. This is the mini-world, not an entity of the mini-world.

For Case Example 2 (Section 2.2), you may find the following entities:

CUSTOMER *(retailers that place orders from LifeStyle LLC)*

EMPLOYEE *(people who work for LifeStyle)*

SUPPLIER *(companies that supply products to LifeStyle)*

PRODUCT *(items LifeStyle buys and sells)*

ORDER *(transactions retailers conduct with LifeStyle)*

Do not feel bad if your list of entities is different from the above. For example, some of you may think that we should have a MANAGER entity. In fact, it's not wrong to have a MANAGER entity. We just decided that we won't add a MANAGER entity because we consider a manager an employee. Also, the MANAGER entity could get complicated when there are middle managers in the company (you would have to add another entity called MIDDLEMANAGER). In summary, do not think of the example as the final answer. The example just gives you a direction so that you can think in the right way.

Another question you may have is, what of "delivery?" If you think of delivery as an entity, you are correct. At this time, though, we will consider delivery as an attribute of PRODUCT.

Still another question is, how about "LifeStyle LLC?" It is the mini-world, not an entity.

The entities we identified above are all called entity types. The specific data within those entities are called entity instances. For example, in Case Example 1, 'EMPLOYEE' is considered an entity type, while a row of data for an employee, including name, date of birth, and so on, is considered an entity instance.

Note that sometimes the word 'entity' is used interchangeably with 'entity instance' and 'entity type.' Under most situations, it is not difficult to differentiate the meaning when we say 'entity'.

A weak entity type is a special type of entity. Sometimes you may find that one entity's existence will completely depend on another's. For example, in a company, if you keep data about each employee's dependents, the DEPENDENT can be a separate entity, but completely depends on the EMPLOYEE entity. So, the DEPENDENT entity is a weak entity. Another example can be a BUILDING entity and a CLASSROOM entity. A classroom completely depends on a building so we say that the CLASSROOM entity is a weak entity.

Entities are represented as a rectangle in ERD with the entity name inside the rectangle. A weak entity has dashed border line.

Figure 2.3 Regular entity and weak entity in ERD.

Review Question 2.20
A(n) _____ is a person, place, object, event, or concept in the mini-world about which we wish to develop the database.
a. entity
b. relationship
c. attribute
d. table

Review Question 2.21
A single occurrence of an entity type is _____
a. a single entity
b. a sole entity

c. an attribute

d. an entity instance

Review Question 2.22

The _____ is an entity type whose existence completely depends on another entity.

a. database

b. object

c. strong entity

d. weak entity

Review Question 2.23

A department has several student clubs. The department needs a database to keep data about the clubs and students. Which of the following is NOT an entity in ERD?

a. department

b. club

c. student

d. department, club, and student are all entities

2.5 Relationship

A relationship is an association between the instances of one or more entity types. For example, Tom Smith (an instance of INSTRUCTOR) teaches Introduction to Computer Science (an instance of COURSE) is an example of a relationship between two entities, the INSTRUCTOR and COURSE entities. Larry Smith (an instance of INSTRUCTOR) teaches sports psychology (an instance of COURSE) is another example of a relationship between the INSTRUCTOR and the COURSE entities.

A relationship type is a collection of the same type of relationships between the same entities. The above two relationship examples are both the relationship type of "INSTRUCTOR teaches COURSE."

The number of entity types in a relationship is called the degree of relationship. If only one entity type participates in the relationship, the degree of relationship is unary. For example, a course (an instance) has a prerequisite of another course (an instance). Both courses are from the COURSE entity. The "a course may have one or more prerequisites" is a unary relationship.

Figure 2.4 Unary Relationship

Another example of a unary relationship is "a manager manages other employees." In this example, both managers and employees are from the EMPLOYEE entity. Still another example is "a person is married to another person." Both are from the PERSON entity. A unary relationship is also called a recursive relationship.

A binary relationship is a relationship between instances of two entity types. For example, "an instructor teaches zero or more courses" is a binary relationship. The instructor is an instance of the INSTRUCTOR entity type and the course is an instance of the COURSE entity type. Binary relationships are the most popular form of relationships. You will see many examples of binary relationships throughout the book.

Figure 2.5 Binary relationship

A ternary relationship is a relationship among instances of three entity types. For example, a supplier ships a product to a retailer. This is a relationship among the instances of three entity types: SUPPLIER, PRODUCT, and RETAILER.

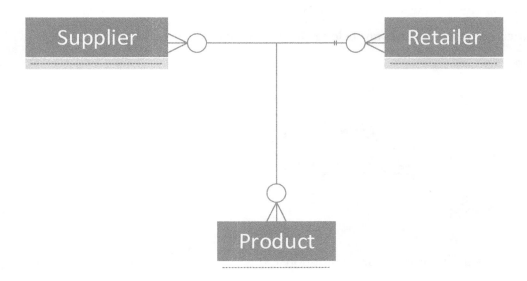

Figure 2.6 Ternary relationship.

The connectivity of a relationship explains the specifics of how two entity types are related. There are three major types of connectivity. The first is one-to-many (1:M). For example, if an instructor can teach many courses and each course can be taught by only one instructor, this is a one-to-many (1:M) relationship. Figure 2.5 shows a one-to-many connectivity between INSTRUCTOR and COURSE. As another example, a customer can place zero or many orders while an order comes from exactly one customer. The connectivity is again 1:M.

Figure 2.7 One-to-many (1:M) relationship.

The second type of connectivity is a many-to-many relationship (M:N). For example, a student can take zero or many courses and each course must have at least one student. This is a many-to-many (M:N) relationship.

Figure 2.8 Many-to-many (M:N) relationship.

The third type of connectivity is a one-to-one relationship (1:1). For example, each student has one computer lab account and each computer lab account belongs to at most one student is an example of a one-to-one (1:1) relationship.

Figure 2.9 One-to-one (1:1) relationship.

If an entity can have zero instances in the relationship, it is optional. It is shown as a small circle in ERD. If an entity has one or many instances in the relationship, it is mandatory. It is shown as a short vertical line in

ERD. For example, if each student can take zero or many courses, the course entity is optional. This is shown in Figure 2.8. If each course must have at least one student, the student entity is mandatory.

If you change the above business rule to "each student must take at least one course (mandatory) and each course must have at least one student (mandatory,)" the relationship will be mandatory on both sides as shown below:

Figure 2.10 Mandatory connectivity on both sides of a relationship.

The cardinality of a relationship is similar to the connectivity, but with more details. It shows the minimum and maximum entity instances possible in the relationship. Continue the above example. If each course is taught by exactly one instructor and each instructor can teach between zero to four courses, then on the INSTRUCTOR side, you add (1, 1). And you add (0, 4) on the COURSE side as shown:

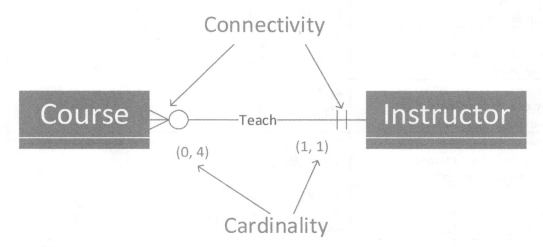

Figure 2.11 Connectivity vs. cardinality.

The cardinality added to which side can be a little bit confusing. While an instructor can teach between 0 and 4 courses, the cardinality is added to the COURSE side. Such notation makes it easy to read the relationship as "Each instructor can teach zero or up to four courses". If there's no upper limit, you can use the letter N to indicate it. For example, if an instructor can teach as many courses as he or she likes, the cardinality would be (0, N).

Knowing the cardinality is very useful for application software programmers. Cardinality cannot be implemented at the table level. As a database developer, you may write triggers to handle it (a topic which will be covered in our next book).

Business rules and connectivity must match. Each business rule shows one side of the connectivity. We recommend two business rules for each relationship. The following example shows 16 possible cases between Instructor and Course entities. The purpose is for you to see the match between rules and ERD, not which university has the rules.

Case 1: Each course is taught by at most one instructor. Each instructor teaches at most one course.	Course ├O──O┤ Instructor
Case 2: Each course is taught by at most one instructor. Each instructor teaches exactly one course.	Course ┤├──O┤ Instructor
Case 3: Each course is taught by at most one instructor. Each instructor teaches zero or more courses.	Course >O──O┤ Instructor
Case 4: Each course is taught by at most one instructor. Each instructor teaches at least one course.	Course >├──O┤ Instructor
Case 5: Each course is taught by exactly one instructor. Each instructor teaches at most one course.	Course ├O──┤├ Instructor
Case 6: Each course is taught by exactly one instructor. Each instructor teaches exactly one course.	Course ┤├──┤├ Instructor
Case 7: Each course is taught by exactly one instructor. Each instructor teaches zero or more courses.	Course >O──┤├ Instructor
Case 8: Each course is taught by exactly one instructor. Each instructor teaches at least one course.	Course >├──┤├ Instructor
Case 9: Each course is taught by zero or more instructors. Each instructor teaches at most one course.	Course ├O──O< Instructor
Case 10: Each course is taught by zero or more instructors. Each instructor teaches exactly one course.	Course ┤├──O< Instructor
Case 11: Each course is taught by zero or more instructors. Each instructor teaches zero or more courses.	Course >O──O< Instructor
Case 12: Each course is taught by zero or more instructors. Each instructor teaches at least one course.	Course >├──O< Instructor

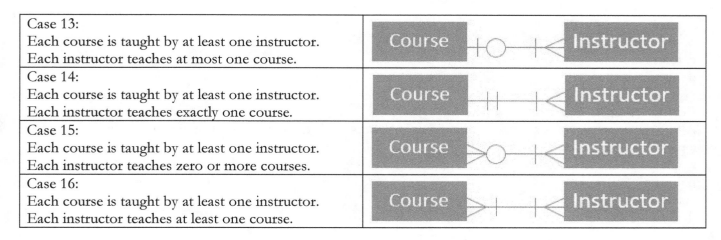

Case 13: Each course is taught by at least one instructor. Each instructor teaches at most one course.	Course — Instructor
Case 14: Each course is taught by at least one instructor. Each instructor teaches exactly one course.	Course — Instructor
Case 15: Each course is taught by at least one instructor. Each instructor teaches zero or more courses.	Course — Instructor
Case 16: Each course is taught by at least one instructor. Each instructor teaches at least one course.	Course — Instructor

Review Question 2.24

A course (an instance) has a prerequisite of another course (an instance). Both courses are from the COURSE entity. The "a course may have one or more prerequisites" is a _____ relationship.

a. unary

b. binary

c. ternary

d. hierarchical

Review Question 2.25

An example of a _____ relationship is "a manager manages other employees." In this example, both managers and employees are from the EMPLOYEE entity.

a. unary

b. binary

c. ternary

d. hierarchical

Review Question 2.26

An example of a _____ relationship is "a person is married to another person." Both are from the PERSON entity.

a. unary

b. binary

c. ternary

d. hierarchical

Review Question 2.27

A _____ relationship is a relationship between instances of two entity types. An example of such a relationship is "an instructor teaches zero or more courses."

a. unary

b. binary

c. ternary

d. hierarchical

Review Question 2.28

According to the author of our textbook, the _____ relationships are the most popular form of relationships. You will see many examples of such relationships throughout the book.

a. unary
b. binary
c. ternary
d. hierarchical

Review Question 2.29
A _____ relationship is a relationship among instances of three entity types. For example, a supplier ships a product to a retailer.
a. unary
b. binary
c. ternary
d. hierarchical

Review Question 2.30
If an instructor can teach many courses and each course can be taught by only one instructor, this is a _____ relationship.
a. 1:1
b. 1:M
c. M:N
d. I:C

Review Question 2.31
If a student can take zero or many courses and each course must have at least one student. This is a _____ relationship.
a. 1:1
b. 1:M
c. M:N
d. I:C

Review Question 2.32
If each student has one computer lab account and each computer lab account belongs to at most one student is an example of a _____ relationship.
a. 1:1
b. 1:M
c. M:N
d. I:C

Review Question 2.33
If an entity can have zero instances in the relationship, it is _____. It is shown as _____ in ERD.
a. 1:M, vertical line
b. mandatory, vertical line
c. zero, a small circle
d. optional, a small circle

Review Question 2.34
If an entity has one or many instances in the relationship, it is _____. It is shown as _____ in ERD.
a. 1:M, a short vertical line
b. mandatory, a short vertical line
c. zero, a small circle
d. optional, a small circle

Review Question 2.35
In the following figure, what label would you use for the symbols pointed by the top two arrows?

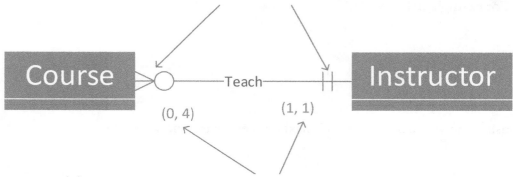

a. connectivity
b. cardinality
c. degree of relationship
d. optional/mandatory

Review Question 2.36
In the following figure, what label would you use for the symbols pointed by the bottom two arrows?

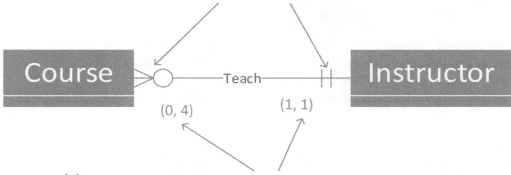

a. connectivity
b. cardinality
c. degree of relationship
d. optional/mandatory

Review Question 2.37
A _____ is an association between the instances of one or more entity types. For example, Tom Smith (an instance of INSTRUCTOR) teaches Introduction to Computer Sciences (an instance of COURSE)
a. connectivity
b. relation
c. relationship
d. cardinality

Review Question 2.38
How many entity types are in the relationship is called the _____ of relationship. Examples include unary, binary, or ternary.
a. degree
b. connectivity
c. cardinality
d. optional/mandatory

Review Question 2.39
The _____ of a relationship is about how many instances of an entity are associated with each instance of the participating entity. For example, 1:1, 1:M, M:N.
a. degree
b. connectivity
c. cardinality
d. optional/mandatory

Review Question 2.40
The _____ of a relationship shows the minimum and maximum entity instances possible in the relationship.
a. degree
b. connectivity
c. cardinality
d. optional/mandatory

Review Question 2.41
What is the business rule for the following ERD?

a. Each student can take zero or many courses and each course can have zero or many students.
b. Each student takes at least one course and each course can have zero or many students.
c. Each student can take zero or many courses and each course has at least one student.
d. Each student takes at least one course and each course has at least one student.

Review Question 2.42
A department has several student clubs. A student can join any number of clubs. A club must have at least three students. The department needs a database to keep data about the clubs and students. What is the connectivity of the relationship between the Club and Student entities in ERD?
a. 1:1
b. 1:M
c. M:1
d. M:N

2.6 Attribute

Attributes are the properties used to describe an entity or a relationship. For example, an INSTRUCTOR entity may have an instructor ID, First name, and last name. The instructor ID, first name, and last name are called attributes of the INSTRUCTOR entity. A relationship such as "a STUDENT takes a COURSE" can have an attribute called final grade. The final grade cannot be an attribute for the STUDENT entity because a student can take many courses. The final grade cannot be an attribute for the COURSE entity because a course can have many students.

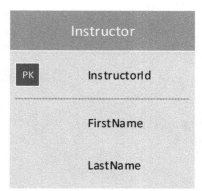

Figure 2.12 The attributes of an entity.

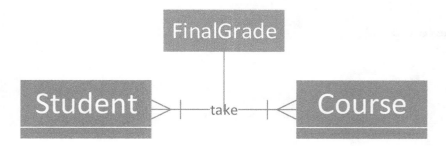

Figure 2.13 The attribute of a relationship.

Each attribute has a value set (data type) associated with it. For example, an instructor ID may be an integer, and the first name and last name should be a string of letters. Finally, each attribute has a set of possible values called a domain. For example, an instructor ID is a 7-digit integer. In other words, an instructor ID cannot be a 6-digit integer, 8-digit integer, nor a string of characters. The domain for the instructor ID is a 7-digit integer. As another example, an unweighted student GPA attribute has the domain of between 0 and 4.0 for many schools.

While an entity is a real-world object of interest to the end user, attributes are characteristics of the entity that are of interest to the end user.

Review Question 2.43
A relationship such as "a STUDENT takes a COURSE" can have a(n) _____ called final grade.
a. attribute
b. entity
c. exam
d. time

Review Question 2.44
In database design, an unweighted student GPA attribute has the _____ of between 0 and 4.0 for many schools.

a. possible value
b. domain
c. single digit value
d. floating point value

Review Question 2.45
The _____ are the properties used to describe an entity or a relationship. For example, an INSTRUCTOR entity may include the instructor ID, first name, and last name.
a. attributes
b. entities
c. relations
d. domains

Review Question 2.46
Each attribute has a set of possible values called a(n) _____.
a. entity
b. relation
c. domain
d. relationship

Review Question 2.47
Each attribute has a value set associated with it. For example, an instructor ID may be an integer, and the first name and last name should be a string of letters. Such a value set is called the attribute's _____ .
a. domain
b. set
c. data type
d. value

Review Question 2.48
In ERD, an entity can have one or more attributes; A _____ can also have attributes.
a. domain
b. connectivity
c. cardinality
d. relationship

2.7 Abstract Level of Data Model

Data models can have different levels of abstraction, which means how much detail we need for the data. Different levels of abstraction can serve different purposes. Business users usually just need a conceptual and logical model, and don't need a physical model, which is less abstract than a conceptual or logical model. A conceptual model will help the users and developers to define the scope of the project. A logical model will help users determine if all data needed are in the model and if no extra data is included in the model. There is no clear line between the levels of abstraction. For example, some books will place both conceptual and logical models on the same level of abstraction, while others won't. All models serve the purpose of communication between the developers and the customers. This book will introduce four levels of abstraction: contextual, conceptual, logical, and physical.

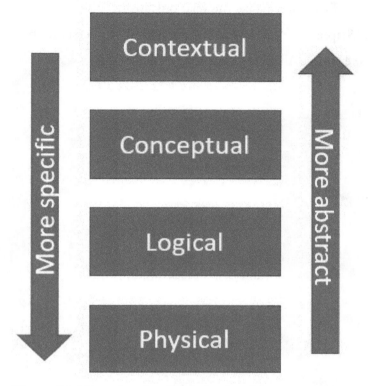

Figure 2.14 Four levels of abstract levels.

The contextual level brings together all business stakeholders with their vision and strategy and their resulting priorities into a set of principles. The model is mainly used during requirement collection. It focuses on why we need to model the data; e.g. student records must be accurate and kept for a long time. This book won't further discuss this level because it is typically covered in systems analysis books.

The conceptual level focuses on data requirements with entities and relationships. It answers 'what' questions, such as 'what are the entities/objects you are going to model? What are the relationships between the entities? What is a course? (Do two sections of the same course count as one or two courses?)' The conceptual model includes all the entities and their relationships.

Based on case example 1 described earlier in the chapter (Section 2.2), you may develop a conceptual model that looks like this:

Figure 2.15 A conceptual model of case example 2 (Section 2.2).

At the logical level, you start to add attributes to each entity and relationship. Determine attribute domains. Decide which attribute(s) can uniquely identify each record. Resolve any many to many relationships, check integrity constraints, convert entities into relations, and finally normalize the relations. More about attributes, keys, and constraints will be explained in Chapter 3, so do not worry if you don't understand the terms used in this paragraph. A logical model of case example 2 (Section 2.2) may look like this:

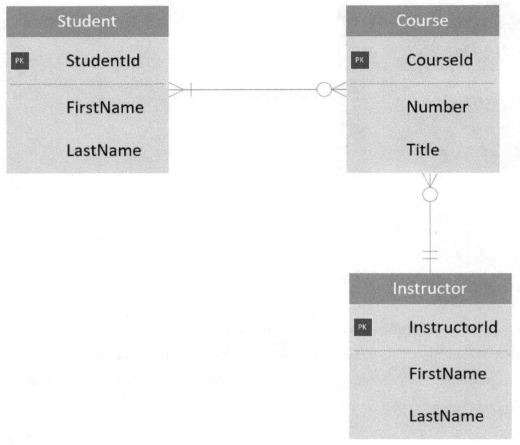

Figure 2.16 A logical model of case example 2.

At the physical level, you first select the DBMS. In this book, you will use SQL Server. Then, add the data type for each field. At this point you may perform denormalization. These topics will be covered in later chapters. You may note that a new entity called enrollment is added in the above model. We will explain this in Chapter 5.

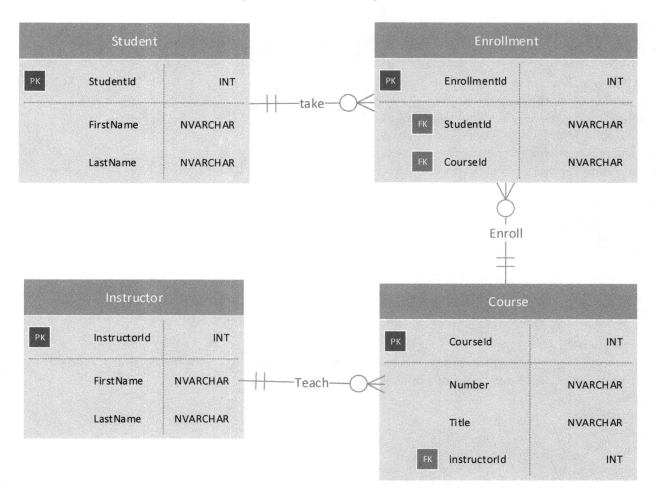

Figure 2.17 A physical model of case example 2.

Review Question 2.49
Different levels of abstraction can serve different purposes. Business users usually just need a _____ and
_____ model, and don't need a _____ model.
a. contextual, conceptual, logical
b. conceptual, logical, physical
c. logical, physical, contextual
d. physical, contextual, conceptual

Review Question 2.50
A _____ model will help the users and developers to define the scope of the project.
a. contextual
b. conceptual
c. logical
d. physical

Review Question 2.51
A _____ model will help users determine if all data needed are in the model and if no extra data is included
in the model.
a. contextual
b. conceptual

c. logical
d. physical

Review Question 2.52
All data models serve the purpose of _____.
a. communication between the developers and the customers
b. having a solid foundation for a robust database design
c. complete requirements from the business users
d. simple coding for the application developers

Review Question 2.53
The _____ model focuses on why we need to model the data; e.g. student records must be accurate and kept for a long time.
a. contextual
b. conceptual
c. logical
d. physical

Review Question 2.54
A model at the _____ level brings together all business stakeholders with their vision and strategy and their resulting priorities into a set of principles.
a. contextual
b. conceptual
c. logical
d. physical

Review Question 2.55
A model at the _____ level focuses on data requirements with entities and relationships, answering "what" questions, such as 'what are the entities/objects you are going to model?'
a. contextual
b. conceptual
c. logical
d. physical

Review Question 2.56
In a model at the _____ level, you start adding attributes to each entity and relationship. Determine attribute domains and decide which attribute(s) can uniquely identify each record.
a. contextual
b. conceptual
c. logical
d. physical

Review Question 2.57
In a model at the _____ level, you first select the DBMS. In this book, you will use SQL Server. Then, add the data type for each field.
a. contextual
b. conceptual
c. logical
d. physical

2.8 Conceptual model

This chapter focuses on the conceptual model of database design. In Section 2.7, you learned that conceptual models have a high level of abstraction. It focuses on the entities and their relationships. Details such as attributes are on purposely omitted to ensure the relationships between entities are correctly modeled from the business description and business rules.

Conceptual model (ERD) Example 1:

The Career Center of Jefferson County offers in-demand IT skill courses to adult learners. They want to keep records of students and courses. Write possible business rules and construct conceptual ERD.

Business rules:

1. A student can take zero or many courses.

2. A course must have at least one student.

Conceptual ERD:

You may notice that the career center is not an entity. It is the mini-world.

Conceptual model (ERD) Example 2:

The Career Center of Jefferson County offers in-demand IT skill courses to adult learners. They want to keep records of students, instructors, and courses. Write possible business rules and construct conceptual ERD.

Business rules:

1. A student can take zero or many courses.

2. A course must have at least one student.

3. An instructor can teach zero or many courses

4. A course has exactly one instructor.

Conceptual ERD:

Conceptual model (ERD) Example 3:

The Career Center of Jefferson County offers in-demand IT skill courses to adult learners. They want to keep records of students, instructors, courses, and classrooms. Write possible business rules and construct conceptual ERD.

Business rules:

1. A student can take zero or many courses.

2. A course must have at least one student.

3. An instructor can teach zero or many courses

4. A course has exactly one instructor.

5. A course is assigned to exactly one classroom.

6. A classroom can be assigned to zero or many courses.

Conceptual ERD:

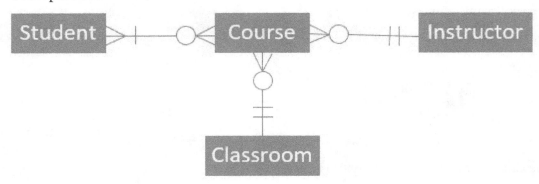

Conceptual model (ERD) Example 4:

Based on the business description and business rules of Case Example 2 (Section 2.2), write possible business rules and construct conceptual ERD.

Business Rules:

An employee may manage zero or many employees.

An employee may be managed by zero or one boss/employee.

An employee can complete zero or many orders.

An order must be completed by exactly one employee.

A customer can place zero or many orders.

An order must come from exactly one customer.

An order contains at least one product.

A product can appear in zero or many orders.

A product is provided by exactly one supplier.

A supplier may provide zero or many products.

Conceptual ERD:

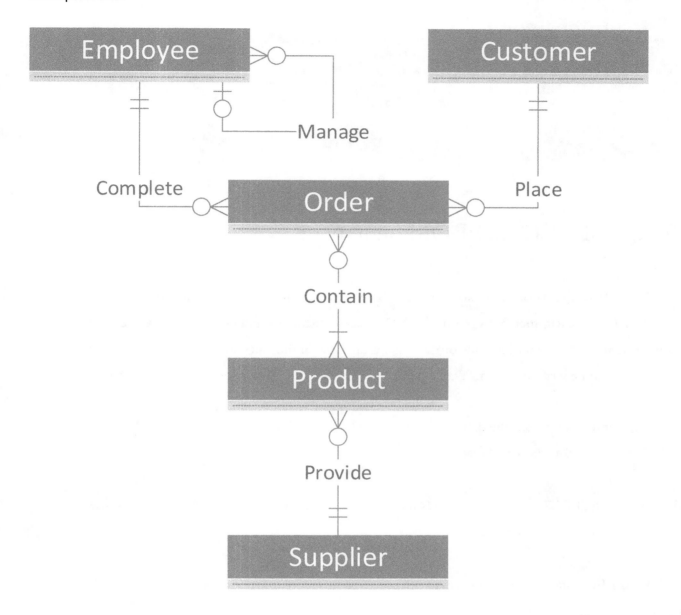

Figure 2.18 Conceptual model for case example 2.

You use this conceptual ERD and the business rules to communicate with the business users, and see whether they agree with you.

Review Question 2.58

A department has several student clubs. A student can join any number of clubs. A club must have at least three students. The department needs a database to keep data about the clubs and students. What is the conceptual ERD?

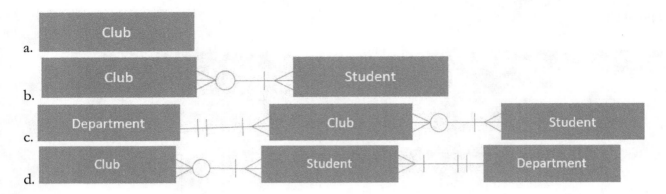

a. Club

b. Club — Student

c. Department — Club — Student

d. Club — Student — Department

2.9 SQL SELECT... FROM Statement

To retrieve data from one or more tables in a database, you can use SELECT ... FROM statement. For example: SELECT CustomerName, Contact FROM Sales.Customers allows you to retrieve data from the CustomerName and Contact columns of the Customers table in the Sales schema. Where you retrieve the data from should be written 'schema'.'table name'. In this case, the Customers table is in the Sales schema.

In the last chapter, you tested the database you installed with the following SQL command:

```
SELECT * FROM Sales.Customers;
```

This is an SQL SELECT statement that tells the DBMS (SQL Server in our case) to return all rows and all columns from the customers table.

The SQL SELECT statement allows you to select one or more columns of all rows from a table. The syntax for a simple SELECT statement is:

```
SELECT ColumnName1, ColumnName2, ...
FROM TableName;
```

SQL statements are case insensitive. However, in this book, we follow the following convention:

SQL keywords are all caps, such as SELECT, FROM.

Table names and column names are capitalized on the first letter of each word, such as Customers, CompanyName.

Note: when working with the examples and exercises, you need to take a look at the list of tables in Appendix B to familiarize yourself with the table structure and the data.

SQL Examples:

To practice SQL statements, you must open the editor and connect it to the LifeStyleDB as you did in Chapter 1.

SQL Example 2.1

Display all customers' names from the Customers table.

SQL Example 2.1 Analysis

Go to Appendix B and find the Customers table. The column name is CustomerName, the table name is Customers, and the schema name is Sales, so you have all input for the SELECT statement.

SQL Example 2.1 statement

```
SELECT CustomerName
FROM Sales.Customers;
```

SQL Example 2.1 Output (Type the above two lines in the editor, highlight both lines, and click on the "execute" button on the top left side to display the following in the output):

	CustomerName
1	Beyond Electronics
2	Beyond Electronics
3	Cheap Electronics
4	E Fun
5	E Fun
6	Electronics4U
7	Just Electronics
8	Overstock E

SQL Example 2.2

Display all customers' names and email addresses from the Customers table.

SQL Example 2.2 Analysis

According to Appendix B, the CustomerName and Email are in the Sales.Customers table. Just add one column to the statement in Example 2.1. Remember to add a comma between column names.

SQL Example 2.2 statement

```
SELECT CustomerName, Email
FROM Sales.Customers;
```

SQL Example 2.2 Output

	CustomerName	Email
1	Just Electronics	jwhite@je.com
2	Beyond Electronics	green@beil.com
3	Beyond Electronics	black1@be.com
4	E Fun	bgold@efun.com
5	Overstock E	dy@os.com
6	E Fun	green@ef.com
7	Electronics4U	smith@e4u.com
8	Cheap Electronics	NULL

SQL Example 2.3

Display all employee's first names, last names, and phone numbers from the Employees table.

SQL Example 2.3 Analysis

According to Appendix B, the column names are FirstName, LastName, and Phone and the table name is HR.Employees, so you have all input for the SELECT statement.

SQL Example 2.3 statement

```
SELECT FirstName, LastName, Phone
FROM HR.Employees;
```

SQL Example 2.3 Output

	FirstName	LastName	Phone
1	Alex	Hall	(434) 290-3322
2	Dianne	Hart	(434) 290-1122
3	Maria	Law	(434) 531-5673
4	Alice	Law	(434) 531-1010
5	Black	Hart	(434) 531-1034
6	Christina	Robinson	NULL
7	Nicholas	Pinkston	NULL

SQL Example 2.4

Display all data from the suppliers table.

SQL Example 2.4 Analysis

For column names, you can either go to Appendix B to write down all column names or just use the wildcard, *, to represent all columns. The table name is Suppliers and the schema is Purchasing, so you have all input for the SELECT statement.

SQL Example 2.4 statement

```
SELECT *
FROM Purchasing.Suppliers;
```

SQL Example 2.4 Output

	SupplierId	SupplierName	StreetAddress	City	State	PostalCode	Country
1	1	Pine Apple	1 Pine Apple St.	Idanha	CA	87201	USA
2	2	IMB	123 International Blvd	Los Angeles	CA	89202	USA
3	3	Lonovo	33 Beijin Square	Beijing	Beijing	100201	China
4	4	Samsong	1 Electronics Road	Yeongtong	Suwon	30174	South Korea
5	5	Canan	12 Camera St	Ota	Tokyo	100-0121	Japan

Review Question 2.59
An SQL SELECT statement allows you to select _____ from a table.
a. one or more rows
b. one or more columns
c. one or more rows or columns
d. any number of cells

Review Question 2.60
What does the following SQL statement do?

```
SELECT FirstName, LastName, GPA
FROM Admission.Student;
```
a. Retrieve all students' first names, last names, and G.P.As from the student table.
b. Select only the first student's first name, last name, and G.P.A from the student table.
c. Retrieve all students who provided their first name, last name, and G.P.A.
d. Select all students' first names, last names, and G.P.As from the admission table.

Review Question 2.61
The * in the SELECT clause of an SQL statement indicates selecting _____.
a. all rows
b. all columns
c. all rows with the * in them
d. all columns with the * in them

2.10 DISTINCT keyword

Sometimes, the SQL command result may contain duplicated rows. For example, if you want to know all the different first names for students at a university, you are sure to see many duplications. To remove all duplications, just add the DISTINCT keyword in the SELECT clause as shown in example 2.5.

SQL Example 2.5

Display all suppliers who have products in LifeStyle's products table. List the product's supplier ID.

SQL Example 2.5 Analysis

Supplier ID appears in two tables. One is the product table and the other is the suppliers table. Since not all suppliers provide a product for LifeStyle, only the products table should be used. The SupplierID is a column in the Products table, so we have all the input to issue the SELECT statement. However, if you execute the following statement:

```
SELECT SupplierId
FROM Purchasing.Products;
```

You will get the following output:

SupplierId
4
4
3
5
2
2
4
2
5

We don't want to see the supplier ID more than once. To remove all duplicate rows, you can use the DISTINCT keyword in SQL as shown in the following statement.

SQL Example 2.5 statement

```
SELECT DISTINCT SupplierId
FROM Purchasing.Products;
```

SQL Example 2.5 Output

	SupplierId
1	2
2	3
3	4
4	5

Review Question 2.62
What does the following SQL statement do?
```
SELECT DISTINCT FirstName, LastName
```
FROM Admission.Student;
a. Retrieve all students' first names and last names.
b. Retrieve all students' first names and last names without duplicates for first names.
c. Retrieve all students' first names and last names without duplicates for both first and last names.
d. Retrieve all students' first names and last names without duplicates for the first name, but duplications may appear for the last name.

2.11 ORDER BY Clause

When a DBMS generates output, there is no guarantee that the result rows will appear in a certain order. You can use the ORDER BY clause to sort results in the column(s) you specified. You can decide whether the results are presented as ascending (default) or descending (for example, in a list of names, whether you prefer it to be alphabetical, or reverse alphabetical.) You may sort multiple columns. In that case, the sorting would be first decided by the first column. If the first column is unable to decide which of two pieces of data should go first, it sorts according to the second column, and so on. In the case of sorting names in alphabetical order, for example, two people could have the same last name (the first column,) and so the ORDER BY clause will move on to the next column, first names, to decide which result goes first.

SQL Example 2.6

Display all employees' first names, last names, and date of births. Sort them from the oldest to the youngest.

SQL Example 2.6 Analysis

By now, it should be easy for you to display all employees' first names, last names, and date of births. The new stuff is the ORDER BY clause which will sort the result in ascending order by default, which is from the oldest to the youngest in this case. This may sound odd, but you sort by the date of birth, not age.

SQL Example 2.6 statement

```
SELECT FirstName, LastName, BirthDate
FROM HR.Employees
ORDER BY BirthDate;
```

SQL Example 2.6 Output

	FirstName	LastName	BirthDate
1	Nicholas	Pinkston	1977-10-05
2	Christina	Robinson	1978-07-13
3	Dianne	Hart	1978-12-03
4	Black	Hart	1982-11-09
5	Maria	Law	1988-07-13
6	Alice	Law	1988-12-13
7	Alex	Hall	1990-02-03

SQL Example 2.7

Display all employees' first names, last names, and date of births. Sort them from the youngest to the oldest.

SQL Example 2.7 Analysis

This is almost the same as Example 2.6. You just need to reverse the order from the ascending to descending by adding the keyword DESC.

SQL Example 2.7 statement

```
SELECT FirstName, LastName, BirthDate
FROM HR.Employees
ORDER BY BirthDate DESC;
```

SQL Example 2.7 Output

	FirstName	LastName	BirthDate
1	Alex	Hall	1990-02-03
2	Alice	Law	1988-12-13
3	Maria	Law	1988-07-13
4	Black	Hart	1982-11-09
5	Dianne	Hart	1978-12-03
6	Christina	Robinson	1978-07-13
7	Nicholas	Pinkston	1977-10-05

SQL Example 2.8

Display all employees' first names and last names. Sort them by how much time he or she has worked for the company, from the longest to the shortest.

SQL Example 2.8 Analysis

The purpose of this example is to demonstrate that you can sort a column that does not appear in the SELECT column list. In the example, you do not list the hire date, but use it in the ORDER BY clause.

SQL Example 2.8 statement

```
SELECT FirstName, LastName
FROM HR.Employees
ORDER BY HireDate;
```

SQL Example 2.8 Output

	FirstName	LastName
1	Dianne	Hart
2	Alice	Law
3	Maria	Law
4	Nicholas	Pinkston
5	Christina	Robinson
6	Black	Hart
7	Alex	Hall

Review Question 2.63

When the DBMS generates output, there is no guarantee that the result rows will appear in a certain order. You can use _____ clause to fix the problem.

a. ORDER
b. SORT
c. ORDER BY
d. SORT BY

2.12 The TOP Keyword

The TOP keyword will select the first however many pieces of data you wish to obtain on the list. TOP is almost always used with an ORDER BY clause so that the results are meaningful, since the ORDER BY clause will sort the list into a meaningful order.

SQL Example 2.9

Display the first two employees who worked for the company and who are still employed now. Show their first names and last names.

SQL Example 2.9 Analysis

This solution needs to use the keyword TOP to limit the results. You should sort the list by hire date before picking the first 2 rows. You can also add PERCENT after the number 2 to limit the number to two percent instead of 2 units.

SQL Example 2.9 statement

```
SELECT TOP 2 FirstName, LastName
FROM HR.Employees
ORDER BY HireDate;
```

SQL Example 2.9 Output

	FirstName	LastName
1	Dianne	Hart
2	Alice	Law

SQL Example 2.10

Display all employees' first names and last names. Sort the results by last name. In the case if two or more last names are the same, sort by the first name.

SQL Example 2.10 Analysis

You just need to add the secondary sort column to the ORDER BY clause. When more than one column is in the ORDER BY clause, they should be separated by a comma.

SQL Example 2.10 statement

```
SELECT firstName, LastName
FROM HR.Employees
ORDER BY LastName, FirstName;
```

SQL Example 2.10 Output

	firstName	LastName
1	Alex	Hall
2	Black	Hart
3	Dianne	Hart
4	Alice	Law
5	Maria	Law
6	Nicholas	Pinkston
7	Christina	Robinson

Review Question 2.64
What does the following SQL statement do?
```
SELECT FirstName, LastName
FROM Admission.Student;
ORDER BY gpa
```
a. Display all students' first names, last names, and GPAs from the student table.
b. Display all students' first names and last names and sort by GPAs with the highest GPA first.
c. Display all students' first names and last names and sort by GPAs with the lowest GPAs first.

d. It has a syntax error because the GPA column was not selected.

Review Question 2.65
Write an SQL statement to display the student with the highest GPA. Show their first name, last name, and GPA.
a. SELECT FirstName, LastName, TOP 1 gpa FROM Admission.Student ORDER BY gpa;
b. SELECT FirstName, LastName, TOP 1 gpa FROM Admission.Student ORDER BY gpa DESC;
c. SELECT TOP 1 FirstName, LastName, gpa FROM Admission.Student ORDER BY gpa;
d. SELECT TOP 1 FirstName, LastName, gpa FROM Admission.Student ORDER BY gpa DESC;

2.13 Chapter Summary

In this chapter, you learned the first few steps for building a data model. You started with writing business descriptions and then extracted business rules from business descriptions. Next, you determined the entities and the relationships among the entities and built the conceptual data model. You learned how to communicate with the business users using the conceptual data model to fix any problems.

You also learned how to display data with certain columns from a table of our LifeStyle Electronic wholesaler by using the SELECT ... FROM statement. You learned how to remove duplication in the output by using the DISTINCT keyword. You applied the ORDER BY clause to sort the result of the SELECT. Finally, you used the TOP keyword to limit the number of rows displayed.

2.14 Discussions

Discussion 2.1.

Think of a model you are familiar with in the real world. Explain the three characteristics of the model.

Discussion 2.2.

Compare and contrast connectivity and cardinality of a relationship in an ERD.

Discussion 2.3.

Why do you need to have different levels of abstraction when modeling data?

2.15 Database Design Exercises

Exercise One:

A small publisher wants to keep data about its books and authors. What are possible business rules (must come from the real world)? Draw a conceptual ERD for the publisher.

Exercise Two:

TourUSA is a small tourism company. It needs a database to store data described here. Its main customers are visitors from other countries. It offers many tours. Each tour includes a list of cities, number of days for the whole tour, and the manager who will be in charge of the tour.

For each city, it lists a brief description of the city and a list of attractions. Each attraction also includes a description and the weather forecast.

Each tour can have zero or many trips. Each trip includes a specific start date and end date, the price, and the guide. The guide information includes first name, last name, date hired, gender, and what languages he or she speaks and with what level of fluency.

A customer can book one or more trips that are announced on TourUSA's website. Each customer provides his or her first name, last name, date of birth, gender, and payment data.

Payment data required by TourUSA includes the name on the credit card, card expiration date, card number, and security code.

Your task:

1. Extract all possible business rules.
2. Construct the conceptual model for the TourUSA.

2.16 SQL Exercises

Exercise 2.1 Display all suppliers' names so the result look like this:

SupplierName
Pine Apple
IMB
Lonovo
Samsong
Canan

Exercise 2.2 Display all suppliers' names and country of origin:

SupplierName	Country
Pine Apple	USA
IMB	USA
Lonovo	China
Samsong	South Korea
Canan	Japan

Exercise 2.3 Display all customers' names, emails, and country.

	CustomerName	Email	Country
1	Just Electronics	jwhite@je.com	USA
2	Beyond Electronics	green@beil.com	USA
3	Beyond Electronics	black1@be.com	USA
4	E Fun	bgold@efun.com	USA
5	Overstock E	dy@os.com	USA
6	E Fun	green@ef.com	UK
7	Electronics4U	smith@e4u.com	UK
8	Cheap Electronics	NULL	Canada

Exercise 2.4 Display all data from the products table.

ProductId	ProductName	supplierid
1	65-Inch 4K Ultra HD Smart TV	4
2	60-Inch 4K Ultra HD Smart LED TV	4
3	3200 Lumens LED Home Theater Projector	3
4	Wireless Color Photo Printer	5
5	6Wireless Compact Laser Printer	2
6	Color Laser Printer	2
7	10" 16GB Android Tablet	4
8	GPS Android Tablet PC	2
9	20.2 MP Digital Camera	5

Exercise 2.5 Display all IDs of employees who have ever made a sale

employeeId
2
3
4
5
6
7

Exercise 2.6 Display all orders sorted by order date, from the earliest to the most recent.

OrderId	CustomerId	EmployeeId	OrderDate
7	5	7	2016-11-08
8	7	2	2016-12-23
1	1	5	2017-01-03
3	2	5	2017-02-23
2	1	3	2017-03-05
4	4	5	2017-04-13
5	1	4	2017-05-03
6	3	6	2017-05-08

Exercise 2.7 Display all orders sorted by order date, from the most recent to the earliest.

OrderId	CustomerId	EmployeeId	OrderDate
6	3	6	2017-05-08
5	1	4	2017-05-03
4	4	5	2017-04-13
2	1	3	2017-03-05
3	2	5	2017-02-23
1	1	5	2017-01-03
8	7	2	2016-12-23
7	5	7	2016-11-08

Exercise 2.8 Display products delivered with the product ID and quantity of each delivery. Sort from the most recent to the oldest.

ProductId	Quantity
1	5
7	18
7	12
6	25
5	15
4	20
3	10
2	10
1	2

Exercise 2.9 Display the three most recent deliveries with the product ID and quantity.

ProductId	Quantity
1	5
7	18
7	12

Exercise 2.10 Display all customers' names and contacts. Sort by the customer name. In the case where two or more customers have the same name, sort by contact.

	CustomerName	Contact
1	Beyond Electronics	Alice Black
2	Beyond Electronics	Scott Green
3	Cheap Electronics	NULL
4	E Fun	Ben Gold
5	E Fun	Frank Green
6	Electronics4U	Grace Smith
7	Just Electronics	John White
8	Overstock E	Daniel Yellow

2.17 Solutions to the Review Questions

2.1 A; 2.2 B; 2.3 A; 2.4 B; 2.5 D; 2.6 A; 2.7 A; 2.8 B; 2.9 C; 2.10 C; 2.11 A; 2.12 D; 2.13 B; 2.14 C; 2.15 B; 2.16 C; 2.17 B; 2.18 B; 2.19 B; 2.20 A; 2.21 D; 2.22 D; 2.23 A; 2.24 A; 2.25 A; 2.26 A; 2.27 B; 2.28 B; 2.29 C; 2.30 B; 2.31 C; 2.32 A; 2.33 D; 2.34 B; 2.35 A; 2.36 B; 2.37 C; 2.38 A; 2.39 B; 2.40 C; 2.41 D; 2.42 D; 2.43 A; 2.44 B; 2.45 A; 2.46 C; 2.47 C; 2.48 D; 2.49 B; 2.50 B; 2.51 C; 2.52 A; 2.53 A; 2.54 A; 2.55 B; 2.56 C; 2.57 D; 2.58 B; 2.59 B; 2.60 A; 2.61 B; 2.62 C; 2.63 C; 2.64 C; 2.65 D;

CHAPTER 3: LOGICAL MODEL AND SQL WHERE CLAUSE

Chapter Learning Objectives

3.1 Construct logical ERD with attributes and primary keys

3.2 Differentiate types of attributes

3.3 Identify attribute domains

3.4 Determine the primary key for an entity

3.5 Interpret entity existence dependence and relationship strength

3.6 Document entities, relationships, and attributes

3.7 Use WHERE clause to retrieve rows that meet certain criteria

3.8 Use BETWEEN and IS NULL operators

3.9 Use AND, OR, and NOT logical operators

3.1 Attributes of an Entity and a Relationship

As you learned in the last chapter, an attribute is a named property or characteristic of an entity or a relationship that is of interest to the user.

After you build the conceptual model of a database, you can move on to the logical design by adding the attributes to the entities and relationships. For example, the INSTRUCTOR entity has the attributes of instructor ID, first name and last name, the COURSE entity has a course ID, course number and course title. In the ERD, you can add them inside the entity box as in Figure 3.1:

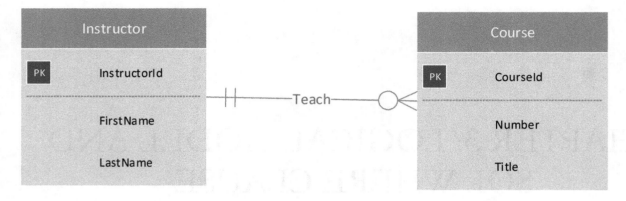

Figure 3.1 ERD entities with attributes added (we will cover PK attribute later in the chapter).

Do not add an attribute to an entity that is an entity in itself. For example, we say every course has an instructor, but we don't add instructor as an attribute to the course entity because an instructor is an entity.

There are many types of attributes you need to know when creating a data model.

A simple attribute has a single atomic value that cannot be subdivided. For example, an instructor's first name is a simple attribute because it cannot be subdivided without losing meaning.

A composite attribute is an attribute that can be further subdivided to yield additional attributes. For example, an instructor's full name is a composite attribute that can be further subdivided into first name, middle initial, and last name, each of which can be its own attribute. Another example is a mailing address, which usually contains street address, city, state, and zip code. Therefore, we can say that a mailing address is a composite attribute.

A single-valued attribute can have only one value for each record. For example, a course can have only one course number. A person can have only one date of birth. Course number and date of birth are single-valued attributes. Do not confuse a simple attribute with a single-valued attribute. Sometimes an attribute can be both, and other times not. For instance, a person's full name is a single-valued attribute, but not a simple attribute.

A multivalued attribute can have more than one value for each record. For example, an instructor's phone number can have multiple values, such as one for a home phone, a work phone, and a cell phone. Many attributes are multivalued attributes, although keep in mind the circumstances of the mini-world. Are those attributes really multivalued in that particular mini-world? For example, if our mini-world is an ordinary business, do you think the employee's last name is multivalued? Unlikely, even though many employees change their last name while employed, whether due to marriage or divorce. In the case that happens, you just update the employee's last name. You don't need to keep track of all his or her last names.

However, if our mini-world was a criminal justice department, you may want the same last name attribute to be multivalued because the entire name history should be kept.

In ERD, you use {LastName} to indicate a multivalued attribute called LastName.

A derived attribute or computed attribute is obtained from other attributes. For example, the student age attribute can be calculated from the date of birth attribute. Storing derived attributes takes storage, so it is preferred to store normal attributes. However, there will be cases in which both a normal attribute and a derived attribute are necessary. For example, if a school wanted to look up the age for one student, they would use a normal attribute. However, if the school frequently needed to look up ages for many students, calculation would take up time, and so it would be more convenient to use a derived attribute.

A required attribute is an attribute that must have a value for every entity instance. For example, an employee's ID, first name, and last name are all required fields to insert a new employee. In ERD, it is often shown as bold.

On the contrary, an optional attribute is an attribute that may not have a value for every entity instance. For example, not all employees will fill out a second phone number for a company's database. In ERD, an optional attribute is often shown as regular text.

Not only can an entity type have attributes, but a relationship type can have attributes as well. For example, there's a relationship between EMPLOYEE and PROJECT. An employee can work on multiple projects and each project has several employees. But then how do you record the hours each employee works on each project? The hours worked on a project is not an attribute of the EMPLOYEE because he or she can work on multiple projects. But, it cannot be an attribute of the project either, because each project has multiple employees. In this case, the attribute actually belongs to the relationship type of "work on project".

As shown in Figure 3.2, hoursWorked is an attribute of the "work on project" relationship. Just like in this example, most relationship attributes apply to M:N relationships.

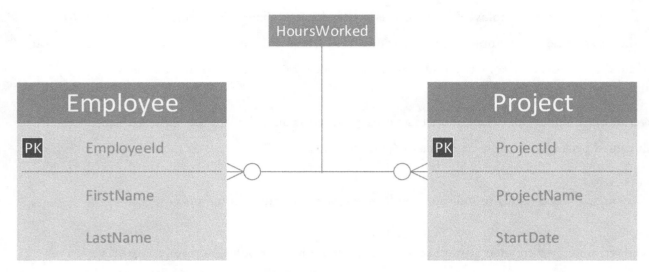

Figure 3.2 An attribute can belong to a relationship.

Review Question 3.1
A(n) _____ is a named property or characteristic of an entity or a relationship that is of interest to the user.
a. attribute
b. variable
c. function
d. piece of data

Review Question 3.2
After you build the conceptual model of a database, you can move on to the logical design by adding the _____ to the entities and relationships.
a. attributes
b. variables
c. tables
d. data

Review Question 3.3
In ERD, you use {LastName} to indicate a(a) _____ attribute called LastName.
a. optional
b. required
c. derived
d. multivalued

Review Question 3.4
Only entities can have attributes.
a. True
b. False

Review Question 3.5

A _____ attribute has a single atomic value that cannot be subdivided.
a. simple
b. composite
c. single-valued
d. multivalued

Review Question 3.6

A _____ attribute is the one that can be further subdivided to yield additional attributes.
a. simple
b. composite
c. single-valued
d. multivalued

Review Question 3.7

A _____ attribute can have only one value for each record.
a. simple
b. composite
c. single-valued
d. multivalued

Review Question 3.8

A _____ attribute can have more than one value for each record.
a. simple
b. composite
c. single-valued
d. multivalued

Review Question 3.9

If the STUDENT entity has an attribute called age, what type of attribute is it most likely to be?
a. composite
b. derived
c. required
d. optional

Review Question 3.10

If the STUDENT entity has an attribute called LastName, what type of attribute is it most likely to be?
a. composite
b. derived
c. required
d. optional

3.2 Attribute Domains

The domain of an attribute is all possible values that are allowed for the attribute. For example, if you have an attribute called GPA, the domain for that attribute would be [0, 4]. In another example, a student's first name is an attribute of the student entity. The domain of that attribute is a set string of alphabetical letters.

In ERD, you usually don't display the domain directly. In the physical model, you will display the data type in the ERD, which partially reflects the domain. A constraint may be added to the physical model due to the attribute domain. For example, you will use DECIMAL data type for the GPA attribute and NVARCHAR data type for FirstName attribute. You may use the CHECK constraint to ensure that a PGA is within the range of 0 and 4.

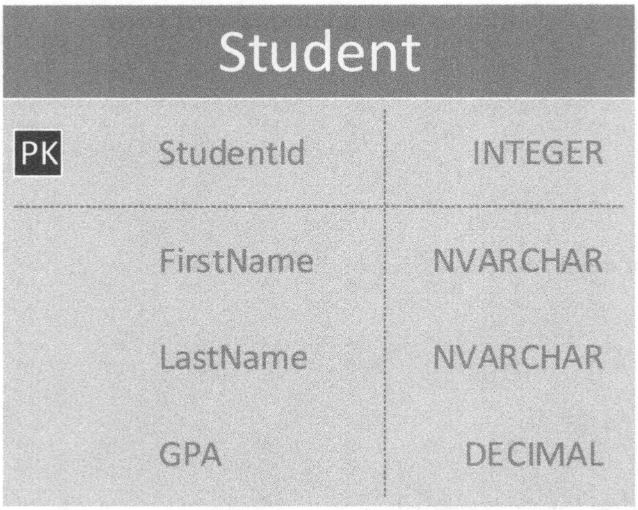

Student		
PK	StudentId	INTEGER
	FirstName	NVARCHAR
	LastName	NVARCHAR
	GPA	DECIMAL

Figure 3.3 Data types are shown in ERD at physical level.

Review Question 3.11
All possible values for an attribute are called the attribute's _____.
a. possibility
b. possible values
c. range
d. domain

Review Question 3.12
If GPA is an attribute of the STUDENT entity and can be values from 0 to 4, what is the set of possible GPA values called?
a. special range
b. possible range
c. domain
d. special domain

Review Question 3.13
If GPA is an attribute of the STUDENT entity and can be values from 0 to 4, you will see a _____ constraint in the physical model if using SQL Server.
a. GPA
b. DOMAIN
c. LIMIT
d. CHECK

3.3 Primary Key

An entity may have one or more attributes that can uniquely identify each instance of the entity type. Such an attribute is called a key of the entity, or an identifier. For example, student ID or social security number is a key of the STUDENT entity. The one key chosen by the database developer is called the primary key (PK). Note that a primary key of an entity does not have to be a single attribute, it can be a few attributes, in which case it is called a composite primary key.

In ERD, primary keys are indicated by underlining or just the PK on the left of the attribute name. All ERD in this book adopts the latter method.

There are a few rules to follow when you choose a primary key.
1. One attribute primary key is better than a composite primary key.

2. A good primary key will not change its value over the life of each instance of the entity type. So, using name and address for primary key is a bad choice because they can change often.

3. A primary key should not have null value. Not even part of the primary key can be null. A null value means no value for the record. For example, not all people have middle names, so middle names should not be included as part of a primary key.

4 A good primary key avoids using an intelligent identifier, meaning parts of the attribute value can be decoded for meaning. For example, some companies use products that contain parts that indicate the manufacturer location, such as US12345 for a product made in the USA, CN23456 for a product made in China.

5. A good primary key uses a single attribute surrogate for large composite identifiers. A surrogate key is a label used to serve as identification that may not have any meaning. For example, companies and schools may use a series of numbers (an ID) to represent an individual. These numbers have no meanings in the mini-world.

6. A good primary key should not use an attribute that can have security or privacy concerns, such as social security number.

When determining the primary key for a weak entity, the primary key of the identifying entity should be included as part of the weak entity's primary key. For example, DEPENDENT is a weak entity. Its identifying entity is EMPLOYEE. Suppose employee ID is the primary key of the EMPLOYEE entity, then the DEPENDENT entity should contain the employee ID as partial key. Then, the primary key for the DEPENDENT can be (EmployeeId, FirstNameOfDependent).

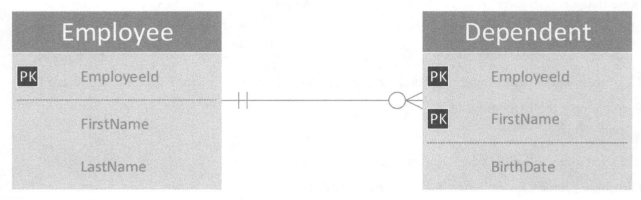

Figure 3.4 Primary key of a weak entity is a composite key.

Review Question 3.14
An entity may have one or more attributes that can uniquely identify each instance of the entity type. Such attribute(s) are called _____ attributes.
a. unique
b. key
c. primary key
d. foreign key

Review Question 3.15
An entity may have multiple keys. The one key chosen by the database developer is called the _____.
a. chosen key
b. major key
c. primary key
d. foreign key

Review Question 3.16
Which of the following statements about primary key is correct?
Statement1: One attribute primary key is better than a composite primary key.
Statement2: A good primary key will not change its value over the life of each instance of the entity type.
a. Statement1 only.
b. Statement2 only.
c. Both Statement1 and Statement2.
d. Neither Statement1 nor Statement2.

Review Question 3.17
Which of the following statements about primary key is correct?
Statement1: A good primary key will not change its value over the life of each instance of the entity type.

Statement2: A primary key may contain null value as long as the value for the column is unique.
a. Statement1 only.
b. Statement2 only.
c. Both Statement1 and Statement2.
d. Neither Statement1 nor Statement2.

Review Question 3.18
Which of the following statements about primary keys is correct?
Statement1: A primary key may contain null value as long as the value for the column is unique.
Statement2: A good primary key is made up of meaningful components. For example, some companies use products that contain parts indicating the manufacturer location, such as US12345 for a product made in the USA, CN23456 for a product made in China.
a. Statement1 only.
b. Statement2 only.
c. Both Statement1 and Statement2.
d. Neither Statement1 nor Statement2.

Review Question 3.19
Which of the following statements about primary key is correct?
Statement1: A good primary key is made up of meaningful components. For example, some companies use products that contain parts indicating the manufacturer location, such as US12345 for a product made in the USA, CN23456 for a product made in China.
Statement2: In the USA, a social security number is a good choice as the primary key for an employee entity because it is always unique.
a. Statement1 only.
b. Statement2 only.
c. Both Statement1 and Statement2.
d. Neither Statement1 nor Statement2.

Review Question 3.20
Sometimes, database developers add a new attribute that is meaningless in the mini-world to an entity to avoid using a large composite primary key. Such a primary key is called _____.
a. simplified key
b. meaningless key
c. single key
d. surrogate key

Review Question 3.21
Which of the following statements about primary key is correct?
Statement1: In the USA, a social security number is a good choice as the primary key for an employee entity because it is always unique.
Statement2: One attribute primary key is better than a composite primary key.
a. Statement1 only.
b. Statement2 only.
c. Both Statement1 and Statement2.
d. Neither Statement1 nor Statement2.

3.4 Existence Dependence

In Chapter 2, you learned that if an entity can exist in the database only when an associated entity exists, then the entity is called a weak entity. The DEPENDENT of EMPLOYEE is an example of a weak entity because a dependent cannot exist without the associated employee in the database. Such an entity is also called an existence-dependent entity.

On the other hand, if an entity can exist by itself, the entity is called existence-independent, also called a strong entity or simply a regular entity. An example of a strong entity can be STUDENT in a university setting.

Review Question 3.22
An ERD contains the BUILDING and CLASSROOM entities. A classroom is always inside a building. What is the CLASSROOM entity called?
a. strong entity
b. existence-dependent entity
c. existence-independent entity
d. regular entity

Review Question 3.23
An ERD contains the BUILDING and CLASSROOM entities. A classroom is always inside a building. What is the CLASSROOM entity called?
a. strong entity
b. weak entity
c. existence-independent entity
d. regular entity

3.5 Relationship Strength

A weak relationship, also known as a non-identifying relationship, exists if the primary key of one entity does not overlap with a primary key of the other entity.

For example, the relationship between the INSTRUCTOR and the COURSE is a weak relationship because the COURSE entity's primary key is CourseID, which does not contain the primary key of the INSTRUCTOR entity.

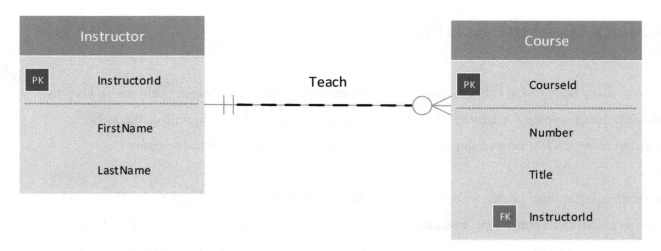

Figure 3.5 A weak relationship using a dashed line.

A strong relationship, or identifying relationship, exists between a strong entity and its associated weak entity. The relationship between EMPLOYEE and DEPENDENT demonstrates a strong relationship.

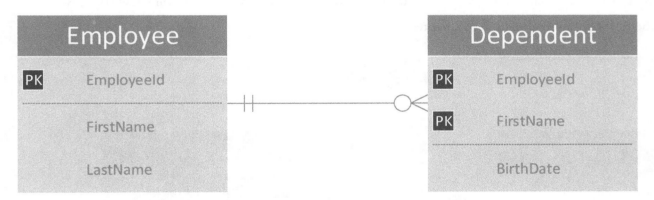

Figure 3.6 A strong relationship between a strong entity and a weak entity.

A strong relationship exists between the strong and weak entity because the primary key of the DEPENDENT entity contains EmployeeID, which is the primary key of the EMPLOYEE entity.

Review Question 3.24
An ERD contains the BUILDING and CLASSROOM entities. A classroom is always inside a building. What is the relationship strength between the BUILDING and CLASSROOM called?
a. a strong relationship
b. a weak relationship
c. a regular relationship
d. a special relationship

3.6 Many-to-Many Relationship

A many-to-many relationship (M:N) is special in relational databases. Some designers choose to keep the relationship until mapping the entities to relations (Chapter 5). Others decide to replace the M:N relationship with two 1:M relationships in the logical model by adding an associative entity.

An associative entity, also known as bridge entity or composite entity, is a relationship that the modeler chooses to model as an entity type. For example, the relationship between the STUDENT and the COURSE is a M:N relationship. We choose to add an associative entity called Enrollment as a bridge entity that makes one M:N relationship into two 1:M relationships (Figure 3.7).

The primary key of the associative entity is usually composed of the primary keys of each of the entities to be connected. In such a case, the primary key of the associative entity has a composite primary key.

As stated earlier, you may just keep the M:N relationship in the logical model. We will show you how to map the relationship to a relation in Chapter 5.

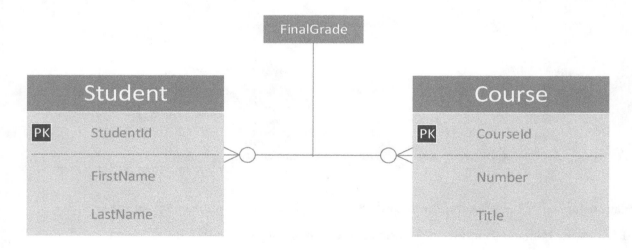

Part A) A many-to-many relationship

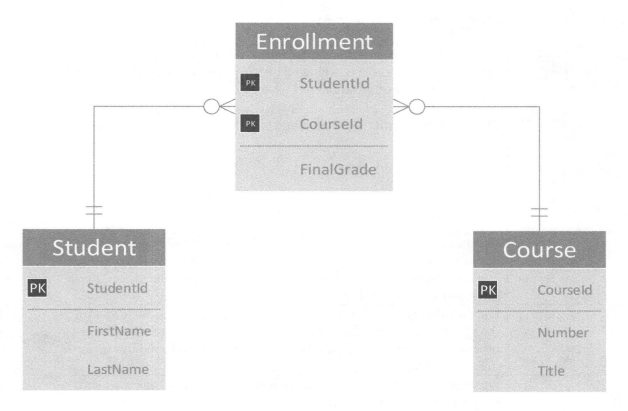

Part B) Two one-to-many relationship

Figure 3.7 Convert a many-to-many relationship into two one-to-many relationships.

Review Question 3.25
A(n) _____ entity is a relationship that the modeler chooses to model as an entity type.
a. relationship
b. special
c. simple
d. associative

3.7 Entity-Relationship Diagram (ERD)

So far, you learned how to develop data models by using entities, relationships, and attributes. It is time to summarize the symbols used. Data models can be represented in many ways. There are four major groups of notations you can use and they are very similar in the ideas behind them. They are Crow's foot, Chen, UML, and IDEF1X database notations. This book will use the Crow's foot notation only. You will see a Chen notation example towards the end of this section. Different notations may fit different purposes. For example, some people prefer to use the Chen notation for conceptual modeling and the UML class diagram for Entity Framework used in .net application development.

Symbol	Meaning
Student **PK** StudentId FirstName LastName	A rectangle shape shows the entity. An entity contains three parts, the entity name is on the top, followed by the primary key attribute(s), and ends with the list of attributes. PK stands for Primary Key attribute.
─┼┼─	Dictates that the relationship of the entity this symbol is next to with the other entities must be 1: M or 1:1. It must be true that there is one and only one participant from the entity this symbol is next to. The participation is mandatory.
─○┼	Dictates that the relationship of the entity this symbol is next to with the other entities must be 1: M or 1:1, but with the possibility that the other entity instances may not have any relationship to the instances of this entity. The participation is optional.
─○<	Dictates that the relationship of the entity this symbol is next to with the other entities must be 1: M or M:N, but with the possibility that the other entity instances may not have any relationship to the instances of this entity. The participation is optional.
─┼<	Dictates that the relationship of the entity this symbol is next to with the other entities must be 1: M or M:N. It must be true that there is at least one participant from the entity this symbol is next to. The participation is mandatory.

Table 3.1: Crow's foot notation

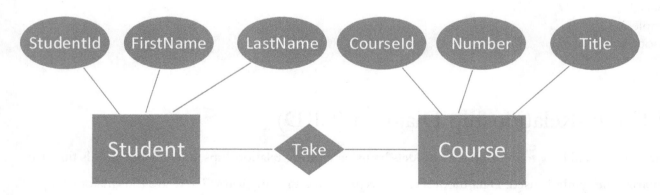

Figure 3.8 Chen's database notation example.

Review Question 3.26
In ERD, what does the following symbol mean?

a. Dictates that the relationship of the entity this symbol is next to with the other entities must be 1: M or 1:1. It must be true that there is one and only one participant from the entity this symbol is next to. The participation is mandatory.
b. Dictates that the relationship of the entity this symbol is next to with the other entities must be 1: M or 1:1, but with the possibility that the other entity instances may not have any relationship to the instances of this entity. The participation is optional.
c. Dictates that the relationship of the entity this symbol is next to with the other entities must be 1: M or M:N, but with the possibility that the other entity instances may not have any relationship to the instances of this entity. The participation is optional.
d. Dictates that the relationship of the entity this symbol is next to with the other entities must be 1: M or M:N. It must be true that there is at least one participant from the entity this symbol is next to. The participation is mandatory.

Review Question 3.27
In ERD, what does the following symbol mean?

a. Dictates that the relationship of the entity this symbol is next to with the other entities must be 1: M or 1:1. It must be true that there is one and only one participant from the entity this symbol is next to. The participation is mandatory.
b. Dictates that the relationship of the entity this symbol is next to with the other entities must be 1: M or 1:1, but with the possibility that the other entity instances may not have any relationship to the instances of this entity. The participation is optional.
c. Dictates that the relationship of the entity this symbol is next to with the other entities must be 1: M or M:N, but with the possibility that the other entity instances may not have any relationship to the instances of this entity. The participation is optional.
d. Dictates that the relationship of the entity this symbol is next to with the other entities must be 1: M or M:N. It must be true that there is at least one participant from the entity this symbol is next to. The participation is mandatory.

Review Question 3.28
In ERD, what does the following symbol mean?

a. Dictates that the relationship of the entity this symbol is next to with the other entities must be 1: M or 1:1. It must be true that there is one and only one participant from the entity this symbol is next to. The participation is mandatory.
b. Dictates that the relationship of the entity this symbol is next to with the other entities must be 1: M or 1:1, but with the possibility that the other entity instances may not have any relationship to the instances of this entity. The participation is optional.
c. Dictates that the relationship of the entity this symbol is next to with the other entities must be 1: M or M:N, but with the possibility that the other entity instances may not have any relationship to the instances of this entity. The participation is optional.
d. Dictates that the relationship of the entity this symbol is next to with the other entities must be 1: M or M:N. It must be true that there is at least one participant from the entity this symbol is next to. The participation is mandatory.

Review Question 3.29
In ERD, what does the following symbol mean?

a. Dictates that the relationship of the entity this symbol is next to with the other entities must be 1: M or 1:1. It must be true that there is one and only one participant from the entity this symbol is next to. The participation is mandatory.
b. Dictates that the relationship of the entity this symbol is next to with the other entities must be 1: M or 1:1, but with the possibility that the other entity instances may not have any relationship to the instances of this entity. The participation is optional.
c. Dictates that the relationship of the entity this symbol is next to with the other entities must be 1: M or M:N, but with the possibility that the other entity instances may not have any relationship to the instances of this entity. The participation is optional.
d. Dictates that the relationship of the entity this symbol is next to with the other entities must be 1: M or M:N. It must be true that there is at least one participant from the entity this symbol is next to. The participation is mandatory.

Review Question 3.30
Which of the following is NOT a popular database modeling notation?
a. Bigfoot
b. Chen
c. UML
d. IDEFX1X

3.8 Documentation

A data model should be accompanied by a document, sometimes called a data dictionary. Good documentation serves at least three purposes. One is as a communication tool between the developers and the customers. The second serves as a facilitator for the deployment of the system to production. The third serves as help to reduce the cost and effort during the maintenance stage of the system.

You should name an entity type so that both the users and developers can understand and interpret it in the same way. Keep in mind that an entity name is typically a noun. A description can help give a better understanding of the entities and the data model as a whole. An alias is also important when different users use different terms to mean the same thing. Finally, how an entity relates with another entity will help the understanding of the entity itself. A sample entity documentation is shown below:

Entity	Description	Alias	Relationship
Customer	All retail customers who buy from LyfeStyle or just registered to be a customer.	Client, Buyer	Each customer place zero or many orders.
Employee	All persons who work at LyfeStyle and still employed	Staff, Manager, Associate	Each employee assists zero or many orders.

Similarly, you should name relationship types so that both users and developers can understand. It usually is a verb or verb phrase. The document typically includes the relationship type names, participating entities and their corresponding cardinalities.

Entity	Cardinality	Relationship	Cardinality	Entity
Customer	(1, 1)	Place	(0, N)	Order
Employee	(1, 1)	Assist	(0, N)	Order
Employee	(0, 1)	Manage	(0, N)	Employee

Finally, you should name an attribute appropriately, organizing them under their entity or relationship. The document should include entity/relationship name, attribute name, description, aliases, data type and size, and attribute type. For ease of reading, the attribute type is often under several columns such as required, composite, multiple value, derived. The following table shows an example:

Customer Entity						
Attribute	Description	Alias	Date Type	Domain	Allow null	Multi-valued
CustomerId	Uniquely identify a customer	Company ID	Integer auto generated by the system	Any integer	No	No
CustomerName	Customer's registered company name	Company name	Up to 50 variable characters	Any alpha-numeric	No	No
StreetAddress	Customer's headquarter street address	Address	Up to 50 variable characters	Any alpha-numeric	Yes	No
City	Customer's headquarter city	Town	Up to 20 variable characters	Any alpha-numeric	Yes	No
State	Customer's headquarter state	Province	Up to 20 variable characters	Any alpha-numeric	Yes	No
PostalCode	Customer's headquarter postal code	Zip code	Up to 10 variable characters	Any alpha-numeric	Yes	No
Country	Customer's headquarter country	Nation	Up to 50 variable characters	Any alpha-numeric	Yes	No
Contact	Customer's liaison person full name	customer	Up to 50 variable characters	Any alpha-numeric	Yes	No
Email	Liaison person's email address	Contact email	Up to 50 variable characters	Any alpha-numeric	Yes	No

Table 3.2 Sample attribute documentation

Note: Many data modeling tools include documentation more or less similar to the one shown. Some companies have their own specific format for collecting data.

Review Question 3.31
Which of the following is NOT a purpose good database modeling documentation can serve?
a. as a communication tool between the developers and the customers.
b. as a facilitator for the deployment of the system to production.
c. as a contract between developers and the customers
d. as help to reduce the cost and effort during the maintenance stage of the system.

3.9 Logical Model

The two major activities in constructing ERD of logical modeling are adding attributes to the entities and relationships and picking primary key for each entity.

In Section 2.8 Conceptual Model of the last chapter, you practiced 4 examples. In this section, you will see how you can make those conceptual models into logical models by adding attributes to each entity and relationship and selecting the primary key for each entity.

Logical model (ERD) Example 1:
The Career Center of Jefferson County offers in-demand IT skill courses to adult learners. They want to keep records of students and courses. A student has an ID, first name, and last name. A course has an ID, number, title, begin date and end date, and class time. Same course may be offered at the same time with different IDs. Each student will receive a grade when the student completes a course. Construct a logical model by adding attributes and selecting PK to the conceptual model example 1 of Chapter 2 (Section 2.8).

Business rules:

1. A student can take zero or many courses.

2. A course must have at least one student.

3. A student has an ID, first name, and last name.

4. A course has an ID, number, title, begin date, end date, and class time.

5. The relationship between a student and a course has a grade.

Logical ERD:

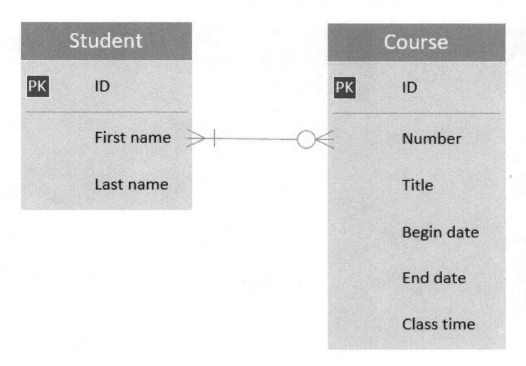

Conceptual model (ERD) Example 2:

The Career Center of Jefferson County offers in-demand IT skill courses to adult learners. They want to keep records of students, instructors, and courses. Write possible business rules and construct conceptual ERD.

Business rules:

1. A student can take zero or many courses.

2. A course must have at least one student.

3. An instructor can teach zero or many courses

4. A course has exactly one instructor.

5. A student has an ID, first name, and last name.

6. A course has an ID, number, title, begin date, end date, and class time.

7. An instructor has an ID, last name, and office.

8. The relationship between a student and a course has a grade.

Logical ERD:

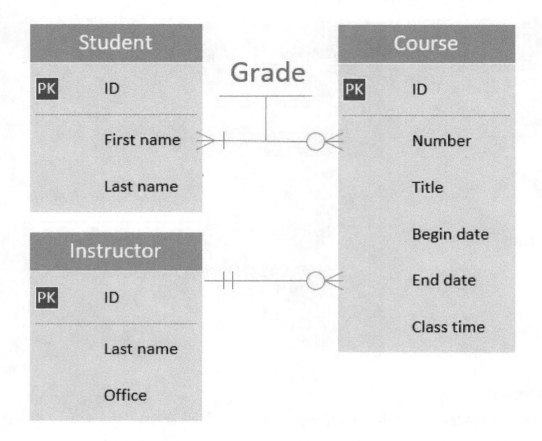

Conceptual model (ERD) Example 3:

The Career Center of Jefferson County offers in-demand IT skill courses to adult learners. They want to keep records of students, instructors, courses, and classrooms. Write possible business rules and construct conceptual ERD.

Business rules:

1. A student can take zero or many courses.

2. A course must have at least one student.

3. An instructor can teach zero or many courses

4. A course has exactly one instructor.

5. A course is assigned to exactly one classroom.

6. A classroom can be assigned to zero or many courses.

7. A student has an ID, first name, and last name.

8. A course has an ID, number, title, begin date, end date, and class time.

9. An instructor has an ID, last name, and office.

10. A classroom has a building name, room number, and seat capacity.

11. The relationship between a student and a course has a grade.

Logical ERD:

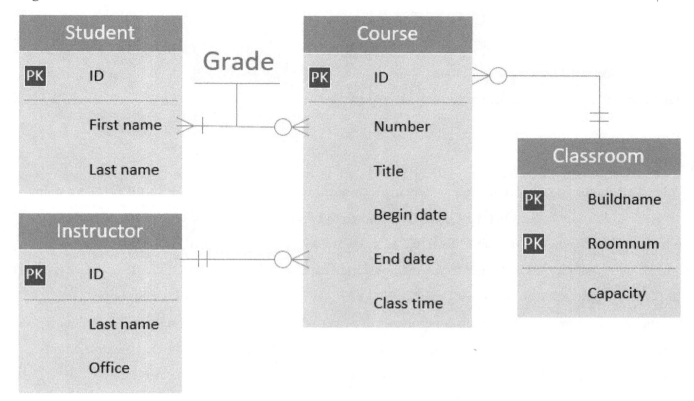

Conceptual model (ERD) Example 4:

Based on the business description and business rules of Case Example 2 (Section 2.2), write possible business rules and construct conceptual ERD.

Business Rules:

An employee may manage zero or many employees.

An employee may be managed by zero or one boss/employee.

An employee can complete zero or many orders.

An order must be completed by exactly one employee.

A customer can place zero or many orders.

An order must come from exactly one customer.

An order contains at least one product.

A product can appear in zero or many orders.

A product is provided by exactly one supplier.

A supplier may provide zero or many products.

An employee has employee ID, first name, last name, birth date, hire date, address, phone, and manager ID.

An order has an order ID and an order date.

A customer has an ID, name, address, contact, and email.

A product has an ID, name, and several deliveries. A delivery has an ID, quantity, price, and delivery date.

A supplier has an ID, name, and address.

The relationship between order and product has quantity and price.

Logical ERD:

Add all attributes and resolve the many-to-many relationship between ORDER and PRODUCT by adding an associative entity called ORDERDETAIL as shown in Figure 3.9. If you prefer, you can keep the M:N relationship between ORDER and PRODUCT. In Figure 3.9, omit the ORDERDETAIL entity and add "price" and "quantity" as attributes to the relationship between ORDER and PRODUCT.

In Figure 3.9, the Address attribute of the EMPLOYEE, CUSTOMER, and SUPPLIER entities are composite attributes which have the components of StreetAddress, City, State, PostalCode, and Country. In reality, you should replace the Address attribute with the five components listed above. However, in this book, we want the ERD to fit on one page, and so we just keep them as composite attributes.

Also, in Figure 3.9, you may notice that the Deliveries attribute of the PRODUCT entity is a composite multiple valued attribute. A delivery is made up of {DeliveryId, Quantity, Price, DeliveryDate} with the {} indicating that it is a multivalued attribute.

The many-to-many relationship between the ORDER and the PRODUCT is now replaced with two 1:M relationships. The following four business rules explain the two relationships:

An ORDER includes at least one ORDERDETAIL.

Each ORDERDETAIL must be included in exactly one ORDER.

A PRODUCT is contained in zero or many ORDERDETAIL.

Each ORDERDETAIL contains exactly one PRODUCT.

You may go back to Chapter 2 for the business rules for the relationship before the replacement.

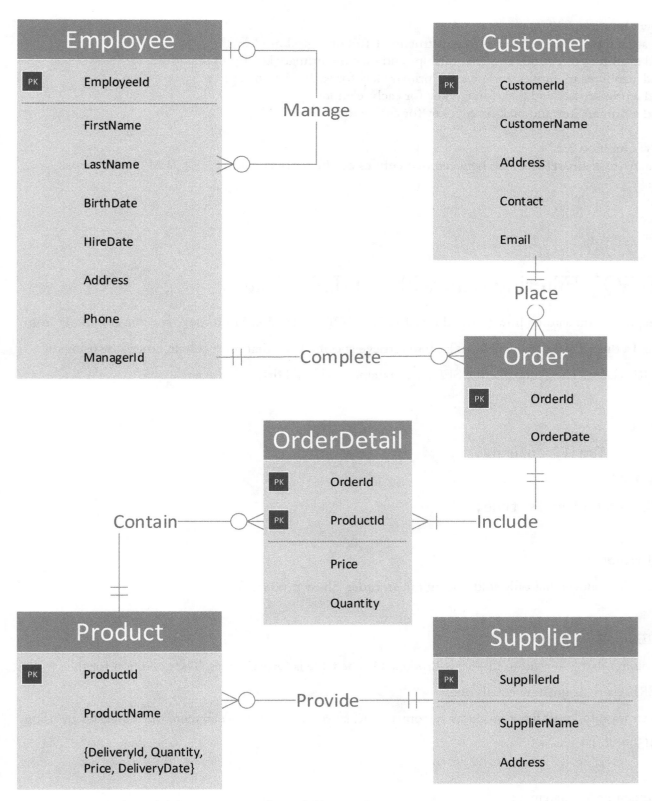

Figure 3.9 Logical model for case example 1 of Chapter 2

Review Question 3.32
What are the two major activities in constructing ERD of logical modeling?
a. Add attributes to entities and relationships and pick the primary key for each entity.
b. Add attributes to entities and pick the primary key for each relationship.
c. Add a primary key and pick foreign key for each relationship.
d. Add a primary key and pick foreign key for each entity.

Review Question 3.33
The many-to-many relationship between two entities can be replaced with _____ 1:M relationships.
a. one
b. two
c. three
d. four

3.10 SQL Filtering data with WHERE Clause

In Chapter 2, you learned how to use the SELECT ... FROM statement to retrieve specific column(s) from a table. In this chapter, you will learn how to retrieve specific rows that meet certain criteria by using the WHERE clause. The syntax for the SELECT statement with WHERE clause is:

```
SELECT Column1, Column2, ...
FROM Table
WHERE condition is true;
```

SQL Example 3.1
Display all products that only sold one unit in an order. Show product ID.

SQL Example 3.1 Analysis
The column that you want to display is ProductID. The table is OrderDetails. The condition for the WHERE clause is quantity equals one.
You just want to know what products customers buy, so you may want to eliminate the duplicates by using the DISTINCT keyword.

SQL Example 3.1 statement

```
SELECT DISTINCT ProductId
FROM Sales.OrderDetails
WHERE quantity = 1;
```

SQL Example 3.1 Output

	ProductId
1	1
2	2
3	6
4	7
5	8
6	9

SQL Example 3.2

Display all products that sold five or more units in an order. Show product ID.

SQL Example 3.2 Analysis

This is almost the same as Example 3.1 except that the filtering condition is different. Instead of finding "quantity = 1", you find "quantity >= 5".

You just want to know what products customers buy, so you may want to eliminate the duplicates by using the DISTINCT keyword.

SQL Example 3.2 statement

```
SELECT DISTINCT ProductId
FROM Sales.OrderDetails
WHERE quantity >= 5;
```

SQL Example 3.2 Output

	ProductId
1	3
2	4
3	6

SQL Example 3.3

Display all USA customers. Show customer name and email. Sort by customer name in alphabetic order.

SQL Example 3.3 Analysis

In order to find customers from the USA, you use the WHERE clause condition country = 'USA'. Note that the quotation mark indicates the value is a string. In the previous two examples, the conditions involved numbers, and didn't use quotation marks. Also note that it is a single quotation mark. You cannot use double quotation marks or no quotation marks.

The ORDER BY clause must appear after the WHERE clause.

SQL Example 3.3 statement

```
SELECT CustomerName, Email
FROM Sales.Customers
WHERE Country = 'USA'
ORDER BY CustomerName;
```

SQL Example 3.3 Output

	CustomerName	Email
1	Beyond Electronics	green@beil.com
2	Beyond Electronics	black1@be.com
3	E Fun	bgold@efun.com
4	Just Electronics	jwhite@je.com
5	Overstock E	dy@os.com

Review Question 3.34
The use of the WHERE clause allows you to _____.
a. retrieve specific rows(s) of a table
b. retrieve specific column(s) of a table
c. insert data in a specific row(s) of a table
d. insert data in a specific column(s) of a table

Review Question 3.35
What's wrong with the following SQL statement:
```
SELECT CustomerName, Email
FROM Sales.Customers
WHERE Country = "Mexico"
```
a. Mexico is not one of the countries for the practice database.
b. The double quotation marks should be removed.
c. Single quotation marks should replace the double quotation marks.
d. No errors.

3.11 SQL BETWEEN and IS NULL operators

You can use the BETWEEN operator for the WHERE condition if you want to select just those rows with a column value between two values, such as selecting all rows with a GPA between 3.0 and 4.0.

SQL Example 3.4

Display all employees who were born in the 1980s. Show first name, last name, and date of birth.

SQL Example 3.4 Analysis

The WHERE clause condition is between January 1, 1980 and December 31, 1989. You can use the BETWEEN operator. The BETWEEN operator includes both ending dates, but only to 12am of the last day, excluding the day. The operator will not cause any problems with the DATE data type. However, if the data type is DATETIME2, you should add an additional day for the ending date. Note how the date is treated like a string with quotation mark and format of 'yyyymmdd', such as '19891231' for December 31, 1989.

How do you know if a data type is DATE or DATETIME2? Go to Appendix B and check the value, does it include the time part in the value? If yes, then it is DATETIME2. Otherwise, it is DATE.

SQL Example 3.4 statement

```
SELECT FirstName, LastName, BirthDate
FROM HR.Employees
WHERE BirthDate BETWEEN '19800101' AND '19891231';
```

SQL Example 3.4 Output

	FirstName	LastName	BirthDate
1	Maria	Law	1988-07-13
2	Alice	Law	1988-12-13
3	Black	Hart	1982-11-09

SQL Example 3.5

Display all products with sale prices between $100.00 and $200.00. Show the product ID and sale price.

SQL Example 3.5 Analysis

This is just another example of using the BETWEEN operator.

SQL Example 3.5 statement

```
SELECT DISTINCT ProductId, Price
FROM Sales.OrderDetails
WHERE price BETWEEN 100.00 AND 200.00;
```

SQL Example 3.5 Output

	ProductId	Price
1	3	149.99
2	3	159.99
3	6	189.99
4	6	199.99
5	7	109.99

SQL Example 3.6

Display all customers that do not provide a contact name. Show customer name.

SQL Example 3.6 Analysis

When a customer does not provide a contact name, the value is NULL. You cannot use the equal sign (=) to compare if a column is NULL. You use the IS NULL operator.

SQL Example 3.6 statement

```
SELECT CustomerName
FROM Sales.Customers
WHERE contact IS NULL;
```

SQL Example 3.6 Output

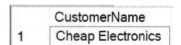

	CustomerName
1	Cheap Electronics

SQL Example 3.7

Display all customers that provide an email. Show customer name and email.

SQL Example 3.7 Analysis

The condition for this example is just the opposite of that in Example 3.6. You can use the IS NOT NULL operator.

SQL Example 3.7 statement

```
SELECT CustomerName, Email
FROM Sales.Customers
WHERE email IS NOT NULL;
```

SQL Example 3.7 Output

	CustomerName	Email
1	Just Electronics	jwhite@je.com
2	Beyond Electronics	green@beil.com
3	Beyond Electronics	black1@be.com
4	E Fun	bgold@efun.com
5	Overstock E	dy@os.com
6	E Fun	green@ef.com
7	Electronics4U	smith@e4u.com

Review Question 3.36
Select the SQL clause that is equivalent to the following SQL clause:
WHERE Price BETWEEN 100.0 And 200.0
a. WHERE Price >= 100.0 AND <= 200.0
b. WHERE Price >= 100.0 AND Price <= 200.0
c. WHERE Price > 100.0 AND < 200.0
d. WHERE Price > 100.0 AND Price < 200.0

Review Question 3.37
Which of the following SQL WHERE clause is correct for retrieving rows without email provided?
a. WHERE Email = NULL
b. WHERE Email IS NULL
c. WHERE Email = ""
d. WHERE Email = " "

Review Question 3.38
Suppose a student's date of birth is "2010-01-01 01:02:03 000001" in a database table. Which of the following filters correctly selects the rows of all students who were born in the first 10 days of 2011?
a. BETWEEN '2011-01-01' AND '2011-01-10'
b. BETWEEN '2010-12-31' AND '2011-01-10'
c. BETWEEN '2011-01-01' AND '2011-01-11'
d. BETWEEN '2010-12-31' AND '2011-01-11'

3.12 SQL Logical Operators, AND, OR, NOT.

When you have more than one condition in the WHERE clause, you can use a logical operator, such as AND, OR, and NOT to combine the conditions. Here's a list to show the result of the operator:

The result of the AND operator is TRUE only if both condition expressions are TRUE.

The result of the OR operator is TRUE if either condition expression is TRUE.

The result of the NOT operator reverses the value of the condition expression.

SQL Example 3.8

Display all products that are sold with unit price under $100.00 and over $1000.00. Show Product ID and sales price.

SQL Example 3.8 Analysis

There are two conditions in the problem. One is the price under $100 and the other is the price over $1000. You want the row if either condition is met. The logical OR operator will combine both in the result set.

SQL Example 3.8 statement

```
SELECT DISTINCT ProductId, Price
FROM Sales.OrderDetails
WHERE Price < 100.00 OR Price > 1000;
```

SQL Example 3.8 Output

	ProductId	Price
1	1	1499.99
2	2	1599.99
3	4	99.99
4	7	79.99
5	8	59.99
6	8	69.99
7	9	1449.99

SQL Example 3.9

Display all employees who were born before January 1, 1990 and hired after January 1, 2014. Show the employee's first name and last name.

SQL Example 3.9 Analysis

There are two conditions expressed in this problem. The first one was born before January 1, 1990 and the second one was hired after January 1, 2014. To meet both conditions, you use the AND logical operator.

SQL Example 3.9 statement

```
SELECT FirstName, LastName
FROM HR.Employees
WHERE BirthDate < '19900101' AND HireDate > '20140101';
```

SQL Example 3.9 Output

	FirstName	LastName
1	Black	Hart
2	Christina	Robinson

SQL Example 3.10

Display all products sold more than 1 unit in an order and that the sales price is either under $100.00 or over $1000.00. Show the product ID, units sold, and unit price.

SQL Example 3.10 Analysis

First, you want to retrieve all products sold from the OrderDetails with a quantity greater than one. Next, you filter out the rows by the price. Keep only those with prices less than $100 or over $1000. If you just put the three conditions expressed like this,

```
SELECT ProductId, Price, Quantity
FROM Sales.OrderDetails
WHERE Quantity > 1 AND Price < 100 OR Price > 1000;
```

You will get the wrong answer as shown below:

	ProductId	Price	Quantity
1	1	1499.99	1
2	1	1499.99	1
3	2	1599.99	1
4	4	99.99	6
5	8	69.99	2
6	9	1449.99	1
7	4	99.99	2
8	1	1499.99	1
9	8	59.99	2

You know the result is incorrect because several of them have a quantity equal to one. The problem is that the "AND" operator is higher ranked than the "OR" operator, which means the DBMS will execute the "AND" before executing the "OR". To solve this problem, you can use a parenthesis to force the OR operator to be performed first as shown below.

SQL Example 3.10 statement

```
SELECT ProductId, Price, Quantity
FROM Sales.OrderDetails
WHERE Quantity > 1 AND (Price < 100 OR Price > 1000);
```

SQL Example 3.10 Output

	ProductId	Price	Quantity
1	4	99.99	6
2	8	69.99	2
3	4	99.99	2
4	8	59.99	2

Review Question 3.39
What is the result of the following:
(5<3) AND (3<2) OR (4>3)
a. TRUE
b. FALSE
c. Cannot tell
d. an error

Review Question 3.40
What is the difference between the following two WHERE clause condition:
```
WHERE Quantity > 1 AND Price < 100 OR Price > 1000
WHERE Quantity > 1 AND (Price < 100 OR Price > 1000)
```
a. You must add a pair of parentheses when logical AND is in the clause.
b. You must add a pair of parentheses when logical OR is in the clause.
c. A pair of parentheses are always required for complicated conditions in the WHERE clause.
d. The "AND" operator is higher ranked than the "OR" operator.

3.13 Chapter Summary

In this chapter, you learned about logical data modeling. After you show the conceptual model to the user, you now add attributes to the entities and relationships, set the primary key to each entity, and optionally, you can result in any many-to-many relationship with two one-to-many relationships.

You also learned how to use SQL WHERE clause to retrieve rows that meet certain criteria. You learned how to use BETWEEN, IS NULL, AND, OR, NOT operators in the WHERE clause.

3.14 Discussion Questions

Discussion 3.1

When developing data models, some people suggest that you should have all entities identified before you add attributes to each entity, while others suggest that you include the attributes in each entity when you start the conceptual model. Explain the pros and cons for each approach.

Discussion 3.2

When determining the primary key for an entity, some people suggest that you should just use a surrogate key to save time. For example, for a STUDENT entity, just use StudentId as the primary key. For a BUILDING just use a BuildingId as a primary key. What are the pros and cons of such an approach?

Discussion 3.3

Many students do not like documentation for data modeling. What are the pros and cons of data modeling documentation?

3.15 Database Design Exercises

Exercise One:

A small publisher wants to keep data about its books and authors. A book has an ISBN, title, author(s), page count, genre(s), edition, retail price, and publishing year. An author has an author ID, first name, last name, and bio. ISBN is unique for books and author ID is unique for authors. Also, royalties are kept for each book and author(e.g. $100 for Book 1 and Author 1, $80 for Book 1 and Author 2). Write all business rules and draw a logical ERD for the publisher.

Exercise Two:

TennisAcademy is a small local tennis club that trains players from all skill levels and ages. The club needs a system to handle its player data.

A player has first name, last name, age, skill level, the date he or she joined the club, and, for some older players, their email and phone number.
A family has at least one player in the club. A family needs to pay an annual membership of $450.00, and provide a contact's first name, last name, email, and phone number.

There are different types of activities a player can participate in and each activity includes a practice fee. For example, a three-time-per-week activity costs $100 a month. An advanced private lesson costs $50 per hour.

All coaches at TennisAcademy are part time employees. They are paid different hourly rates based on their experience and their time with the club. A coach may be qualified to coach one or more activities and each activity may have more than one qualified coach.

Most players also participate in different types of tournaments. Each tournament can have none or multiple players in it. A tournament includes a name, start date and end date, fee, and location. The club also keeps record of the points (e.g. the first place in a more competitive tournament may earn 500 points while a local tournament champion may only count for 100 points) a player earns for a tournament.

Finally, the club encourages all players to play with each other for practice at a location and time of their own choice. However, one of the players needs to report the winner and date played.

Your task:

1. Extract all possible business rules.

2. Construct the logical model for the TennisAcademy.

3.16 SQL Exercises

Exercise 3.1

Display all products sold with the unit price of $149.99. Show product ID and unit price.

	ProductId	Price
1	3	149.99

Exercise 3.2

Display all products that are delivered more than 10 units at a time. Show product ID and units delivered in that delivery.

	ProductId	Quantity
1	4	20
2	5	15
3	6	25
4	7	12
5	7	18

Exercise 3.3

Display all UK customers. Show customer name and email. Sort customer name in alphabetic order.

	CustomerName	Email
1	E Fun	green@ef.com
2	Electronics4U	smith@e4u.com

Exercise 3.4

Display all products delivered in the first 9 days of October, 2016. Show product ID, quantity, and date.

	ProductId	Quantity	DeliveryDate
1	1	2	2016-10-01 09:30:00.0000000
2	2	10	2016-10-02 11:10:00.0000000
3	3	10	2016-10-05 09:15:00.0000000
4	4	20	2016-10-07 14:00:00.0000000
5	5	15	2016-10-07 15:30:00.0000000

Exercise 3.5

Display all products with supplier price between $100.00 and $200.00. Show the product ID, quantity, and price.

	ProductId	Quantity	Price
1	3	10	129.99
2	5	15	139.99
3	6	25	169.99

Exercise 3.6

Display all employees who do not provide a phone number. Show the employee's first name and last name.

	FirstName	LastName
1	Christina	Robinson
2	Nicholas	Pinkston

Exercise 3.7

Display all employees who provide a phone number. Show the employee's first name, last name, and phone number.

	FirstName	LastName	Phone
1	Alex	Hall	(434) 290-3322
2	Dianne	Hart	(434) 290-1122
3	Maria	Law	(434) 531-5673
4	Alice	Law	(434) 531-1010
5	Black	Hart	(434) 531-1034

Exercise 3.8

Display all products with supplier unit price under $100.00 or over $1000.00. Show Product ID and supplier price.

	ProductId	Price
1	1	1099.99
2	1	1199.99
3	2	1199.99
4	4	79.99
5	7	79.99
6	7	69.99

Exercise 3.9

Display all customers that placed orders before January 1, 2017 or After May 1, 2017. Show customer id and order date.

	CustomerId	OrderDate
1	1	2017-05-03
2	3	2017-05-08
3	5	2016-11-08
4	7	2016-12-23

Exercise 3.10

Display all products that are delivered more than 5 units at a time and the supplier price is either under $100.00 or over $1000.00. Show the product ID, supplier price, and delivery date.

	ProductId	Price	DeliveryDate
1	2	1199.99	2016-10-02 11:10:00.0000000
2	4	79.99	2016-10-07 14:00:00.0000000
3	7	79.99	2016-10-11 11:10:00.0000000
4	7	69.99	2016-10-12 09:50:00.0000000

3.17 Solutions to Review Questions

3.1 A; 3.2 A; 3.3 D; 3.4 B; 3.5 A; 3.6 B; 3.7 C; 3.8 D; 3.9 B; 3.10 C; 3.11 D; 3.12 C; 3.13 D; 3.14 B; 3.15 C; 3.16 C; 3.17 A; 3.18 D; 3.19 D; 3.20 D; 3.21 B; 3.22 B; 3.23 B; 3.24 A; 3.25 D; 3.26 A; 3.27 B; 3.28 C; 3.29 D; 3.30 A; 3.31 C; 3.32 A; 3.33 B; 3.34 A; 3.35 C; 3.36 B; 3.37 B; 3.38 C; 3.39 A; 3.40 D;

CHAPTER 4: ENHANCED DATA MODEL AND SQL FUNCTIONS

Chapter Learning Objectives

4.1 Construct enhanced entity relationship diagrams (EERD).

4.2 Explain entity inheritance.

4.3 Implement disjointness and completeness constraints on EERD.

4.4 Apply supertype subtype discriminator.

4.5 Use LIKE operator with single character and multiple character wildcards.

4.6 Use concatenations and aliases in the SELECT clause.

4.7 Use calculated fields in the SELECT clause.

4.8 Use functions to handle numbers and strings.

4.9 Use functions to handle date and time.

4.1 Enhanced Entity Relationship Diagram (EERD)

In the last two chapters, you learned how to model a database with an Entity Relationship Diagram (ERD). However, sometimes you may find the attributes and relationships to have many duplications. It is wise, then, to use an enhanced entity relationship diagram (EERD). EERD is an extension of ERD and allows you to model more complex data requirements than ERD can do.

Suppose there are two types of students in the mini-world: GRADUATE and UNDERGRADUATE. You have three options to model the mini-world.

The first option is to use just a STUDENT entity that includes both undergraduate students and graduate students. There will be two issues in this approach. One is that there will be many null values. For example, if you have an attribute called GRE score (Graduate Record Examination), then the field value will be null for all undergraduate students. Another issue pertains to relationships. For example, a certain relationship may only exist for undergraduate students, which also results in more null values.

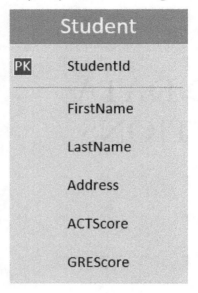

The second option is to replace the STUDENT entity with two entities, UNDERGRADUATE and GRADUATE? If you use this two-entity approach, you will have a model like this:

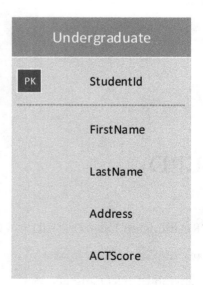 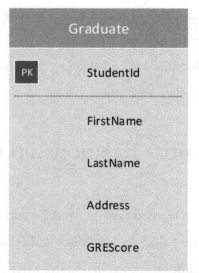

Figure 4.1 Use Undergraduate and graduate entities to replace the Student entity.

The problem for this approach is that there are many duplicated fields. As shown in Figure 4.1, you see that both entities contain FirstName, LastName, and Address attributes. In reality, there would be even more duplications. Duplication is often the major problem for maintenance.

To solve this problem, you can have a third option of modeling by choosing a third entity with all the common fields from UNDERGRADUATE and GRADUATE and put them in this new third entity. The new three-entity model looks like Figure 4.2. The duplication problem is solved because you have only one place to update.

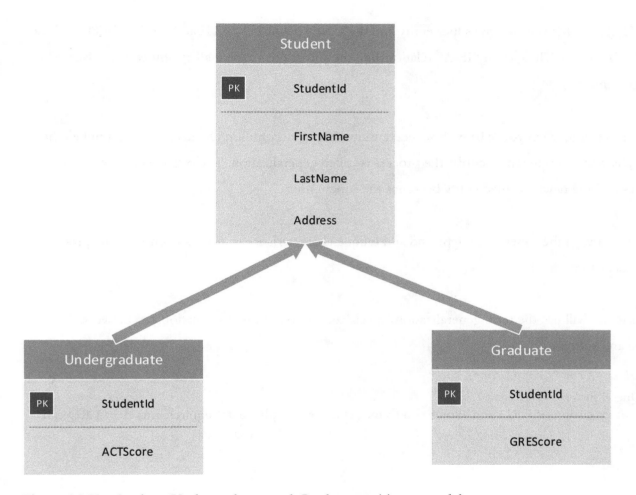

Figure 4.2 Use Student, Undergraduate, and Graduate entities to model.

Compare the model in Figure 4.2 and Figure 4.1. You can see that the duplicated attributes are all gone. The common/duplicated attributes are now only in the STUDENT entity. The UNDERGRADUATE and GRADUATE entities have their own unique attributes (except for the primary key, in this case student ID, which is expected to be shared.)

Such an arrangement allows the UNDERGRADUATE and GRADUATE entities to inherit attributes from the STUDENT entity. Both attributes and relationships of the STUDENT entity are inherited by UNDERGRADUATE and GRADUATE entities. And, the UNDERGRADUATE or GRADUATE entity can have its own relationship with other entities.

The relationship between the STUDENT and the UNDERGRADUATE and GRADUATE entities is called an "IS-A" relationship. In other words, an undergraduate student is a student, and a graduate student is a student, therefore allowing the UNDERGRADUATE and GRADUATE entities to inherit all attributes and relationships from the STUDENT entity.

The STUDENT entity is called the super entity and the UNDERGRADUATE and GRADUATE entities are called sub entities. Thus, in an "IS-A" relationship, the sub entities inherit all attributes and relationships of the super entity.

In EERD modeling, when you start with several entities that have common characteristics and put all those common characteristics in a new entity, the process is called generalization. The original entities become the sub entities and the newly formed entity becomes the super entity.

When you start with the super entity type and add unique characteristics to form sub entities, the process is called specialization.

In this book, we will use the term generalization/specialization to indicate the relationship between the super type and subtypes.

Review Question 4.1
EERD is an extension of ERD and allows you to model more complex data requirements than ERD can do.
a. True.
b. False

Review Question 4.2
Suppose there are UNDERGRADUATE and GRADUATE entities in the mini-world. What might be a problem if you combine the two entities into just one entity called STUDENT?
a. not enough entities to hold all attributes.
b. there may be many null values.
c. more entities are better than fewer entities.
d. too many attributes in just one entity.

Review Question 4.3
Suppose there are UNDERGRADUATE and GRADUATE entities in the mini-world. What might be a problem if you combine the two entities into just one entity called STUDENT?
a. There are not enough entities to hold all attributes.
b. This is not possible when a relationship is unique to the UNDERGRADUATE entity.
c. More entities are better than fewer entities.
d. There are too many attributes in just one entity.

Review Question 4.4

Suppose there are UNDERGRADUATE and GRADUATE entities in the mini-world. What might be a problem if you model with just the two entities?

a. There are not enough entities to hold all attributes.

b. This is not possible when a relationship is unique to the UNDERGRADUATE entity.

c. More entities are better than fewer entities.

d. Many duplicated attributes can cause maintenance issues.

Review Question 4.5

Suppose there are UNDERGRADUATE and GRADUATE entities in the mini-world. What might be an advantage if you model with three entities: UNDERGRADUATE, GRADUATE, and STUDENT?

a. There are fewer null values.

b. More attributes can be held with three entities.

c. More entities are better than fewer entities.

d. Three is a good number.

Review Question 4.6

Suppose there are UNDERGRADUATE and GRADUATE entities in the mini-world, and you pick all common attributes from both UNDERGRADUATE and GRADUATE entities and put them into a new entity called STUDENT. What do you call this new STUDENT entity?

a. associative entity

b. super entity

c. sub entity

d. composite entity

Review Question 4.7

Suppose there are UNDERGRADUATE and GRADUATE entities in the mini-world. You pick all common attributes from both UNDERGRADUATE and GRADUATE entities and put them into a new entity called STUDENT. What do you call the UNDERGRADUATE entity?

a. associative entity

b. super entity

c. sub entity

d. composite entity

Review Question 4.8

If you start with several entities that have common characteristics and put all those common characteristics in a new entity, the process is called _____.

a. common flow

b. one-to-many relationship

c. generalization

d. specialization

Review Question 4.9

If you start with the super entity type and add unique characteristics to form sub entities, the process is called _____.

a. common flow

b. one-to-many relationship

c. generalization

d. specialization

Review Question 4.10
When you model two entities as supertype and subtype, the subtype entity inherits _____.
a. all attributes and relationships of the super type entity.
b. some attributes and relationships of the super type entity.
c. all attributes of the super type entity.
d. all relationships of the super type entity.

Review Question 4.11
Suppose there are UNDERGRADUATE and GRADUATE entities in the mini-world. You pick all common attributes from both UNDERGRADUATE and GRADUATE entities and put them into a new entity called STUDENT. What is the relationship between the STUDENT the UNDERGRADUATE entities called?
a. EERD relationship
b. ERD relationship
c. STUDENT relationship
d. IS-A relationship

Review Question 4.12
Which of the following statements about EERD is correct?
a. A supertype is always a subtype
b. A subtype is always a supertype
c. A supertype is a subtype if you generalize
d. A subtype is a supertype if you generalize

4.2 Constraints

There are two types of constraints, or limitations, that can apply to a specialization/generalization between supertype and subtype entities. They are the disjointness constraint and the completeness constraint.

The disjointness constraint has two possible values: disjoint (specified by a character "d" in the circle in the diagram) or overlapping (specified by a character "o" in the circle in the diagram.) For a disjoint constraint, a super type entity instance can be a member of at most one of the subtypes of the specialization/generalization, while for an overlapping constraint, a super type entity instance can be a member of more than one subtype of the specialization/generalization relationship.

For example, if a student cannot be considered as both an undergraduate and graduate at the same time, then the constraint is disjoint. If a student can be considered as both an undergraduate and graduate at the same time, then the constraint is overlapping (some universities allow 5th year undergraduate students to be counted as both an undergraduate or graduate student.)

A completeness constraint is about whether a supertype instance must be one of the subtype instances. There are two possibilities. If a super type instance must be one of the subtype instances, the constraint is called total completeness, specified by a double line under the circle in the diagram. On the other hand, if a super type instance can be none of the subtype instances, the constraint is called partial completeness, specified by a single line under the circle in the diagram. For example, if a student must be one or both undergraduate and graduate, then the constraint is total completeness. On the other hand, if a student has not registered for any classes yet, they are neither an undergraduate nor graduate student, and so the constraint is partial completeness.

An example of EERD is displayed below assuming the following business rules: A student cannot be both an undergraduate and a graduate at the same time (this is a disjoint constraint and is indicated as a letter "d" inside the circle.) A student can also be neither undergraduate nor graduate (a student that does not register for any course for the current semester is still a student, but not an undergraduate nor graduate. This is a partial completeness constraint and is indicated as a single line under the circle in the figure.)

Similar to regular ERD, EERD should also be based on business rules. The business rules for the following EERD are: A student cannot be both an undergraduate and a graduate.

A student can be neither an undergraduate nor a graduate.

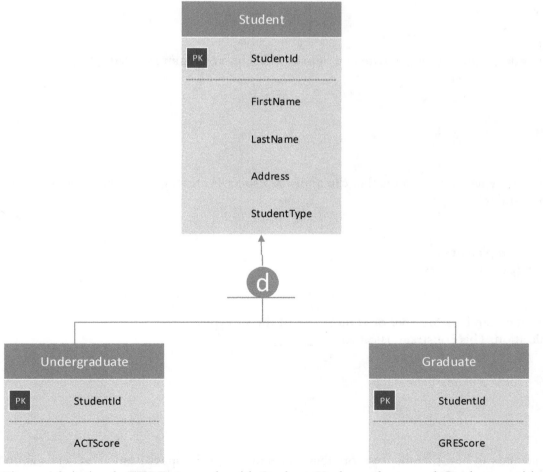

Figure 4.3 A simple EERD example with Student, Undergraduate, and Graduate entities.

Review Question 4.13
A student cannot be both an undergraduate and a graduate in a mini-world. This constraint is called
_____.
a. disjoint
b. overlapping
c. total completeness
d. partial completeness

Review Question 4.14
A student can be both an undergraduate and a graduate in a mini-world. This constraint is called _____.
a. disjoint
b. overlapping
c. total completeness
d. partial completeness

Review Question 4.15
A student can be neither an undergraduate nor a graduate in a mini-world. This constraint is called
_____.
a. disjoint
b. overlapping
c. total completeness
d. partial completeness

Review Question 4.16
A student must be an undergraduate or a graduate in a mini-world. This constraint is called _____.
a. disjoint
b. overlapping
c. total completeness
d. partial completeness

Review Question 4.17
Which of the following are types of constraints that can apply to a specialization/generalization between
supertype and subtype entities?
a. disjointness
b. completeness
c. both disjointness and completeness
d. neither disjointness nor completeness

Review Question 4.18
A super type entity instance can be a member of at most one of the subtypes of the
specialization/generalization. This constraint is called _____.
a. disjoint
b. overlapping
c. total completeness
d. partial completeness

Review Question 4.19
A super type entity instance can be a member of more than one subtype of the specialization/generalization
relationship. This constraint is called _____.
a. disjoint

b. overlapping
c. total completeness
d. partial completeness

Review Question 4.20
If a super type instance must be one of the subtype instances, the constraint is called _____.
a. disjoint
b. overlapping
c. total completeness
d. partial completeness

Review Question 4.21
If a super type instance can be none of the subtype instances, the constraint is called _____.
a. disjoint
b. overlapping
c. total completeness
d. partial completeness

Review Question 4.22
In EERD, the character d in the circle indicates _____.
a. disjoint
b. overlapping
c. total completeness
d. partial completeness

Review Question 4.23
In EERD, the character o in the circle indicates _____.
a. disjoint
b. overlapping
c. total completeness
d. partial completeness

Review Question 4.24
In EERD, a double line under the circle indicates _____.
a. disjoint
b. overlapping
c. total completeness
d. partial completeness

Review Question 4.25
In EERD, a single line under the circle indicates _____.
a. disjoint
b. overlapping
c. total completeness
d. partial completeness

4.3 Subtype Discriminator

One problem with creating a supertype is that it can be hard to identify which subtype a supertype instance belongs to. For example, along with the undergraduate/graduate example, an instance under the student entity gives the student's name and identification, but does not indicate which subtype the student belongs to, undergraduate or graduate. Therefore, you need a discriminator, which is an attribute for the supertype entity used to identify which subtype an instance belongs to. In the student example, the discriminator could be an attribute under the student entity called StudentType, in which the student is either shown to be an 'undergraduate', 'graduate', both or neither. In the case of Figure 4.3, the domain for the student type is "undergraduate" and "graduate".

The connectivity between the supertype and each subtype is 1:1. This 1:1 relationship only exists between the supertype and each subtype. In other words, we cannot label relationships between the supertype and multiple subtypes. Thus, a student who is both an undergraduate and a graduate experiences two connectivity relationships: a 1:1 between student and undergraduate, and a 1:1 between student and graduate.

A discriminator is a single attribute when the disjointness constraint between the supertype and subtype is disjoint. The discriminator is a multivalued attribute when the disjointness constraint is overlapping. For example, if a student can only be an undergraduate or a graduate (a disjoint constraint,) a discriminator is a single attribute called studenttype with the attribute domain of "undergraduate" and "graduate". The example in Figure 4.3 illustrates the situation.

If a student can be both undergraduate and graduate at the same time (an overlapping constraint,) the discriminators are two attributes, an undergraduate attribute and a graduate attribute, in which both have the attribute domain of "yes" and "no".

Review Question 4.26
In order to know which subtype the supertype instance belongs to, the supertype needs a _____ as an attribute.
a. subtype indicator
b. supertype indicator
c. subtype discriminator
d. supertype discriminator

Review Question 4.27
The connectivity between the supertype and subtype is _____.
a. one-to-one
b. one-to-many
c. many-to-many

d. one-to-two

Review Question 4.28
How many subtype discriminators are needed when the disjointness constraint between the supertype and subtype is disjoint?
a. 1
b. 2
c. 3
d. cannot tell
Review Question 4.29
Suppose a supertype has two subtypes. If the disjointness constraint is overlapping, how many subtype discriminators are needed?
a. 1
b. 2
c. 3
d. cannot tell

4.4 An Example of Using EERD

LearningByDoing University needs a database to keep track of its personnel. It has the following business description:

The university has several colleges, such as College of Business and College of Engineering. Each person is associated with only one college. There are three types of persons: employee, student, and alumni. A person can belong to one, two, or all three types. For example, an alumnus can be an employee of the university and also take courses as a student to update knowledge. A person must be at least one of the three. Each person has a name, social security number, address, date of birth, and email. Every person works for one of the colleges (Arts and Sciences, the engineering school, etc.)

There are two types of employees: faculty and staff. An employee must be either faculty or staff, but cannot be both. Each employee has a date hired. A faculty member has a rank level, such as full professor. A staff member has a staff position, such as student advisor. Staff members also have a salary.

An alumna/alumnus has a degree year, such as 2022.

There are two types of students, undergraduate and graduate. A student can be neither undergraduate nor graduate, for example, a non-degree student. A student can be undergraduate or graduate. And, a student can be both undergraduate and graduate. Each student has a GPA.

An undergraduate student has a class standing which determines what courses she or he can take. A graduate student has major research interests.

A logical EERD may look like:

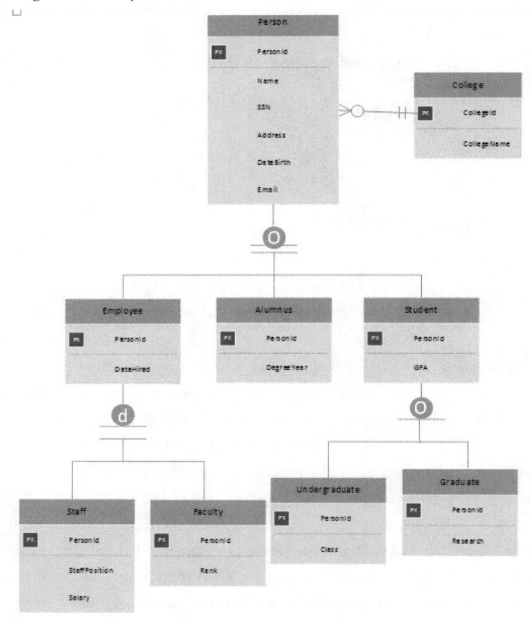

Figure 4.4. An example of EERD.

4.5 Figure 4.4 Example Explanation:

A person has to be at least one of the three types (Employee, Alumnus, Student) which suggests that the disjointness constraint is overlapping (character "o" in the figure) and the completeness constraint is total completeness (double lines under the circle in the figure).

An employee has to be exactly one of the two types (staff and faculty) which suggests that the disjointness constraint is disjoint (character "d" in the figure) and the completeness constraint is total completeness (double lines under the circle in the figure).

A student can be neither or both types (undergraduate and graduate) which suggests that the disjointness constraint is overlapping (character "o" in the figure) and the completeness constraint is partial completeness (single line under the circle in the figure).

4.6 SQL LIKE Operator

Sometimes, the filtering condition in the WHERE clause may not be an exact match for a string. For example, if you search for a customer name, you may only know part of their name. In this case, you may still use the WHERE clause to filter the rows by using the LIKE operator.

SQL Example 4.1

Display all customers that have the word "Electronics" in its name. Show the customer name and their country of origin.

SQL Example 4.1 Analysis

In the WHERE clause, instead of using WHERE CustomerName = 'Electronics', you can use WHERE CustomerName LIKE '%electronics%'. LIKE is a keyword that you use when you don't have an exact string. The percentage % sign indicates that there may be any number of characters.

So in this case, the rows with customer names containing anything before and after the word "electronics" will be displayed. The string is not case sensitive in SQL Server by default.

SQL Example 4.1 statement

```
SELECT CustomerName, Country
```

```
FROM Sales.Customers
WHERE CustomerName LIKE '%electronics%';
```

SQL Example 4.1 Output

	CustomerName	Country
1	Just Electronics	USA
2	Beyond Electronics	USA
3	Beyond Electronics	USA
4	Electronics4U	UK
5	Cheap Electronics	Canada

SQL Example 4.2

Display all customers that are in the USA, and if their state abbreviation has an 'A' as the second letter. Show customer name and country.

SQL Example 4.2 Analysis

Similar to Example 4.1, this time you know exactly how many letters are missing and where the missing letter is (the first letter is missing). In this case, you can use an underscore (_) to indicate a missing letter. You can use an underscore to indicate one missing character in any string. You can use the underscore as many times as you like, each one indicating one unknown character.

SQL Example 4.2 statement

```
SELECT CustomerName, Country
FROM Sales.Customers
WHERE Country = 'USA' AND State LIKE '_A';
```

SQL Example 4.2 Output

	CustomerName	Country
1	Beyond Electronics	USA
2	E Fun	USA
3	Overstock E	USA

Review Question 4.30
In the SQL SELECT statement, when the filtering condition in the WHERE clause is not an exact match for a string, you can use the _____ operator.
a. partial match
b. equal
c. wildcard
d. LIKE

Review Question 4.31
In the SQL SELECT statement, when the filtering condition in the WHERE clause has LIKE operator, the % stands for _____.
a. one unknown character
b. any number of unknown characters
c. percentage
d. really like

Review Question 4.32
In the SQL SELECT statement, when the filtering condition in the WHERE clause has LIKE operator, the "_" stands for _____.
a. one unknown character
b. any number of unknown characters
c. one variable
d. really like

4.7 SQL Concatenate Fields and Use Alias

Sometimes you may want to combine fields as you retrieve them. For example, you can combine the first name and last name of an employee and make it a full name. This is called concatenating. You use the + sign to concatenate, such as FirstName+ ' ' + LastName. You combine the first name and last name with a space in between. You are not limited to using a space. For example, FirstName+'-'+LastName will add a dash sign between the first name and last name

When you do the concatenation, you often need to rename the column head. In the above example, it is no longer appropriate to call the combined result either first name or last name. Instead, you may want to call it 'full name.' This is called using an alias. You use the keyword AS to add an alias. For example, FirstName + ' ' + LastName AS FullName.
If you want the column head to have more than one word, such as Full Name with a space in it, you will have to use either a quotation mark (either single or double) or a square bracket [] surrounding the alias words, for example FirstName + ' ' + LastName AS 'Full Name' or FirstName + ' ' + LastName AS "Full Name", or FirstName + ' ' + LastName AS [Full Name].

SQL Example 4.3
Display all employees' full names, which is the first name plus the last name with a space in between.

SQL Example 4.3 Analysis

You will need two columns, the FirstName and LastName columns. Then use a plus sign to combine them. Remember to add a space in the middle.

SQL Example 4.3 statement

```
SELECT FirstName + ' ' + LastName
FROM HR.Employees;
```

SQL Example 4.3 Output

	(No column name)
1	Alex Hall
2	Dianne Hart
3	Maria Law
4	Alice Law
5	Black Hart
6	Christina Robinson
7	Nicholas Pinkston

SQL Example 4.4

Same as SQL Example 4.3, but this time use a more meaningful column head called "Full Name".

SQL Example 4.4 Analysis

The only thing new is that you add the alias by using the keyword AS. Note that the AS keyword is optional. We suggest that you use it to make it read easier.

SQL Example 4.4 statement

```
SELECT FirstName + ' ' + LastName AS "Full Name"
FROM HR.Employees;
```

SQL Example 4.4 Output

	Full Name
1	Alex Hall
2	Dianne Hart
3	Maria Law
4	Alice Law
5	Black Hart
6	Christina Robinson
7	Nicholas Pinkston

Review Question 4.33
Suppose a table has a postalCode field, which is a five-digit string and a plus4 field which is a four-digit string. Write the SELECT clause that will display the zip+4 in the format of 12345-1234.
a. SELECT 12345-1234
b. SELECT postalCode, plus4
c. SELECT postalCode, -, plus4
d. SELECT postalCode + '-' + plus4

Review Question 4.34
Suppose a table has studentName and nickName fields. Write the SELECT clause that will display the name and nickname in the format of Lisa Smith (Liz).
a. SELECT studentName, nickName
b. SELECT studentName (nickName)
c. SELECT studentName + (nickName)
d. SELECT studentName + ' ('+nickName+')'

Review Question 4.35
Suppose a table has a postalCode field and you want the field header to display Postal Code. What is the correct SELECT clause?
a. SELECT postalCode
b. SELECT Postal Code
c. SELECT postalCode AS "Postal Code"
d. SELECT postalCode AS Postal Code

4.8 Calculated Fields

You not only can concatenate several fields into one with any strings (e.g. space) added, but you can also operate on these fields. For example, every product delivery includes the quantity and unit price. You can calculate the monetary value of each delivery by multiplying the quantity with the unit price.

SQL Example 4.5
Calculate the monetary value of each product delivery. Show all delivery IDs, product IDs, quantities, unit prices, and delivery monetary values (quantity x price.)

SQL Example 4.5 Analysis
Similar to the concatenation, you just add quantity * price AS "Monetary Value" in the column list of the SELECT. Remember to add the alias to make the display more meaningful. The keyword "AS" is optional.

SQL Example 4.5 statement

```
SELECT DeliveryId, ProductId, Quantity, Price, Quantity*Price AS "Monetary
Value"
FROM Purchasing.Deliveries;
```

SQL Example 4.5 Output

	DeliveryId	ProductId	Quantity	Price	Monetary Value
1	1	1	2	1099.99	2199.98
2	2	1	5	1199.99	5999.95
3	3	2	10	1199.99	11999.90
4	4	3	10	129.99	1299.90
5	5	4	20	79.99	1599.80
6	6	5	15	139.99	2099.85
7	7	6	25	169.99	4249.75
8	8	7	12	79.99	959.88
9	9	7	18	69.99	1259.82

SQL Example 4.6

The product 1's supplier decided to give Product 1 a 10% discount. Show delivery ID, product ID, regular price and discounted price.

SQL Example 4.6 Analysis

In the SELECT columns, you should add a new calculated column which is Price * 0.9.

SQL Example 4.6 statement

```
SELECT DeliveryId, ProductId, Price AS "Regular Price", Price *0.9 AS "Sale
Price"
FROM Purchasing.Deliveries
WHERE ProductId = 1;
```

SQL Example 4.6 Output

	DeliveryId	ProductId	Regular Price	Sale Price
1	1	1	1099.99	989.99100
2	2	1	1199.99	1079.99100

Review Question 4.36
If a table has two numeric fields, X1 and X2, which of the following SELECT clauses is NOT valid?
a. SELECT X1+X2 AS Sum
b. SELECT 2X1 AS DoubleValue

c. SELECT X1-X2 AS DifferentValue

d. SELECT 2X1

4.9 Use Functions to Handle Number and Strings

In SQL Example 4.6's output, you may notice that the "Sale Price" contains five decimal places. To display only two decimal places, you may need a function called CAST(). There are many such functions in SQL. For example: An UPPER() function will change a string to all uppercase.

The CHARINDEX() function allows you to search for a specific expression in another expression. The return will be the starting position. For example, you can search for "go" in "go to a good school". The result will be 1. Every character counts, including the space. You can also specify where to start your search. In the above example, if you want to start the search from position 2, the result will be 9 because the first "go" will be ignored as it starts the search at position 2. By default, the search is case-insensitive.

Syntax:

CHARINDEX('expression to find', 'expression to search', start_location)

For example:

CHARINDEX('e', CustomerName, 3) will return the position of the first "e" in the customer's name beginning from the third letter. If the customerName is "electronic store", the returned value will be 3. If a match is not found, the returned value will be 0.

SUBSTRING() function can be used to return part of a character, binary, text, or image expression.

Syntax:

SUBSTRING('expression', start, length)

The 'expression' is the string you want to extract from.

The start is an integer number that specifies where the returned string starts.

The length is an integer number that specifies how many characters are in the returned string.

For example:

SUBSTRING('George Washington', 8, 10) will return the string of "Washington"

SUBSTRING('George Washington', 1, 6) will return the string of "George".

SQL Example 4.7

Same as SQL Example 4.6. This time, you should display only two decimal places for the "Sale Price" column.

SQL Example 4.7 Analysis

The syntax for CAST() function is

CAST(expression AS DataType)

In this example, you cast the sale price to a numeric data type that can take up to 7 digits with 2 decimal places.

SQL Example 4.7 statement

```
SELECT DeliveryId, ProductId, Price AS "Regular Price", CAST(Price *0.9 AS
NUMERIC(7, 2)) AS "Sale Price"
FROM Purchasing.Deliveries
WHERE ProductId = 1;
```

SQL Example 4.7 Output

	DeliveryId	ProductId	Regular Price	Sale Price
1	1	1	1099.99	989.99
2	2	1	1199.99	1079.99

SQL Example 4.8

Display customer name and its headquarter country with the country name in all capital letters.

SQL Example 4.8 Analysis

Use UPPER() function to convert the country name to all capital letters.

SQL Example 4.8 statement

```
SELECT CustomerName, UPPER(Country) AS Country
FROM Sales.Customers;
```

SQL Example 4.8 Output

	CustomerName	Country
1	Just Electronics	USA
2	Beyond Electronics	USA
3	Beyond Electronics	USA
4	E Fun	USA
5	Overstock E	USA
6	E Fun	UK
7	Electronics4U	UK
8	Cheap Electronics	CANADA

SQL Example 4.9

Find the position of the first "e" in a customer's name. Show customer name and the position of "e".

SQL Example 4.9 Analysis

Use the CHARINDEX() function to find the position. The search starts from the first position so you don't need to specify the starting position. Just provide the string to search for

SQL Example 4.9 statement

```
SELECT CustomerName, CHARINDEX('e', CustomerName) AS "Position of e"
FROM Sales.Customers;
```

SQL Example 4.9 Output

	CustomerName	Position of e
1	Just Electronics	6
2	Beyond Electronics	2
3	Beyond Electronics	2
4	E Fun	1
5	Overstock E	3
6	E Fun	1
7	Electronics4U	1
8	Cheap Electronics	3

SQL Example 4.10

Find the position of the first "e" and second "e" in a customer's name. Show customer name and the position of the first "e" and second "e" in the customer's name. If the name does not contain one or two e's, show 0.

SQL Example 4.10 Analysis

Display the customer name and the position of the first "e" is the task of SQL Example 4.9. The only new task is to add a new column to display the position of the second "e". You will still use the CHARINDEX() function, but this time, you cannot begin the search from position 1. You have to start the search after the position of the first "e". You already know the location of the first "e", so just add a number 1 to it as CHARINDEX('e', CustomerName)+1 for start_location.

SQL Example 4.10 statement

```
SELECT CustomerName, CHARINDEX('e', CustomerName) AS "Position of e",
CHARINDEX('e', CustomerName, CHARINDEX('e', CustomerName)+1) AS "Position of
second e"
FROM Sales.Customers;
```

SQL Example 4.10 Output

	CustomerName	Position of e	Position of second e
1	Just Electronics	6	8
2	Beyond Electronics	2	8
3	Beyond Electronics	2	8
4	E Fun	1	0
5	Overstock E	3	11
6	E Fun	1	0
7	Electronics4U	1	3
8	Cheap Electronics	3	7

SQL Example 4.11

Display all characters between the first two e's in a customer's name. For example, for the customer "Cheap Electronics", the characters between the first two e's are "ap ". Show customer name and the characters between the first two e's.

SQL Example 4.11 Analysis

Use SUBSTRING() function to extract all characters between the first two e's. You need to know the start location, which is the example in SQL Example 4.9. You also need the number of characters between the two e's which is the location of the second "e" minus the location of the first "e" minus 1.

For example, the number of characters between the two e's in "Cheap Electronics" is 3 (include a space). The location of the second "e" is 7. The location of the first "e" is 3. So the number of characters between the two e's are 7-3-1 = 3.

SQL Example 4.10 is about the location of the second "e".

You cannot show the characters between the two e's for customers who don't have two e's. So, you need to add a WHERE clause to filter out those who don't have two e's in the name by using
WHERE CustomerName LIKE '%e%e%';

SQL Example 4.11 statement

```
SELECT CustomerName, SUBSTRING(CustomerName, CHARINDEX('e', CustomerName)+1,
CHARINDEX('e', CustomerName, CHARINDEX('e', CustomerName)+1)-CHARINDEX('e',
CustomerName)-1 ) AS "Characters between the two e"
FROM Sales.Customers
WHERE CustomerName LIKE '%e%e%';
```

SQL Example 4.11 Output (Note that it is difficult to see the ending space in the string)

	CustomerName	Characters between the two e
1	Just Electronics	l
2	Beyond Electronics	yond
3	Beyond Electronics	yond
4	Overstock E	rstock
5	Electronics4U	l
6	Cheap Electronics	ap

Review Question 4.37
What is the purpose of the following WHERE clause?
WHERE CustomerName LIKE '%e%e%'
a. Retrieve only rows with a percentage sign in a customer name.
b. Retrieve only rows with three percentage signs in a customer name.
c. Retrieve only rows with two "e"s in a customer name.
d. Retrieve only rows with both "e"s and percentage signs in a customer name.

Review Question 4.38
What will be the result of the following function?
SUBSTRING('Lucy Scott', 1, 6)
a. Lucy
b. Lucy S
c. ucy S
d. ucy Sc

Review Question 4.39
What will be the result of the following function?
CHARINDEX('t', 'Lucy Scott', 3)
a. 2
b. 3

c. 9

d. 10

4.10 Use Functions to Handle Date and Time

The GETDATE() function will return today's date. You can often use it to calculate how many years/days/weeks have passed.

You can use the DATEDIFF() function to calculate the difference between two dates. The syntax is DATEDIFF(day, startdate, enddate)

The function will return the difference in days between the two dates. If you change the day to month, it will return the difference in number of months between the two dates. However, the calculation only considers the difference of months, not how much time is between. For example, between January 31st and February 1st, there is a one month difference. Between January 1st and January 31st, there is a zero month difference, so the actual time passed is not necessarily considered.

DATEDIFF(month, '20170601', '20170630') will return zero because the two dates are in the same month, while DATEDIFF(month, '20170630', '20170701') will return 1 because the two dates are in different months.

You can also change the day to year so that the function will return the number of years between two dates.

YEAR(date) will return the year of the date value. For example: YEAR('20160912') will return 2016. Similarly, MONTH('20160912') will return 9 and DAY('20160912') will return 12.

DATEFROMPARTS(year, month, day) function allows you to construct a new date from the three integers of year, month, and day as long as the three integers are valid (for example, you cannot insert 42 for the day value.)

SQL Example 4.12

Display today's date and the number of months the employee has worked for the company. Show the employee's first name, last name, today's date, and the number of months the employee has worked.

SQL Example 4.12 Analysis

In order to get today's date, you will use the GETDATE() function. To get the month difference between the date the employee was hired and today's date, you use the DATEDIFF() function.

SQL Example 4.12 statement

```
SELECT FirstName, LastName, HireDate, GETDATE() AS "Today's Date",
DATEDIFF(month, HireDate, GETDATE()) AS "Months Worked"
FROM HR.Employees;
```

SQL Example 4.12 Output (Note: the number of months worked will be different from yours because it depends on today's date)

	FirstName	LastName	HireDate	Today's Date	Months Worked
1	Alex	Hall	2015-08-09	2021-01-30 09:45:20.507	65
2	Dianne	Hart	2010-08-01	2021-01-30 09:45:20.507	125
3	Maria	Law	2012-08-21	2021-01-30 09:45:20.507	101
4	Alice	Law	2012-04-22	2021-01-30 09:45:20.507	105
5	Black	Hart	2015-04-12	2021-01-30 09:45:20.507	69
6	Christina	Robinson	2014-06-15	2021-01-30 09:45:20.507	79
7	Nicholas	Pinkston	2013-05-22	2021-01-30 09:45:20.507	92

SQL Example 4.13

Same as SQL Example 4.14. This time, show today's date without the time part.

SQL Example 4.13 Analysis

No new functions are necessary to accomplish this task. Recall the use of CAST() function in SQL Example 4.7. You just need to cast the data type to date.

SQL Example 4.13 statement

```
SELECT FirstName, LastName, HireDate, CAST(GETDATE() AS DATE) AS "Today's
Date", DATEDIFF(month, HireDate, GETDATE()) AS "Months Worked"
FROM HR.Employees;
```

SQL Example 4.13 Output (Note: the number of months worked will be different from yours because it depends on today's date)

	FirstName	LastName	HireDate	Today's Date	Months Worked
1	Alex	Hall	2015-08-09	2021-01-30	65
2	Dianne	Hart	2010-08-01	2021-01-30	125
3	Maria	Law	2012-08-21	2021-01-30	101
4	Alice	Law	2012-04-22	2021-01-30	105
5	Black	Hart	2015-04-12	2021-01-30	69
6	Christina	Robinson	2014-06-15	2021-01-30	79
7	Nicholas	Pinkston	2013-05-22	2021-01-30	92

SQL Example 4.14

Display all employees who were born in December of any year. Show the employee's first name, last name, and date of birth.

SQL Example 4.14 Analysis

To find out the month of an employee's date of birth, use the MONTH() function by passing the date of birth to the function.

SQL Example 4.14 statement

```
SELECT FirstName, LastName, BirthDate
FROM HR.Employees
WHERE MONTH(BirthDate) = 12;
```

SQL Example 4.14 Output

	FirstName	LastName	BirthDate
1	Dianne	Hart	1978-12-03
2	Alice	Law	1988-12-13

SQL Example 4.15

Display all employees' birth month and year. Show employees' first name, last name, and the month and year of birth. To hide the day of birth, use the first day of the month for all employees.

SQL Example 4.15 Analysis

You can still use the BirthDate column of the employees table. Just replace the day of the month with the first day of the month and keep the actual month and year. The DATEFROMPARTS() function can be used.

SQL Example 4.15 statement

```
SELECT FirstName, LastName, DATEFROMPARTS(YEAR(BirthDate), MONTH(BirthDate),
1) AS BirthMonth
FROM HR.Employees;
```

SQL Example 4.15 Output

	FirstName	LastName	BirthMonth
1	Alex	Hall	1990-02-01
2	Dianne	Hart	1978-12-01
3	Maria	Law	1988-07-01
4	Alice	Law	1988-12-01
5	Black	Hart	1982-11-01
6	Christina	Robinson	1978-07-01
7	Nicholas	Pinkston	1977-10-01

Review Question 4.40
Which T-SQL function returns today's date?
a. TODAY()
b. GETDATE()
c. CURRENT()
d. TODAYDATE()

4.11 Chapter Summary

In this chapter, you learned how to use an enhanced entity relationship diagram to model the mini-world with entities that allow inheritance of attributes and relationships. When you have two or more entities that share many attributes or relationships, you should consider using EERD.

You also learned how to use functions in the SQL SELECT clause. You can use t-sql functions to change data format, retrieve data, and manipulate fields for displaying. The functions covered in this chapter are only a small part of all t-sql functions. Also note that functions in SQL are one of the least versatile (it may or may not work with other DBMS).

4.12 Discussion Questions

Discussion 4.1

Compare the EERD you learned in this chapter with the ERD you learned in the previous chapters. What do you think are the advantages and disadvantages of EERD?

Discussion 4.2

Explain the differences between specialization and generalization in EERD design. Which one would you recommend under which situation? Why?

Discussion 4.3

A subtype discriminator is one or more attributes of the supertype. When would you just add one attribute for the discriminator and when would you add multiple attributes for the discriminator?

Discussion 4.4

Suppose the Graduate entity has a GRE attribute and the Undergraduate entity has an ACT attribute. Is it possible to count the two attributes as the same attribute in the supertype entity, say, Student, as TestScore? Why or why not?

4.13 Database Design Exercises

Exercise One:

A small publisher wants to keep data about its books. A book has an ISBN, title, author(s), page count, genre(s), edition, retail price, and publishing year. An author has an author ID, first name, last name, and bio. Also, royalties are kept for each book and author. A book has three to four reviewers but only one editor. A reviewer is a volunteer who has a reviewer ID, first name, last name, and date that he or she reviews a book. An editor is an employee who has an employee ID, first name, last name, and all the books he or she edits. Write all business rules and draw a logical EERD for the publisher.

Exercise Two:

The following narrative describes a simplified version of a local bank. There are about two dozen branches of the bank located in a Midwest state. Each branch has an address and a branch manager. Each branch also has 10 to 30 employees. Employee data includes name, office, and supervisor. Each branch offers several different types of accounts for its customers.

There are four different types of accounts. Three of them bear interest. They are savings accounts, money market deposit accounts (MMDAs), and certificates of deposits (CDs). The MMDA and CD includes a penalty if minimum requirements are not met. The non-interest account is the checking account.

All accounts have account numbers and balance. The interest-bearing accounts include the interest rate and the amount of interest earned. For the MMDA and CD account, the penalty amount is tracked. The checking account keeps track of each check written. A check has an amount and date. A CD account has a maturity date.

Each branch also offers several different types of loans for its customers. All loans have a loan amount and maturity date.

A CD secured loan includes the CD account number. Vehicle loans have a VIN number and purchase amount. Customer data includes name, social security number, address, and phone.

Your tasks:

1. Extract all possible business rules.
2. Construct a logical EERD for the bank.

4.14 SQL Exercises

Exercise 4.1

Display all products that have the word "LED" in its name. Show product ID and product name.

	ProductId	ProductName
1	2	60-Inch 4K Ultra HD Smart LED TV
2	3	3200 Lumens LED Home Theater Projector

Exercise 4.2

Display all suppliers that have the letter "a" as its second letter in the name. Show supplier ID and supplier name.

	SupplierId	SupplierName
1	4	Samsong
2	5	Canan

Exercise 4.3

Display all suppliers with the supplier name followed by the country in parentheses, such as Pine Apple (USA).

	(No column name)
1	Pine Apple (USA)
2	IMB (USA)
3	Lonovo (China)
4	Samsong (South Korea)
5	Canan (Japan)

Exercise 4.4

Same as Exercise 4.3, but this time use a more meaningful column head called "Supplier (Country)".

	Supplier (Country)
1	Pine Apple (USA)
2	IMB (USA)
3	Lonovo (China)
4	Samsong (South Korea)
5	Canan (Japan)

Exercise 4.5

Calculate the monetary value of each order detail. Show order ID, product ID, price, quantity, and order detail monetary value (quantity x price.)

	OrderId	ProductId	Price	Quantity	Monetary Value
1	1	1	1499.99	1	1499.99
2	1	3	149.99	2	299.98
3	2	1	1499.99	1	1499.99
4	2	2	1599.99	1	1599.99
5	2	4	99.99	6	599.94
6	2	6	189.99	5	949.95
7	3	3	159.99	2	319.98
8	3	6	199.99	1	199.99
9	3	7	109.99	2	219.98
10	3	8	69.99	2	139.98
11	3	9	1449.99	1	1449.99
12	4	4	99.99	2	199.98
13	4	8	69.99	1	69.99
14	5	3	149.99	6	899.94
15	5	6	199.99	3	599.97
16	6	1	1499.99	1	1499.99
17	7	2	999.99	1	999.99
18	8	7	79.99	1	79.99
19	8	8	59.99	2	119.98

Exercise 4.6

The LifeStyle manager decides to give customers who bought three or more units of the same product in the same order a 20 percent discount. Show order ID, product ID, price, quantity, and discounted price for those discounted in the orderdetails.

	OrderId	ProductId	Price	Quantity	Discounted Price
1	2	4	99.99	6	79.99200
2	2	6	189.99	5	151.99200
3	5	3	149.99	6	119.99200
4	5	6	199.99	3	159.99200

Exercise 4.7

Same as Exercise 4.6. This time, you should display only two decimal places for the "Discounted Price" column.

	OrderId	ProductId	Price	Quantity	Discounted Price
1	2	4	99.99	6	79.99
2	2	6	189.99	5	151.99
3	5	3	149.99	6	119.99
4	5	6	199.99	3	159.99

Exercise 4.8

Display employees' first name and last name with the last name in all capital letters.

	FirstName	LastName
1	Alex	HALL
2	Dianne	HART
3	Maria	LAW
4	Alice	LAW
5	Black	HART
6	Christina	ROBINSON
7	Nicholas	PINKSTON

Exercise 4.9

Find the position of the first blank space in a supplier's street address. Show supplier street address and the position of the first blank space.

	StreetAddress	Position of space
1	1 Pine Apple St.	2
2	123 International Blvd	4
3	33 Beijin Square	3
4	1 Electronics Road	2
5	12 Camera St	3

Exercise 4.10

Find the position of the first blank space and second blank space in a supplier's street address. Show supplier's street address and the position of first blank space and second blank space in the supplier's street address.

	StreetAddress	Position of space	Position of 2nd space
1	1 Pine Apple St.	2	7
2	123 International Blvd	4	18
3	33 Beijin Square	3	10
4	1 Electronics Road	2	14
5	12 Camera St	3	10

Exercise 4.11

Display the first word after the street number in a supplier's street address. For example, for the supplier "1 Pine Apple St", the first word after the street number is "Pine". Show the supplier's street address and the first word after the street number.

	StreetAddress	First word after street number
1	1 Pine Apple St.	Pine
2	123 International Blvd	International
3	33 Beijin Square	Beijin
4	1 Electronics Road	Electronics
5	12 Camera St	Camera

Exercise 4.12

Display today's date and the number of days that have passed since the order date. Show order ID, customer ID, employee ID, order date, today's date, and the order's age in days.

	OrderId	CustomerId	EmployeeId	OrderDate	Today's Date	Order's Age
1	1	1	5	2017-01-03	2017-06-11 14:16:14.610	159
2	2	1	3	2017-03-05	2017-06-11 14:16:14.610	98
3	3	2	5	2017-02-23	2017-06-11 14:16:14.610	108
4	4	4	5	2017-04-13	2017-06-11 14:16:14.610	59
5	5	1	4	2017-05-03	2017-06-11 14:16:14.610	39
6	6	3	6	2017-05-08	2017-06-11 14:16:14.610	34
7	7	5	7	2016-11-08	2017-06-11 14:16:14.610	215
8	8	7	2	2016-12-23	2017-06-11 14:16:14.610	170

Exercise 4.13

Same as Exercise 4.12. This time, show today's date without the time part.

	OrderId	CustomerId	EmployeeId	OrderDate	Today's Date	Order's Age
1	1	1	5	2017-01-03	2017-06-11	159
2	2	1	3	2017-03-05	2017-06-11	98
3	3	2	5	2017-02-23	2017-06-11	108
4	4	4	5	2017-04-13	2017-06-11	59
5	5	1	4	2017-05-03	2017-06-11	39
6	6	3	6	2017-05-08	2017-06-11	34
7	7	5	7	2016-11-08	2017-06-11	215
8	8	7	2	2016-12-23	2017-06-11	170

Exercise 4.14

Display all orders placed in May of any year. Show the order's order ID, customer ID, employee ID, and order date.

	OrderId	CustomerId	EmployeeId	OrderDate
1	5	1	4	2017-05-03
2	6	3	6	2017-05-08

Exercise 4.15

Display all orders by month and year. Show the order's order ID, customer ID, employee ID, and order date as the first day of that month and year.

	OrderId	CustomerId	EmployeeId	OrderMonth
1	1	1	5	2017-01-01
2	2	1	3	2017-03-01
3	3	2	5	2017-02-01
4	4	4	5	2017-04-01
5	5	1	4	2017-05-01
6	6	3	6	2017-05-01
7	7	5	7	2016-11-01
8	8	7	2	2016-12-01

4.15 Solutions to Review Questions

4.1 A; 4.2 B; 4.3 B; 4.4 D; 4.5 A; 4.6 B; 4.7 C; 4.8 C; 4.9 D; 4.10 A; 4.11 D; 4.12 B; 4.13 A; 4.14 B; 4.15 D; 4.16 C; 4.17 C; 4.18 A; 4.19 B; 4.20 C; 4.21 D; 4.22 A; 4.23 B; 4.24 C; 4.25 D; 4.26 C; 4.27 A; 4.28 A; 4.29 B; 4.30 D; 4.31 B; 4.32 A; 4.33 D; 4.34 D; 4.35 C; 4.36 B; 4.37 C; 4.38 B; 4.39 C; 4.40 B;

CHAPTER 5: ERD TO RELATION MAPPING AND SQL AGGREGATE FUNCTIONS

Chapter Learning Objectives

5.1 Explain the need for ERD to relation mapping.

5.2 Implementing the objectives of ERD to relation mapping.

5.3 Exemplify ERD to relation mapping.

5.4 Use aggregate functions in SQL statements.

5.5 Use GROUP BY clauses.

5.6 Use HAVING clauses.

5.7 Differentiate WHERE clause and HAVING clause.

5.8 Use simple subquery in SQL statements.

5.1 What is ERD to Relations Mapping?

The end product of database development is to have the tables constructed. Tables are called relations (that's where the word "relational" in relational databases comes from.) at the logical level. The purpose of mapping is to convert the entities and relationships in the ERD into relations/tables so that SQL statements can be written to actually create the database and the tables in the database server.

Under most situations, one entity will be mapped into one relation. The relationship between two entities will be represented as a foreign key. A foreign key is an attribute of one entity that is a primary key for another entity. Adding the foreign key allows the constraints of the relationship to be transferred to the relations.

An example of a constraint is the relationship between sales and employees of a commission-based retail store, in which every sale is handled by an employee and each employee can handle any number of sales. The ERD is shown in Figure 5.1a.

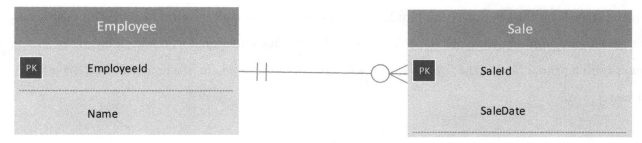

Figure 5.1a ERD of Employee and Sale.

In the example, you will use two tables, one to hold data about the employee, such as employee ID and name, and one to hold data about the sales, such as sale ID and sale date. However, we have yet to add a foreign key to represent the relationship between the two entities. This chapter will show you how to create relations to store the data and keep the constraints of the relationships.

There is more than one way to add a foreign key. Which way you use is dependent on the situation. Keep in mind that you should avoid or minimize null values (a null value is a value you do not know or a value that doesn't exist.) For example, an employee who just got hired and hasn't moved to the new town may not have a local address yet. The address for that employee is a null value.

In the rest of the chapter, you will learn the methods for mapping ERD to relations. No matter which method you use to map ERD to relations, the method must follow these three general rules:

1. All attributes of an entity are transferred over to the attributes of a relation.
2. Relationship constraints in ERD are kept in relations, which means that foreign keys are added.

3. Minimize null values whenever possible. This applies when you have more than one option for mapping.

In this book, we will represent a relation in three ways to help you understand the relations better. The first one is a table with two dimensional values (We show the column head row only for simplicity.):

Student Table

StudentId	FirstName	LastName	MiddleInitial

The second way is a relational schema:

Student (StudentId, FirstName, LastName, MiddleInitial)

The schema starts with the relation name (Student in this case), and then all the attributes in the parentheses with the primary key underlined with a solid line and the foreign key underlined with a dash line. If an attribute is both a primary key and a foreign key, it will have both the solid and dashed underline (so two underlines.)

The third way is to keep everything in the original ERD. You may see additional foreign attributes added to a relation by following the mapping rules. A foreign key attribute will be labeled FK on the left side of an attribute.

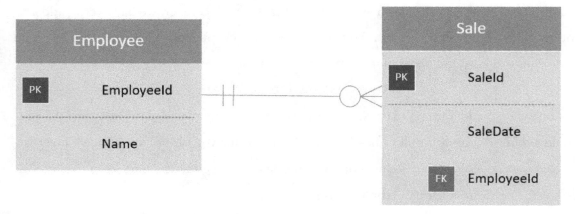

Figure 5.1b Relations of Employee and Sale.

Compared to Figure 5.1a, Figure 5.1b has an additional attribute called EmployeeId in the Sale relation with the FK labeled on the left. The added attribute is called foreign key (FK) because it is a primary key (PK) in the related relation of Employee. You will learn how to add FK in the following sections of this chapter.

Review Question 5.1
Tables are called _____ at the logical level.
a. spreadsheets
b. two dimensional tables
c. relations
d. logical tables

Review Question 5.2
Under most situations, one entity will be mapped into _____.
a. one relation
b. two relations
c. three relations
d. four relations

Review Question 5.3
Under most situations, a relationship between two entities will be represented as a _____.
a. primary key
b. foreign key
c. relation
d. mapped relation

Review Question 5.4
A foreign key is an attribute of one entity that is a _____ for another entity.
a. primary key
b. foreign key
c. relation
d. mapped relation

Review Question 5.5
Which of the following is a general rule for mapping ERD to relations?
a. All attributes of an entity are transferred over to the attributes of a relation.
b. Relationship constraints in ERD are kept in relations, which means that primary keys are added.
c. Minimize numeric values whenever possible. This applies when you have more than one option for mapping.
d. All primary keys of an entity are transferred over to the foreign keys of a relation.

Review Question 5.6
Which of the following is a general rule for mapping ERD to relations?
a. All attributes of an entity are transferred over to the primary keys of a relation.
b. Relationship constraints in ERD are kept in relations, which means that foreign keys are added.
c. Minimize numeric values whenever possible. This applies when you have more than one option for mapping.
d. All primary keys of an entity are transferred over to the foreign keys of a relation.

Review Question 5.7
Which of the following is a general rule for mapping ERD to relations?
a. All attributes of an entity are transferred over to the primary keys of a relation.
b. Relationship constraints in ERD are kept in relations, which means that primary keys are added.
c. Minimize null values whenever possible. This applies when you have more than one option for mapping.
d. All primary keys of an entity are transferred over to the foreign keys of a relation.

Review Question 5.8
What does "relational" in "relational database" mean?
a. relationship
b. database
c. table
d. column

Review Question 5.9
What is the "ERD to relations mapping"?
a. converting entities to relations
b. converting relationships to relations
c. converting entities and relationships in ERD to relations so that tables can be created.
d. converting one ERD to one relation.

Review Question 5.10
What is a null value in relational database design?
a. an empty string value
b. a zero numeric value
c. an empty string value or a zero numeric value
d. an unknown value

Review Question 5.11
Which of the following is NOT one of the ERD to relation mapping objectives?
a. No data duplication.
b. All attributes in ERD are kept in relations.
c. Keep relationship constraints from ERD to relations.
d. Minimize the null values in the relations whenever possible.

Review Question 5.12
In a relation schema, how do you represent a primary key?
a. put the attribute as the first one in the list.
b. solid underline the attribute.
c. dash underlines the attribute.
d. put the attribute as the last one in the list.

Review Question 5.13
In a relation schema, how do you represent a foreign key?
a. put the attribute as the first one in the list.
b. solid underline the attribute.
c. dash underlines the attribute.
d. put the attribute as the last one in the list.

Review Question 5.14
What is the table name if you see the relation schema? Movie (MovieId, Title, Duration)
a. Movie
b. MovieId
c. Title
d. Duration

5.2 Mapping a Regular/Strong Entity in ERD to a Relation

This is the simplest case. One relation from one entity. All attributes of the entity become column headers in the relation. For example, to map a regular entity to a relation, just make the entity name to relation name and keep all attributes of the entity in the relation.

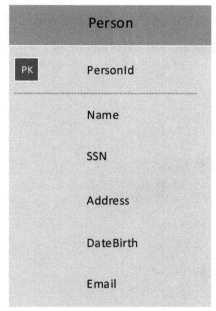

Figure 5.2 A regular entity.

A corresponding relation/table would look like this:

Person Table

PersonId	Name	SSN	Address	DateBirth	Email

A relation schema would look like this:

Person (PersonId, Name, SSN, Address, DateBirth, Email)

There would be no changes in the original ERD when a regular entity is converted to a relation.

Review Question 5.15
How do you map a regular entity in the ERD to a relation?
a. The entity name becomes the relation name and the entity attributes become the relation column headers. There is no change in the primary key.
b. The relation is given no name, and entity attributes become relation column headers.
c. Each attribute in the entity becomes a relation.

d. Add the primary key of the owner entity as a foreign key to the entity and set both the owner primary key and current entity primary key as a composite primary key.

5.3 Mapping a Weak Entity in ERD to a Relation

In Chapter 2, you learned that a weak entity is a special type of entity in which its existence depends entirely on another entity. An example of a weak entity is the dependents of an employee. The DEPENDENT entity instance completely depends on the EMPLOYEE entity.

Let's see an example:

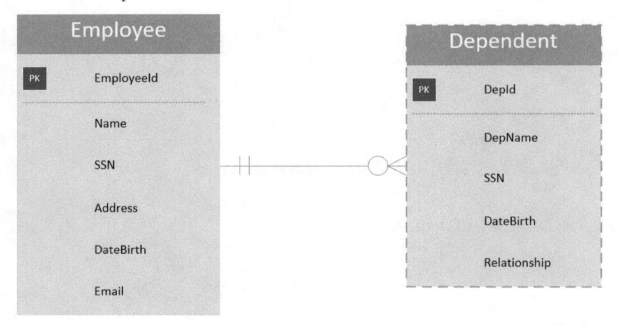

Figure 5.3 A weak entity mapping.

The Figure 5.3 shows the ERD of EMPLOYEE and the DEPENDENT. The EMPLOYEE is a strong entity and you learned how to map a strong entity to a relation in last section. The DEPENDENT is a weak entity. To map the DEPENDENT entity to a relation, 1) add the primary key of the owner entity (Employee in this case) as a foreign key in the weak entity, and 2) set both the primary keys of the owner entity and the weak entity as a composite primary key (EmployeeId and DepId in this case).

The following demonstrates the relations in three formats:

1) Table format:

Employee Table

EmployeeId	Name	SSN	Address	DateBirth	Email

Dependent Table

EmployeeId	DepId	DepName	SSN	DateBirth	Relationship

2) Schema format:

Employee (EmployeeId, Name, SSN, Address, DateBirth, Email)

Dependent (EmployeeId, DepId, DepName, SSN, DateBirth, Relationship)

3) ERD format:

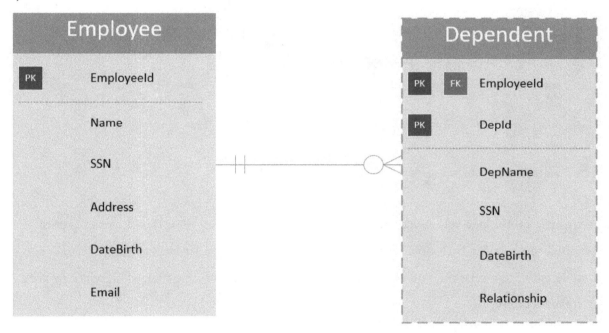

Figure 5.4 Relation for a weak entity.

Review Question 5.16
What is the rule for mapping a weak entity in an ERD to a relation?
a. Add the PK of the owner entity as a FK in the weak entity. Set the two keys as a composite PK.
b. Add the FK of the owner entity as a FK in the weak entity. Set the two keys as a composite PK.
c. Add the PK of the owner entity as a FK in the weak entity. Set the two keys as a composite FK.
d. Add the FK of the owner entity as a FK in the weak entity. Set the two keys as a composite FK.

Review Question 5.17
Suppose Dependent is a weak entity with the Employee entity as its owner. If EmployeeId is the primary key of the Employee entity and DependentName is the primary key of the Dependent entity, what is the primary key of the mapped relation of the Dependent entity?
a. EmployeeId

b. DependentName
c. EmployeeId, DependentName
d. None of the above

5.4 Map a Binary 1:M Relationship to Relations

The one-to-many relationship is perhaps the most popular relationship in the ERD. To map such a relationship, just add the primary key from the one side as a foreign key on the "many" side. Let's see an example:

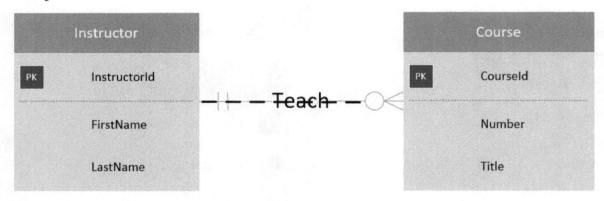

Figure 5.5 A one-to-many relationship (1:M).

The Instructor entity is on the one side while the Course entity is on the many side. The Instructor entity can be easily mapped to a relation by following section 5.2 on mapping a regular entity to a relation. When mapping the course entity to a relation, you should add the IntructorId as a foreign key. The relations are shown in three formats below.

Instructor Table

InstructorId	FirstName	LastName

Course Table

CourseId	Number	Title	InstructorId

Instructor (InstructorId, FirstName, LastName)

Course (CourseId, Number, Title, InstructorId)

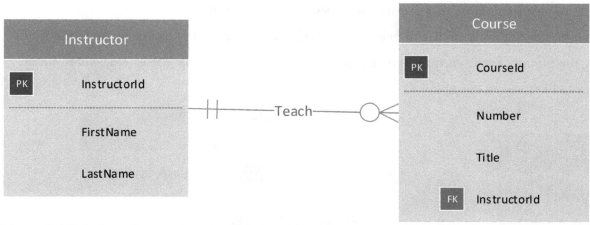

Figure 5.6 Relations for one-to-many relationships.

Review Question 5.18
Given the following ERD, the left side is the _____side while the right side is the _____ side.

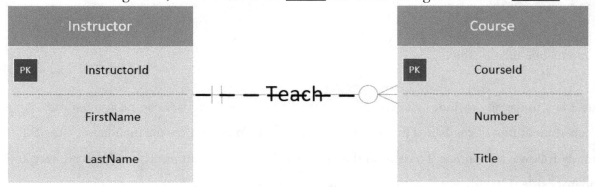

a. one, one
b. many, many
c. one, many
d. many, one

Review Question 5.19
To map a one-to-many relationship to relations, just add the primary key from the _____ side as a foreign key on the _____ side
a. one, one
b. one, many
c. many, one
d. many, many

5.5 Map a Binary 1:1 Relationship to a relation

Mapping a binary 1:1 relationship is very similar to mapping a binary 1:M relationship as in section 5.4. To map a binary one-to-one relationship to relations, add the primary key from the mandatory side as a foreign key to the optional side (remember that the mandatory side is the side with the two vertical dashes, while the optional side is the side with one circle and one vertical line.) Such mapping will reduce the number of null values (adding the primary key from the optional side as a foreign key to the mandatory side will result in more null values.) Let's see an example:

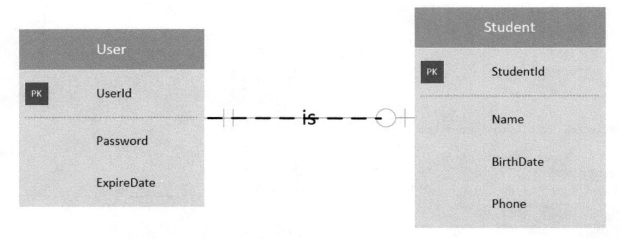

Figure 5.7 A one-to-one relationship.

A computer user in a university includes students, faculty, and staff, thus each user can be at most one student and each student must be a user. This relationship is 1:1. The mapping on the mandatory side (the user entity) simply follows section 5.2. To map on the optional side (the student entity,) add the primary key from the mandatory side (UserId) as a foreign key on the optional side (the student entity).

User Table

UserId	Password	ExpireDate

Student Table

StudentId	Name	BirthDate	Phone	UserId

User (UserId, Password, ExpireDate)
Student (StudentId, Name, BirthDate, Phone, UserId)

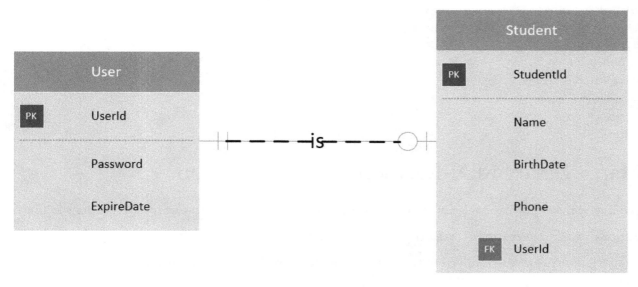

Figure 5.8 Relations for one-to-one relationship.

Review Question 5.20
Given the following ERD, the left side is the _____side while the right side is the _____ side.

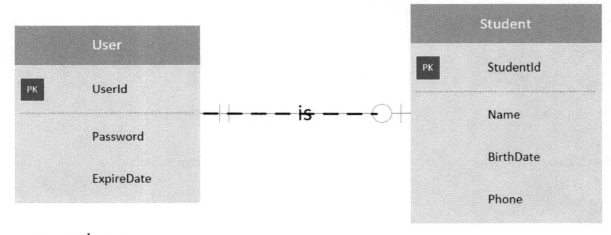

a. one, mandatory
b. one, optional
c. optional, mandatory
d. mandatory, optional

Review Question 5.21
To map a binary 1:1 relationship to relations, add the primary key from the _____ side as a foreign key to the _____ side.
a. optional, mandatory
b. mandatory, optional
c. optional, optional
d. mandatory, mandatory

Review Question 5.22

When mapping a binary 1:1 relationship to relations, adding the primary key from the optional side as a foreign key to the mandatory side results in _____.
a. more null values
b. fewer null value
c. more columns
d. fewer columns

5.6 Map a Binary M:N Relationship to a Relation

To map a binary many-to-many relationship, you need to create three relations. For the two entities in the M:N relationship, simply create two relations as demonstrated in Section 5.2. Additionally, create a third relation (also known as an associative entity, as from Chapter 3) with at least two attributes -- the primary keys from each participating entity. The primary key of this new relation is a composite key of these two attributes. The two attributes also serve as foreign keys because they are primary keys of related relations. Add any attributes of the relationship to this new relation. Let's see an example:

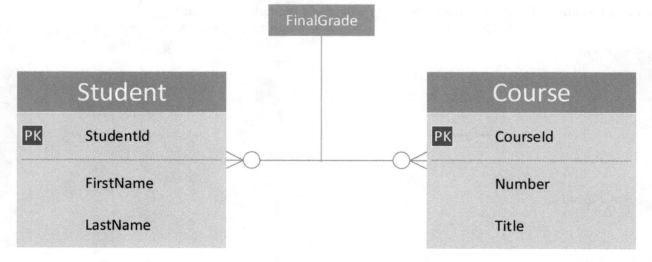

Figure 5.9 A many-to-many relationship.

There will be three relations mapped to the above M:N relationship

Student Table

StudentId	FirstName	LastName

Course Table

CourseId	Number	Title

Enrollment Table

StudentId	CourseId	FinalGrade

Student (StudentId, FirstName, LastName)

Course (CourseId, Number, Title)

Enrollment (StudentId, CourseId, FinalGrade)

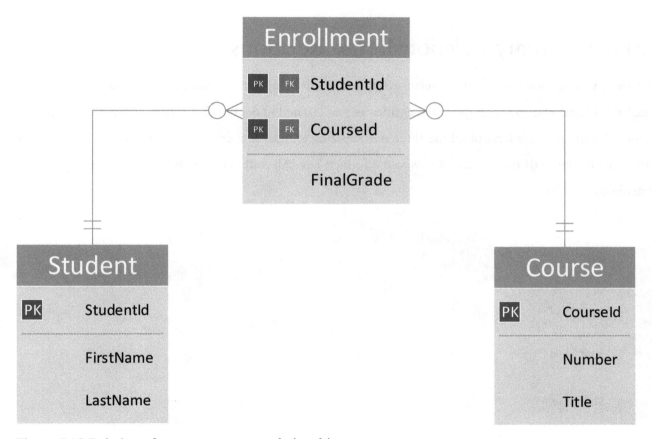

Figure 5.10 Relations for many-to-many relationships.

Review Question 5.23
To map a binary many-to-many relationship, you will create a total of _____ relation(s).
a. one
b. two
c. three
d. four

Review Question 5.24
To map a binary many-to-many relationship, you add a new relation to the database. This new relation is mapped to the _____.
a. associative entity
b. third entity
c. additional entity

d. backup entity

Review Question 5.25
The associative entity/relation added in a many-to-many relationship mapping contains at least two attributes _____.
a. from one of the participating entities.
b. from both of the participating entities.
c. composite of the primary key attributes of the participating entities
d. composite of all attributes from both entities.

5.7 Map a Ternary Relationship to Relations

In Chapter 2, you learned that a ternary relationship is a relationship among three entities. To map a ternary relationship to relations, you map the three entities as you learned in Section 5.2. Then, add a new relation which includes the primary keys of all the three participating entities as a composite primary key for this new relation. Each attribute of the primary key is also a foreign key. Also add any attributes of the ternary relationship to this new relation.

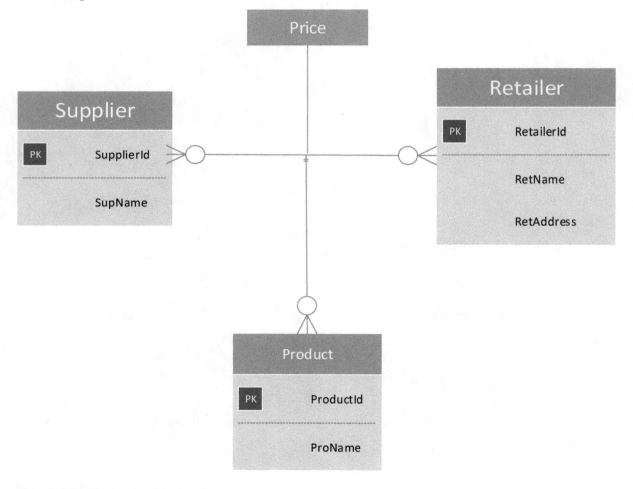

Figure 5.11 A ternary relationship.

This ERD shows that the mini-world includes data on which supplier ships which products to which retailers. Each delivery includes the quote price. The mapped relations are as follows:

Supplier Table

SupplierId	SupName

Retailer Table

RetailerId	RetName	RetAddress

Product Table

ProductId	ProName

Delivery Table

SupplierId	RetailerId	ProductId	Price

Supplier (SupplierId, SupName)

Retailer (RetailerId, RetName, RetAddress)

Product (ProductId, ProName)

Delivery (SupplierId, RetailerId, ProductId, Price)

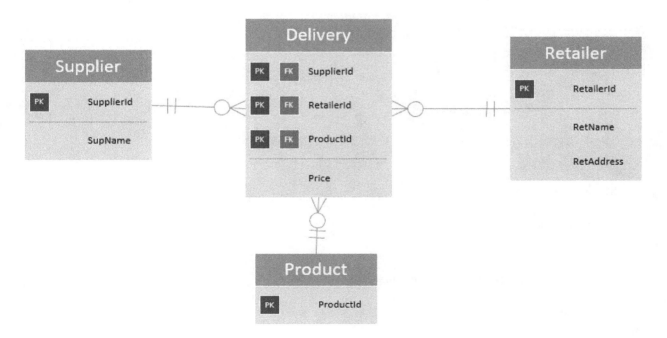

Figure 5.12 Relations for a ternary relationship.

Review Question 5.26
A ternary relationship will be mapped into a total of _____ relation(s).
a. one
b. two
c. three
d. four

5.8 Map Generalization/Specialization Relationship to Relations

You learned generalization/specialization relationships in Chapter 4. For generalization/specialization mapping, simply convert each entity into a relation, add the primary key of the super entity as a foreign key in each sub entity, then set the foreign key in the sub entity as also a primary key. Let's see an example:

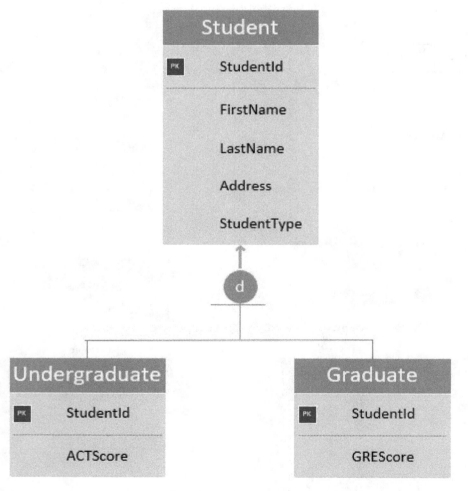

Figure 5.13 A generalization/specialization relationship.

The mapped relations are:

Student Table

StudentId	FirstName	LastName	Address	StudentType

Undergraduate Table

StudentId	ACTScore

Graduate Table

StudentId	GREScore

Student (StudentId, FirstName, LastName, Address, StudentType)

Undergraduate (StudentId, ACTScore)

Graduate (StudentId, GREScore)

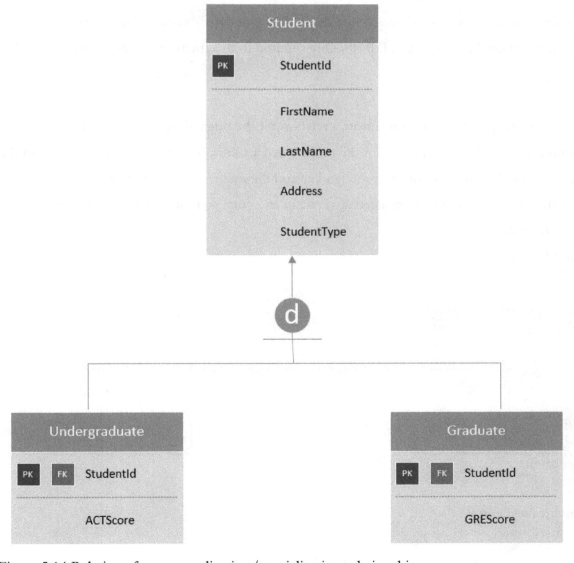

Figure 5.14 Relations for a generalization/specialization relationship.

Review Question 5.27
To map a generalization/specialization relationship to relations, create a relation for each entity, set the primary key of the _____ entity as a foreign key in each _____ entity, and then set the foreign key in the _____ entities as also the primary key.
a. sub, super, sub
b. super, sub, sub
c. super, super, sub
d. sub, super, super

5.9 Map a Multivalued-attribute Entity to a Relation

The multivalued attribute was introduced in Chapter 3. A multivalued attribute has more than one value. For example, if an employee has worked for a company and then left the company and then returned, what is the hire date? If the company wants to keep all hire dates, then hire date is a multivalued attribute. Multivalued attributes cannot be created in a DBMS. One solution to this then is to create a relation for the attribute(s).

To map an entity with a multivalued attribute, create a relation for the original entity without the multivalued attribute, then add a new relation for the multivalued attribute(s), with the primary key from the original entity as a foreign key, setting both this foreign key and the multivalued attribute as a composite primary key. If there is more than one multivalued attribute in an entity, you can group them in one new relation if they are related.

Let's see an example:

Figure 5.15 A multivalued entity.

The HireDate attribute of the Employee entity is a multivalued attribute. The two relations are:

Employee Table

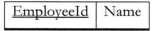

EmployeeId	Name

EmploymentHistory Table

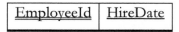

EmployeeId	HireDate

Employee (EmployeeId, Name)

EmploymentHistory (EmployeeId, HireDate)

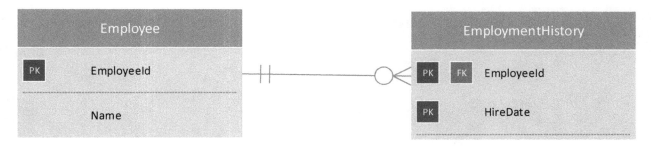

Figure 5.16 Relations for a multivalued entity.

Review Question 5.28

When mapping an entity with multivalued attributes, _____.

a. there is no difference from mapping a strong entity.

b. there is no difference from mapping a weak entity.

c. add a new attribute for the multivalued attributes.

d. add a new relation for the multivalued attributes.

5.10 An Example of Mapping ERD to Relations

Given the ERD as shown in Figure 5.17, map it to relations by following the rules described in this chapter.

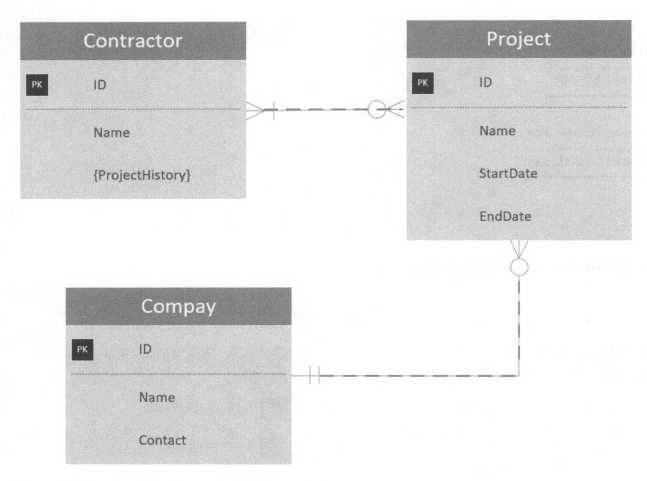

Figure 5.17 An example of mapping ERD to relations.

Step 1: Map each entity to a relation by keeping every attribute and PK.

```
Contractor (ID, Name, ProjectHistory)
Project (ID, Name, StartDate, EndDate)
Company (ID, Name, Contact)
```

Step 2: Is there any weak entities?

No. Skip this step.

Step 3: Is there any multi-value attribute?

Yes, ProjectHistory is one. Ask the client what data is in the project history. Suppose there is just a project name in this case. Add a new relation by following the rule described in Section 5.9:

```
Contractor (ID, Name)
ProjectHistory(ContractorID, ProjectName)
Project (ID, Name, StartDate, EndDate)
```

```
Company (ID, Name, Contact)
```

Step 4: Map each relationship

1. The relationship between Contractor and Project is a M:N relationship. Follow the rule described in Section 5.6:

```
Contractor (ID, Name)
ProjectHistory(ContractorID, ProjectName)
Project (ID, Name, StartDate, EndDate)
ContractorProject (ContractorID, ProjectID)
Company (ID, Name, Contact)
```

2. The relationship between Project and Company is 1:M relationship. Follow the rule described in Section 5.4:

```
Contractor (ID, Name)
ProjectHistory(ContractorID, ProjectName)
Project (ID, Name, StartDate, EndDate, CompanyID)
ContractorProject (ContractorID, ProjectID)
Company (ID, Name, Contact)
```

The above five relations are the final mapped relations for the given ERD.

5.11 SQL Aggregate Functions

An aggregate function performs a calculation on a column and returns a single value. It includes one or more rows in a column as input and returns a single value as output. For example, if a table has a column called GPA, then AVG(GPA) will return the average GPA of all GPAs selected. The difference between the regular functions you learned in the last chapter and the aggregate functions you will learn in this section is that the former has one row value as input and the latter has one or more row values as input.

Aggregate functions ignore null values. So, if you have four students but only three of them have a GPA, then only three GPAs will be averaged even though you selected four students.

SQL Example 5.1

Display the average price of all products in the OrderDetails table.

SQL Example 5.1 Analysis

Use the AVG() function to show the average of all prices.

SQL Example 5.1 statement

```sql
SELECT CAST(AVG(Price) AS NUMERIC(7, 2)) AS "Average Price"
FROM Sales.OrderDetails;
```

SQL Example 5.1 Output

	Average Price
1	536.31

SQL Example 5.2

Display number of customer emails in the customers table.

SQL Example 5.2 Analysis

Use the COUNT() function to show the number of customer emails. Note that the null value in the Email column won't count as one.

SQL Example 5.2 statement

```sql
SELECT COUNT(Email) AS "Number of customer emails"
FROM Sales.Customers;
```

SQL Example 5.2 Output

	Number of customer emails
1	7

SQL Example 5.3

Display the total number of units of products in the order with the ID 3. From Appendix B Sales.OrderDetails table, you can find that the number is 2 units of Product Three +1 unit of Product Six +2 units of Product Seven + 2 units of Products Eight + 1 unit of Product Nine = 8 units of all products.

SQL Example 5.3 Analysis

Use the SUM() function to total all numbers in the quantity column of the OrderDetails table. Remember to keep this only to the order with ID 3.

SQL Example 5.3 statement

```
SELECT SUM(Quantity) AS "Total units in order id 3"
FROM Sales.OrderDetails
WHERE OrderId = 3;
```

SQL Example 5.3 Output

	Total units in order id 3
1	8

SQL Example 5.4

Display total sales value in the order with ID 3.

SQL Example 5.4 Analysis

In order to find out the total sales value, you need to use the OrderDetails table. The following table shows all items in the order with ID 3.

	OrderId	ProductId	Price	quantity
1	3	3	159.99	2
2	3	6	199.99	1
3	3	7	109.99	2
4	3	8	69.99	2
5	3	9	1449.99	1

The total value of the order with ID 3 will be 159.99×2 + 159.99×1 + 109.99×2 + 69.99×2 + 1449.99×1 = 2329.92. The SQL for calculating the total is SUM(Price*Quantity).

SQL Example 5.4 statement

```
SELECT SUM(Quantity*Price) AS "Total sales in order id 3"
FROM Sales.OrderDetails
WHERE OrderId = 3;
```

SQL Example 5.4 Output

	Total sales in order id 3
1	2329.92

SQL Example 5.5

Display the highest priced item on sale. Show the price.

SQL Example 5.5 Analysis

Use the MAX() function to display the highest priced item from the OrderDetails table.

SQL Example 5.5 statement

```
SELECT MAX(Price) AS "Highest priced item"
FROM Sales.OrderDetails;
```

SQL Example 5.5 Output

	Highest priced item
1	1599.99

Review Question 5.29
A(n) _____ function performs a calculation on a column and returns a single value.
a. mathematic
b. aggregate
c. normal
d. single

Review Question 5.30
The difference between the regular functions you learned in the last chapter and the aggregate functions you will learn in this section is that the former has _____ as input and the latter has _____ as input.
a. one row value, one or more row values
b. one or more row values, one row values
c. one row value, zero or one row value
d. zero or one row value, one row value

Review Question 5.31
Which of the following is an aggregate function in Transact SQL?
a. UPPER()
b. SUBSTRING()
c. CAST()
d. MAX()

5.12 The GROUP BY Clause

The normal SELECT statement will return a result selected from rows. For example, if you want to return all students whose GPA are higher than 3.0, it will return, for example, 25 rows if there are 25 students whose GPA are higher than 3.0.

If you want to use the SELECT statement to return a result from a certain group of rows, you need to use the GROUP BY clause. For example, if you want to return the average GPA of all freshmen, you will need to group them by the class cohort using the GROUP BY clause as shown in the following example.

SQL Example 5.6

Display total number of units in each order. Show order ID and the corresponding total units in the order. Like this:

OrderId	Total units in the order
1	3
2	13
3	8
4	3
5	9
6	1
7	1
8	3

SQL Example 5.6 Analysis

In SQL Example 5.3, you learned how to retrieve the total number of units in order ID 3.

You may be tempted to try the following SQL statement:

```
SELECT OrderId, SUM(Quantity)
FROM Sales.OrderDetails;
```

You will get the following error:

"Msg 8120, Level 16, State 1, Line 28

```
Column 'Sales.OrderDetails.OrderId' is invalid in the select list because it is not contained in
either an aggregate function or the GROUP BY clause."
```

To put it simply, SQL Server won't allow you to select OrderId and an aggregate function, SUM() in this case, together. This is because OrderId is an individual row value while SUM() is a result of multiple row values. The solution is to add the GROUP BY clause so that the SQL Server knows which rows to add together and will use just one OrderId value for all those rows.

SQL Example 5.6 statement

```
SELECT OrderId, SUM(Quantity) AS "Total units in the order"
FROM Sales.OrderDetails
GROUP BY OrderId;
```

SQL Example 5.6 Output

	OrderId	Total units in the order
1	1	3
2	2	13
3	3	8
4	4	3
5	5	9
6	6	1
7	7	1
8	8	3

SQL Example 5.7

Display one of the highest priced items on sale. Show the product ID and the price.

SQL Example 5.7 Analysis

SQL Example 5.5 asks for the highest price item on sale. This time you need to show which product has that price. If you simply add the product ID in the SELECT, like this

```
SELECT ProductId, MAX(Price) AS "Highest priced item"
FROM Sales.OrderDetails;
```

You will receive an error message similar to the error message in SQL Example 5.6. The solution is to add the GROUP BY clause. Now the SQL statement will run and display all orders and their price as shown:

	ProductId	Highest priced item
1	1	1499.99
2	2	1599.99
3	3	159.99
4	4	99.99
5	6	199.99
6	7	109.99
7	8	69.99
8	9	1449.99

To display the highest price only, you can use ORDER BY with DESCENDING and then pick the first one with the TOP keyword.

If there are more than one highest priced item, this method will only show one of them and SQL cannot guarantee which one. You will learn more in our second book on SQL.

SQL Example 5.7 statement

```
SELECT TOP 1 ProductId, MAX(Price) AS "Highest priced item"
FROM Sales.OrderDetails
GROUP BY ProductId
ORDER BY "Highest priced item" DESC;
```

SQL Example 5.7 Output

	ProductId	Highest priced item
1	2	1599.99

SQL Example 5.8

Display the total value of each order. For example, with the following data of the order with Id 1

	OrderId	ProductId	Price	quantity
1	1	1	1499.99	1
2	1	3	149.99	2

The total value of Order id 1 is 1499.99×1 + 149.99×2 = 1799.97

Show order ID and total value

SQL Example 5.8 Analysis

The total value of each item in an order is calculated as Price * Quantity. The total value of an order will be the sum of each item value in that order, which is SUM(Price*Quantity). You should also group the total value by order ID using the GROUP BY clause.

SQL Example 5.8 statement

```
SELECT OrderId, SUM(Price * Quantity) AS "Order total"
FROM Sales.OrderDetails
GROUP BY OrderId;
```

SQL Example 5.8 Output

	OrderId	Order total
1	1	1799.97
2	2	4649.87
3	3	2329.92
4	4	269.97
5	5	1499.91
6	6	1499.99
7	7	999.99
8	8	199.97

Review Question 5.32
If you want to use the SELECT statement to return the result by a group of rows, you will use the
_____ clause.
a. GROUP
b. WHERE
c. GROUP BY
d. ORDER BY

Review Question 5.33
What is the output of executing the following SQL statement on our LifeStyleDB database?
```
SELECT OrderId, SUM(Quantity)
FROM Sales.OrderDetails;
```
a. All order ID and the total number of quantities in that order.
b. All order ID and the total number of quantities in the Sales.OrderDetails table.
c. An error because the Sales.OrderDetails table does not have a column called Quantity.
d. An error because OrderId returns individual rows while SUM(Quantity) returns the aggregation value of multiple rows.

5.13 The HAVING Clause

In Chapter 3, you learned how to use the WHERE clause to filter out certain rows. For example, if you have a table called Students that holds data about all students, and you want to display only students with GPA of 3.5 or higher, you have something like this:

```
SELECT FirstName, LastName, GPA
FROM Students
WHERE GPA >= 3.5;
```

Suppose you want to display students' GPA average by cohort (that is, Freshman, Sophomore, Junior, and Senior) and only display the cohort with Average GPA of 3.5 or higher. You cannot use the WHERE clause. The following example won't work.

```
SELECT Cohort, AVG(GPA)
FROM Students
GROUP BY Cohort
WHERE AVG(GPA) >= 3.5;
```

To make it work, you will use HAVING clause like this:

```
SELECT Cohort, AVG(GPA)
FROM Students
GROUP BY Cohort
HAVING AVG(GPA) >= 3.5;
```

In short, WHERE is used to filter out individual rows while HAVING is used to filter out individual groups.

SQL Example 5.9

Display all orders with more than $2000.00 value. Display Order ID and corresponding order total.

SQL Example 5.9 Analysis

This is similar to SQL Example 5.8 except that you don't want any orders with a total of $2000.00 or less to be displayed. Because each order is a group of order items, you cannot use the WHERE clause to filter out the rows. Instead, you need to use the HAVING clause to filter out individual orders.

SQL Example 5.9 statement

```
SELECT OrderId, SUM(Price * Quantity) AS "Order total"
FROM Sales.OrderDetails
GROUP BY OrderId
HAVING SUM(Price * Quantity) > 2000;
```

SQL Example 5.9 Output

	OrderId	Order total
1	2	4649.87
2	3	2329.92

SQL Example 5.10

Display any orders with a total number of more than 2 units in each order. Show order ID and the corresponding total units in the order.

SQL Example 5.10 Analysis

This is similar to SQL Example 5.6 except that you don't show any order with total units of 2 or less. As can be seen in the SQL Example 5.6 result table, there are 8 orders in all. Only 6 of those 8 orders have more than 2 units of items in them.

Because an order is a group, so you will use the HAVING clause instead of the WHERE clause to filter the rows.

SQL Example 5.10 statement

```
SELECT OrderId, SUM(Quantity) AS "Total units in order"
FROM Sales.OrderDetails
GROUP BY OrderId
HAVING SUM(Quantity) > 2;
```

SQL Example 5.10 Output

	OrderId	Total units in order
1	1	3
2	2	13
3	3	8
4	4	3
5	5	9
6	8	3

SQL Example 5.11

Display all products costing more than $1000.00 per unit with ten or more units delivered. Show product ID and the total units delivered.

SQL Example 5.11 Analysis

First, take a look at all deliveries from the deliveries table:

	DeliveryId	ProductId	Quantity	Price	DeliveryDate
1	1	1	2	1099.99	2016-10-01 09:30:00.0000000
2	2	1	5	1199.99	2016-11-01 10:20:00.0000000
3	3	2	10	1199.99	2016-10-02 11:10:00.0000000
4	4	3	10	129.99	2016-10-05 09:15:00.0000000
5	5	4	20	79.99	2016-10-07 14:00:00.0000000
6	6	5	15	139.99	2016-10-07 15:30:00.0000000
7	7	6	25	169.99	2016-10-10 10:30:00.0000000
8	8	7	12	79.99	2016-10-11 11:10:00.0000000
9	9	7	18	69.99	2016-10-12 09:50:00.0000000

Next, pick all rows with price of more than $1000.00, which gives the following table:

	DeliveryId	ProductId	Quantity	Price	DeliveryDate
1	1	1	2	1099.99	2016-10-01 09:30:00.0000000
2	2	1	5	1199.99	2016-11-01 10:20:00.0000000
3	3	2	10	1199.99	2016-10-02 11:10:00.0000000

Now, Product ID 1 has only 7 units delivered while Product ID 2 has 10 units. Only Product ID 2 meets the condition and should be displayed.

The reasoning above requires two steps. First is filtering out all prices lower than or equal to $1000.00. Second is filtering out all total units less than 10. The first filter is at the row level so you should use the WHERE clause and the second filter is at the group level (e.g. Product ID 1 is 7, not 2 and 5) so you should use the HAVING clause.

SQL Example 5.11 statement

```
SELECT ProductId, SUM(Quantity) AS "Total quantity"
FROM Purchasing.Deliveries
WHERE Price > 1000.0
GROUP BY ProductId
HAVING SUM(Quantity) >= 10;
```

SQL Example 5.11 Output

	ProductId	Total quantity
1	2	10

SQL Example 5.12

Display products that are delivered between Oct 1, 2016 and Oct. 10, 2016. Show product ID, total quantity and average price (not weighted average price) of each product delivered during that time.

SQL Example 5.12 Analysis

First, you will use the WHERE clause to select products delivered between Oct. 1, 2016 and Oct. 10, 2016. Because the delivery date is a DateTime2 data type, you have to include one extra day in the ending date. Then, use the SUM() function for total quantity and AVG() function for average price. Finally, because there are aggregate functions used, you must GROUP BY all non-aggregate fields in the SELECT clause.

SQL Example 5.12 statement

```
SELECT ProductId, SUM(Quantity) AS "Total units", AVG(Price) AS "Average
price"
FROM Purchasing.Deliveries
WHERE DeliveryDate BETWEEN '20161001' AND '20161011'
GROUP BY ProductId;
```

SQL Example 5.12 Output

	ProductId	Total units	Average price
1	1	2	1099.99
2	2	10	1199.99
3	3	10	129.99
4	4	20	79.99
5	5	15	139.99
6	6	25	169.99

SQL Example 5.13

Display products that are delivered between Oct 1, 2016 and Oct. 10, 2016 with total units delivered being 10 or more units during the time period. Show total quantity and average price of each product delivered during that time. Sort by total units delivered in descending order.

SQL Example 5.13 Analysis

This example is very similar to SQL Example 5.12 except that 1) you are only interested in products with a total unit of 10 or more and 2) you want to sort by total units. To answer 1) above, use the HAVING clause. To answer 2) above, use the ORDER BY clause.

Note that this example uses all clauses in the SELECT statement. You should pay attention to the sequence each clause is presented as shown:

```
SELECT
FROM
WHERE
GROUP BY
HAVING
ORDER BY
```

Note that the sequence they are actually executed always follows the following order, and not the order you typed them in:

```
FROM
WHERE
GROUP BY
HAVING
SELECT
ORDER BY
```

Knowing the order of execution is important. For example, you can use the column alias in the ORDER BY clause, but cannot use the column alias in the GROUP BY nor HAVING clause. This is because ORDER BY is executed after the SELECT so that DBMS knows what the alias is, while GROUP BY and HAVING clauses are executed before the SELECT so the DBMS does not know what the alias is.

SQL Example 5.13 statement

```
SELECT ProductId, SUM(Quantity) AS "Total units", AVG(Price) AS "Average price"
FROM Purchasing.Deliveries
WHERE DeliveryDate BETWEEN '20161001' AND '20161011'
GROUP BY ProductId
HAVING SUM(Quantity) >= 10
ORDER BY 'Total units' DESC;
```

SQL Example 5.13 Output

	ProductId	Total units	Average price
1	6	25	169.99
2	4	20	79.99
3	5	15	139.99
4	2	10	1199.99
5	3	10	129.99

Review Question 5.34
In SQL, the WHERE clause is used to filter out individual rows while the _____ clause is used to filter out individual groups.
a. BOOLEAN
b. WHERE GROUP
c. LOGICAL AND
d. HAVING

Review Question 5.35
Which of the following is the correct execution sequence (not syntax sequence) of SQL statements?
a. SELECT, FROM, WHERE
b. FROM, WHERE, SELECT
c. SELECT, WHERE, FROM
d. FROM, SELECT, WHERE

Review Question 5.36
Which of the following is the correct execution sequence (not syntax sequence) of SQL statements?
a. FROM, WHERE, GROUP BY, HAVING, SELECT
b. SELECT, FROM, WHERE, GROUP BY, HAVING
c. SELECT, FROM, HAVING, GROUP BY, WHERE
d. SELECT, FROM, WHERE, HAVING, GROUP BY

Review Question 5.37
Which of the following is the correct execution sequence (not syntax sequence) of SQL statements?
a. SELECT, FROM, WHERE, GROUP BY, HAVING, ORDER BY
b. FROM, WHERE, GROUP BY, HAVING, ORDER BY, SELECT
c. FROM, WHERE, HAVING, GROUP BY, SELECT, ORDER BY
d. FROM, WHERE, GROUP BY, HAVING, SELECT, ORDER BY

5.14 Subquery

Subqueries are queries inside another query. The result of a SELECT statement is a table even though sometimes this table has only one value or even no values at all. You can use the result of a query in another query.

SQL Example 5.14

Display orders that contain product ID 1. Show Order ID.

SQL Example 5.14 Analysis

This is a simple SQL example to introduce a subquery.

SQL Example 5.14 statement

```
SELECT OrderId
FROM Sales.OrderDetails
WHERE ProductId = 1;
```

SQL Example 5.14 Output

	OrderId
1	1
2	2
3	6

SQL Example 5.15

Display customers who placed the order ID 1, 2, or 6. Show customer ID.

SQL Example 5.15 Analysis

The OrderDetails table includes both customer ID and order ID. Use the WHERE clause and IN operator to filter the rows. The IN operator limits the column value to a set of values.

SQL Example 5.15 statement

```
SELECT DISTINCT CustomerId
FROM Sales.Orders
WHERE OrderId IN (1, 2, 6);
```

SQL Example 5.15 Output

	CustomerId
1	1
2	3

SQL Example 5.16

Display customers whose orders contain product ID 1. Show customer ID.

SQL Example 5.16 Analysis

This is almost the same as Example 5.15. Just replace the literal OrderId inside the IN parentheses with the query from Example 5.14. You don't need to manually enter the order ID. Let the SQL SELECT statement do that. The SELECT statement inside the IN parentheses is called the subquery or inner query. Note that the subquery is executed before the outer query is executed.

SQL Example 5.16 statement

```
SELECT DISTINCT CustomerId
FROM Sales.Orders
WHERE OrderId IN (SELECT OrderId
            FROM Sales.OrderDetails
            WHERE ProductId = 1);
```

SQL Example 5.16 Output

	CustomerId
1	1
2	3

SQL Example 5.17

Similar to Example 5.7, display all highest priced item(s) on sale. Show the product ID and the price.

SQL Example 5.17 Analysis

The subquery should find the highest price. The outer query displays all items that match that price.

SQL Example 5.17 Statement

```
SELECT ProductId, Price AS "Highest price"
FROM Sales.OrderDetails
WHERE Price = (SELECT Max(Price)
               FROM Sales.OrderDetails);
```

SQL Example 5.17 Output

	ProductId	Highest price
1	2	1599.99

Review Question 5.38

In SQL statements, a query can be built on the result of another query. This is called _____.

a. query on query
b. subquery
c. result query
d. super query

5.15 Chapter Summary

In this chapter, you learned how to map entities and relationships in ERD to relations in databases. A relation is just another name for a table. You will learn more about relations in the next chapter. Mapping makes it possible to move models to databases.

You also learned how to retrieve scale values by using aggregate functions in SQL. Usually these SELECT statements are accompanied by the GROUP BY clause and HAVING clause. You should pay more attention to the differences between the WHERE and HAVING clauses. This chapter introduces all the major clauses used in a SELECT statement. Finally, the concept of subquery was explained.

5.16 Discussion Questions

Discussion 5.1

If you compare an entity to a relation, you may notice there is almost no change most of the time. Yet, the mapping from ERD to relation is an important process. Explain what the significance of mapping is.

Discussion 5.2

This chapter introduces three formats of a relation. Which one is the easiest for beginners to understand? Why do you think so?

Discussion 5.3

One of the objectives for mapping from ERD to relations is the minimization of null values. In your opinion, what are some concerns of null values?

Discussion 5.4

When you write a SELECT statement with all the clauses, it looks like this:

SELECT

FROM

WHERE

GROUP BY

HAVING

ORDER BY

However, when DBMS executes the statement, it changes the sequence to this:

FROM

WHERE

GROUP BY

HAVING

SELECT

ORDER BY

What are some advantages of this design?

5.17 Database Design Exercise

Exercise One:

Map the following ERD into relations. Each customer can have many shipping addresses (including a name for each address). The account holder is just one of the many. Must include the final mapping list.

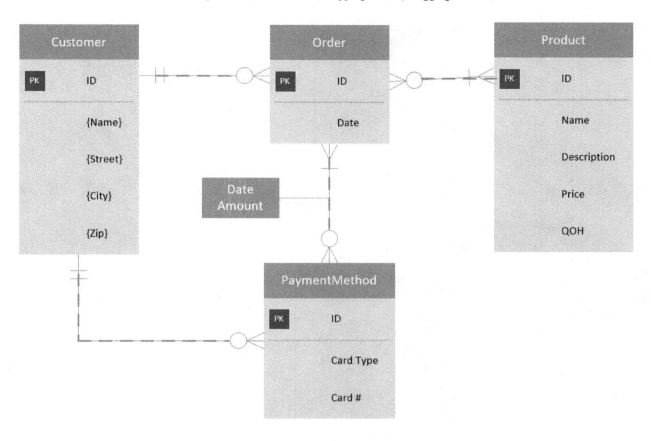

Exercise Two:

Map the following ERD into relations:

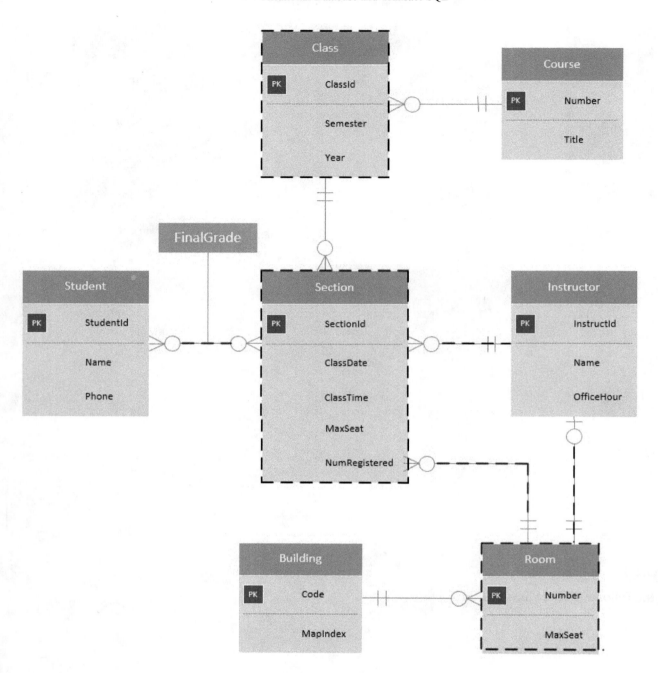

5.18 SQL Exercises

Exercise 5.1

Display the average price of all products in the Deliveries table.

	Average Price
1	463.32

Exercise 5.2

Display the number of employees who provide a phone number in the employees table.

	Number of employees with phone number
1	5

Exercise 5.3

Display the total number of units of products ID 1 delivered. From Appendix B, you may find that product ID 1 is delivered twice: the first one delivered on Oct. 1, 2016 of 2 units. The second was delivered on Nov. 1, 2016 of 5 units for a total of 7 units of product ID 1 delivered.

	Total units of product id 1 delivered
1	7

Exercise 5.4

Display the total value for product ID 7 in the deliveries table. Note that Product ID 7 was delivered twice. The first one is on Oct. 11, 2016 -- 12 units of $79.99 per unit. The second one is on Oct. 12, 2016 -- 18 units of $69.99 per unit. The displayed total value for product ID 7 should be 12X79.99 + 18X69.99 = $2219.70.

	Total value of Product ID 7 delivered
1	2219.70

Exercise 5.5

Display the lowest priced item on sale. Show the price.

	Lowest priced item
1	59.99

Exercise 5.6

Display the total number of units delivered for each product. Show product ID and the corresponding total units delivered, like this:

	ProductId	Total units delivered
1	1	7
2	2	10
3	3	10
4	4	20
5	5	15
6	6	25
7	7	30

Exercise 5.7

Display one of the highest priced items in the deliveries table. Show the product ID and the price.

	ProductID	Highest priced item
1	2	1199.99

Exercise 5.8

Display the total value delivered for each product. For example, with the following data about Product Id 1,

	DeliveryId	ProductId	Quantity	Price	DeliveryDate
1	1	1	2	1099.99	2016-10-01 09:30:00.0000000
2	2	1	5	1199.99	2016-11-01 10:20:00.0000000

The total delivered value of Product Id 1 is 2X1099.99 + 5X1199.99 = 1799.97

Show product ID and corresponding total price

	ProductId	Delivery total
1	1	8199.93
2	2	11999.90
3	3	1299.90
4	4	1599.80
5	5	2099.85
6	6	4249.75
7	7	2219.70

Exercise 5.9

Display all products with a total value delivered of more than $3,000.00. By looking at the result in Exercise 5.8, you can see Product ID 1, 2, and 6 meet this criterion. Display Product ID and the corresponding delivery total.

	ProductId	Delivery total
1	1	8199.93
2	2	11999.90
3	6	4249.75

Exercise 5.10

Display the total units of each product delivered, but only those with a total unit more than 15. Referring to the results table in Exercise 5.6, you can see that only 3 of the 7 products meet this criterion. Show product ID and the corresponding total units delivered.

	ProductId	Total units delivered
1	4	20
2	6	25
3	7	30

Exercise 5.11

Display orders that contain three or more units of items that cost more than $150.00 each. Show order ID and the total units of the item.

	OrderId	Total quantity
1	2	7
2	3	4
3	5	3

Exercise 5.12

Display orders that contain product ID 1 or 3. Show order ID, total quantity of product, and average price (not weighted average price) for each order.

	OrderId	Total units	Average price
1	1	3	824.99
2	2	1	1499.99
3	3	2	159.99
4	5	6	149.99
5	6	1	1499.99

Exercise 5.13

Display orders that contain 3 or more units of product ID 1 or 3. Show order ID, total quantity of product, and average price (not weighted average price) of each order. Sort by quantity from high to low.

	OrderId	Total units	Average price
1	5	6	149.99
2	1	3	824.99

Exercise 5.14

Display products that are delivered between Oct. 5, 2016 and Oct. 10, 2016. Show product ID.

	ProductId
1	3
2	4
3	5

Exercise 5.15

Display suppliers who provide product ID 3, 4, or 5. Show supplier ID.

	SupplierId
1	3
2	5
3	2

Exercise 5.16

Display suppliers whose products are delivered between Oct. 5, 2016 and Oct. 10, 2016. Show supplier ID.

	SupplierId
1	3
2	5
3	2

SQL Exercise 5.17

Similar to Exercise 5.7, display all highest priced item(s) in the deliveries table. Show the product ID and the price.

	ProductId	Highest price
1	1	1199.99
2	2	1199.99

5.19 Solutions to Review Questions

5.1 C; 5.2 A; 5.3 B; 5.4 A; 5.5 A; 5.6 B; 5.7 C; 5.8 C; 5.9 C; 5.10 D; 5.11 A; 5.12 B; 5.13 C; 5.14 A; 5.15 A; 5.16 A; 5.17 C; 5.18 C; 5.19 B; 5.20 D; 5.21 B; 5.22 A; 5.23 C; 5.24 A; 5.25 C; 5.26 D; 5.27 B; 5.28 D; 5.29 B; 5.30 A; 5.31 D; 5.32 C; 5.33 D; 5.34 D; 5.35 B; 5.36 A; 5.37 D; 5.38 B;

CHAPTER 6: NORMALIZATION AND SQL JOIN

Chapter Learning Objectives

6.1 Differentiate a good relation from a bad one.

6.2 Explain different types of anomalies.

6.3 Recognize the problems caused by null values.

6.4 Exemplify functional dependency in a relation.

6.5 Execute normalization on relations.

6.6 Recognize the need for denormalization.

6.7 Critique on entity integrity and referential integrity.

6.8 Retrieve data from multiple tables with JOIN and UNION in SQL.

6.1 What Is a Good Relation?

In the last chapter, you learned how to map an ERD to relations. Technically, you can start to write SQL statements to create tables for a database. In fact, there are many types of software that can automatically generate SQL statements and thus create the database for you based on given ERD and relations.

However, just like how there are many ways to construct a four-bedroom house, there are many ways to design a database. Are they all of the same quality? No. Then how do we know which way is better than the others? In this chapter, we will show you how to check if a relation is good and how to make it better through a process called normalization.

A good relation should reflect what's in the ERD, and, of course, the ERD should reflect the mini-world. The relations should contain all the data needed by the business. For example, if the business needs the total years an employee has worked, then the database should have employment history for each employee. All the attributes, entities, and relationships in an ERD should be carried over to relations (how to meet this requirement was covered in the last chapter.)

A good relation should also minimize the data redundancy. When you have the same data stored in more than one place, it takes extra storage, and, more importantly, it can cause inconsistency or data anomalies (for example, you might update the data in one place and forget to update it in another.) Minimizing data redundancy is the topic of this chapter.

Review Question 6.1
You can check if a relation is good and how to make it better through a process called _____.
a. improvement
b. relation enhancement
c. normalization
d. denormalization

Review Question 6.2
All databases developed using ERD will end up with the same quality.
a. True.
b. False.

Review Question 6.3
What does a good relation do?
a. It reflects what is in the ERD.
b. It allows minimum redundancy.
c. both reflecting what is in the ERD and allowing minimum redundancy.
d. none of the options.

Review Question 6.4
Which of the following is the most serious issue with data redundancy in relations?
a. extra storage.
b. data inconsistency.
c. longer retrieval time.
d. confusion for the user.

6.2. What are anomalies?

Let's see an example. The following table contains data about employees in a company.

EmployeeId	FirstName	LastName	Department
111	Victoria	Gibson	Accounting
112	Justin	Smith	Accounting
113	Melisa	Martin	Marketing
114	Roy	Rocha	Sales
115	Jonathan	Williams	Accounting

Table 1: Employees in one table.

Now, assume the company wants to establish a new department, say, Business Intelligence. This new department currently has no employees. The new table will look like this:

EmployeeId	FirstName	LastName	Department
111	Victoria	Gibson	Accounting
112	Justin	Smith	Accounting
113	Melisa	Martin	Marketing
114	Roy	Rocha	Sales
115	Jonathan	Williams	Accounting
Null	Null	Null	Business Intelligence

Table 2: A new department is added to the table.

The problem with this table is that the primary key (EmployeeId) cannot accept null values. However, making up employee IDs, such as 116, to fill in for the null values will also result in issues, in that even though there are only five employees, the table implies that there are six.

This is called an insertion anomaly and can be avoided if you use two tables as shown below. Here, you just add a new row called "Business Intelligence" to the department table.

EmployeeId	FirstName	LastName	DepartmentId
111	Victoria	Gibson	1
112	Justin	Smith	1
113	Melisa	Martin	2
114	Roy	Rocha	3
115	Jonathan	Williams	1

Table 3. New employee table

DepartmentId	Department
1	Accounting
2	Marketing
3	Sales

Table 4. New Department table.

Back to Table 1, also consider if employee Roy Rocha left the company. We would have to remove his record, and since he is the only employee in Sales, all data on Sales would be gone if using the single table approach. This is called the deletion anomaly and can be avoided if you use two tables as shown above (Table 3 and 4).

Let's see one more anomaly. Back to Table 1, suppose the accounting department is renamed as the finance department. You would have to update the name in three locations, row 1, 2, and 5, if using the single table approach. The more times you make a correction, the more susceptible you are to making mistakes (note: in terms of SQL, this is a less serious problem since updates can be corrected in one statement, but it is still possible to have a mistake.)

This is called a modification anomaly and can be avoided through the two-table approach (Table 3 and 4). In the two-table approach, you will only need to update one row in the department table.

Review Question 6.5

The following employee table may cause anomalies. You can avoid the problem by _____.

EmployeeId	FirstName	LastName	Department
111	Victoria	Gibson	Accounting
112	Justin	Smith	Accounting

a. not inserting abnormal rows
b. not deleting a whole row
c. not providing a null value
d. breaking up the table into an employee table and a department table

Review Question 6.6

Which of the following is not a type of relation anomaly discussed in this chapter?
a. Insertion anomalies
b. Deletion anomalies
c. Modification anomalies
d. Creation anomalies

Review Question 6.7

With the following employee table, an insertion anomaly may happen when _____.

EmployeeId	FirstName	LastName	Department
111	Victoria	Gibson	Accounting
112	Justin	Smith	Accounting

a. a new employee without a department is inserted
b. a new employee for a new department is inserted
c. a new department is inserted
d. a new department without any employees is inserted

Review Question 6.8
With the following employee table, a deletion anomaly may happen when _____.

EmployeeId	FirstName	LastName	Department
114	Roy	Rocha	Sales
115	Jonathan	Williams	Accounting

a. an employee is deleted
b. when more than one employee is deleted
c. when an employee who is the single person in a department is deleted
d. when more than one employee in the same department is deleted

Review Question 6.9
With the following employee table, a modification anomaly may happen when _____.

EmployeeId	FirstName	LastName	Department
114	Roy	Rocha	Sales
115	Jonathan	Williams	Accounting

a. a department changes its name
b. an employee changes his or her last name
c. an employee changes his or her first name
d. an employee changes both his or her first name and last name

6.3 Problems with Null Value

There are some situations in which a value for an attribute (of an entity instance) cannot be entered in the database. This could be due to three types of situations. The first situation is that the attribute is not applicable. For example, if your current job is your first job, then the attribute of the previous job title is not applicable. The second situation is that the attribute value exists, but the information is not yet available for the database. It is a missing value. For example, all employees have a date of birth, but when entering data for a new employee, you may not know that data yet. The third situation is that a value for an attribute may not be known. For example, a new employee's marital status may not be known. The employee may be already married or may still be single. A null value in the database may indicate the presence of any of the above situations.

As a result, the logical operation for null values is different from a known value. When a null value is in the operation, the operation is often called three-valued logic. These operators are often used in the WHERE and HAVING clauses of SQL SELECT statements.

One Operand value is:		The Other Operand value is:		
		True	*False*	*Null*
	True	**True**	**False**	**Null**
	False	**False**	**False**	**False**
	Null	**Null**	**False**	**Null**

Table 6.5 Three-valued AND logical operator

For example, suppose you want to see whether an employee meets a requirement of being born before Jan. 1 1990 and is a Texas resident. If it is true that an employee's date of birth is before Jan. 1, 1990 and their hometown is unknown/null, then it would therefore be unknown/null whether they meet the requirement of being born before Jan. 1 1990 and being a Texas resident.

However, if it is false that an employee's date of birth is before Jan. 1 1990 (meaning they were born after Jan. 1 1990) and their hometown is still unknown/null, it can be confidently declared that they do not meet the requirement of being born before Jan. 1 1990 and being a Texas resident.

Similarly, the following table shows the three-valued OR operator.

One Operand value is:		The Other Operand value is:		
		True	*False*	*Null*
	True	**True**	**True**	**True**
	False	**True**	**False**	**Null**
	Null	**True**	**Null**	**Null**

Table 6.6 Three-valued OR logical operator

Finally, the following table shows the three-logic NOT operator. Keep in mind that the three-valued NOT logical operator can only be used for one variable unlike for the AND and OR operator.

The Operand value is:	The result of the NOT operation
True	**False**
False	**True**
Null	**Null**

Table 6.7 Three-valued NOT logical operator

You cannot compare a null value to a Boolean value by using an equal sign. It is either IS NULL or IS NOT NULL. Also, when null values are in the column of a JOIN operation (an SQL topic on combining two tables later in the chapter), the result can be difficult to predict.

Review Question 6.10

If your current job is your first job, then the attribute of the previous job title is not applicable. The value for such a situation in a relational table is _____.
a. N/A
b. not relevant
c. blank
d. null

Review Question 6.11
All employees have a date of birth, but when entering data for a new employee, you may not know that data yet. The value for such a situation in a relational table is _____.
a. N/A
b. not known
c. blank
d. null

Review Question 6.12
A new employee's marital status may not be known. The value for such a situation in a relational table is _____.
a. N/A
b. not known
c. blank
d. null

Review Question 6.13
When null values are in the column of a JOIN operation, _____.
a. the SQL statement won't work
b. the SQL statement will run slow
c. the result can be difficult to predict
d. the result can contain many more null values

Review Question 6.14
Which of the following is NOT a possible situation for null values in a database?
a. the database server is down
b. the attribute is not applicable for the entity instance.
c. the data has been not entered in the database table
d. the data is not known

Review Question 6.15
What is the result of the following three-valued logic expression?
True AND Null
a. True
b. False
c. Null

Review Question 6.16
What is the result of the following three-valued logic expression?
False AND Null
a. True
b. False
c. Null

Review Question 6.17
What is the result of the following three-valued logic expression?
False OR Null
a. True
b. False
c. Null

Review Question 6.18
What is the result of the following three-valued logic expression?
True OR Null
a. True
b. False
c. Null

Review Question 6.19
In SQL statements, which of the following is the correct way to write the WHERE clause?
a. WHERE SecondPhone = Null
b. WHERE SecondPhone = 'Null'
c. WHERE SecondPhone IS Null
d. WHERE SecondPhone LIKE Null

6.4 Functional Dependency in a Relation

Functional dependency refers to when one attribute determines another. Say you have two columns of a relation, Column1 and Column2. If we say that Column2 is functionally dependent on Column1, we mean that if any two rows in Column1 have the same value, then the corresponding two rows in Column2 must also be equal to each other.

For example, if whenever two students have the same ID they also have the same first name, it can be stated that student first name is functionally dependent on student ID.

However, if two students have the same first name, they don't necessarily have the same last name, and therefore it can be stated that student last name is not functionally dependent on student first name.

The above functional dependency definition can be extended to include more than one column. In other words, this relationship can exist between two groups of columns, or even a group of columns and one column.

The functional dependency conclusion should not be made based on limited records in a relation. It should be based on the mini-world data. For example,

Course	Classroom
CS101	Lincoln311
CS102	Lincoln312
CS103	Lincoln313

Table 6.8 A partial data for course and classroom table.

Based on the limited data sample, you may conclude that Course is functionally dependent on Classroom since with a given classroom, you can find only one course. However, in reality, this is often not true.

Let's see an example of functional dependency in a relation:

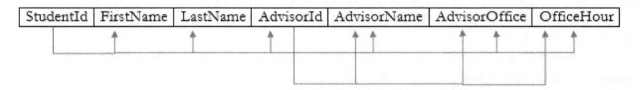

Figure 6.1 Functional dependency diagram

In the above dependency diagram, studentId is called a determinant because if you know the student ID, you can find out all the remaining columns that the arrows point to. AdvisorId is also a determinant, which points to its dependents: AdvisorName, AdvisorOffice, and OfficeHour.

Review Question 6.20
If you want to prove that an attribute is NOT functionally dependent on another attribute, you need _____ examples.
a. one
b. two
c. three
d. many

Review Question 6.21
Say you have two columns of a relation, Column1 and Column2. If two rows in Column1 are equal to each other, then the two corresponding values of Column2 must also be equal to each other. Thus, Column2 is _____ on Column1.
a. functionally dependent
b. over dependent
c. composite primary key
d. equal

Review Question 6.22
If two students have the same ID, they must have the same first name. Which of the following is true?
a. ID is the primary key
b. ID is a determinant
c. First name is the primary key
d. First name is a determinant

Review Question 6.23
To find out if a column is functionally dependent on another column, you only need a small sample of the database table.
a. True
b. False

6.5 Normalization

As stated in section 6.2, anomalies are caused by duplicated data. There is a process that can reduce the data redundancy called normalization. Normalization is based on functional dependency.

The normalization process begins with examining the dependency diagram to break up a relation based on its determinants, thus achieving first normal form. This process can be repeated to achieve second normal form, third normal form, and so on, if necessary.

6.5.1 First Normal Form

A relation is a two-dimensional table with unique rows. In other words, any table with a primary key is a relation. A relation is said to be in the first normal form if all cells are atomic and no repeating group. Let's see an example:

StudentId	Name	DateBirth	CourseId	Title	Grade	Semester	Location
111	Alice	1/4/2001	CS101, CS211	Intro CS, Java	A, A	Fall 2017	Lincoln311, 312
112	Tom	2/6/2000	CS201, CS211	Algorithm, Java	B, B	Fall 2017	Lincoln311, 312

Table 6.9 Student registration table without atomic cell values.

Table 6.9 is not in the first normal form because it contains multivalued data. The course id, title, grade, and location fields have more than one value in a cell. One solution to make Table 6.9 in the first normal form is to make each simple value in its own row as shown in Table 6.10.

StudentId	Name	DateBirth	CourseId	Title	Grade	semester	Location
111	Alice	1/4/2001	CS101	Intro CS	A	Fall 2017	Lincoln311
112	Tom	2/6/2000	CS201	Algorithm	B	Fall 2017	Lincoln311
111	Alice	1/4/2001	CS211	Java	A	Fall 2017	Lincoln312
112	Tom	2/6/2000	CS211	Java	B	Fall 2017	Lincoln312

Table 6.10 Student registration table with atomic cell values

Table 6.10 is in the first normal form because all cells of the table contain atomic values and any attribute depends on the composite primary key of studentID and courseID.

If you follow the steps for database design from the previous chapters, you won't get a relation like Table 6.9 because multivalued attributes are mapped into a separate relation.

Atomic also means a value is not composite, or that it cannot be further broken down into smaller parts. For example, a student name is not atomic in many cases because the value can be broken down into first name, last name, and middle name. However, sometimes, you may be happy with just a student name. In short, we treat "atomic" as "a single thing". If a school always uses a student name as a single thing, it is ok to treat it as atomic.

6.5.2 Second Normal Form

A relation is said to be in the second normal form if it is in the first normal form and every non- primary key attribute is functionally dependent on the whole primary key. Compared to the first normal form, the new part in the second normal form is the "dependent on the whole primary key". For a single attribute primary key relation, this is automatically satisfied because all non-key attributes are dependent on the whole key.

Is the student table of Table 6.10 in the second normal form? First, you need to find out what the primary key is. It is a composite primary key of StudentId and CourseId. The question is, "Is every non-primary key attribute functionally dependent on the whole primary key?" The answer is no. For example, Title is not dependent on both StudentId and CourseId. It is dependent on only CourseId. Thus the "dependent on the whole key" is violated.

Let's draw the dependency diagram for Table 6.10.

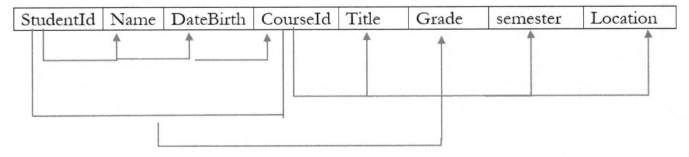

Figure 6.2 Dependency Diagram for Table 6.9

Based on the dependency diagram of Figure 6.2, the relation can be broken into three relations because there are three determinants. The first one is StudentId, the second one is CourseId, and the third one is the composite determinant of StudentId and CourseId.

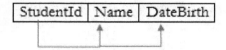

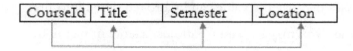

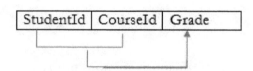

Figure 6.3 Dependency diagram after breakup of a relation.

ALL three relations in Figure 6.3 are in second normal form.

Let's see another relation that is in the first normal form, but not in the second normal form. Below, you can see that the primary key is both StudentId and CourseId. However, Location does not depend on StudentId (only on CourseId) and so it is in the first normal form but not the second normal form.

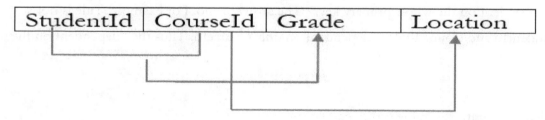

Figure 6.4 Dependency diagram for a relation in first normal form, but not second normal form.

6.5.3 Third Normal Form

A relation is in third normal form if it is in second normal form and has no transitive dependency. A transitive dependency is a dependent relationship between two non-primary key attributes.

Suppose a university allows any students to take at most one course for free. They may have a relation like this below:

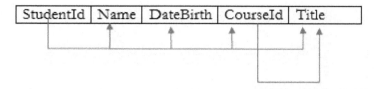

Figure 6.5 A relation with transitive dependency.

In Figure 6.5, the Title attribute is functionally dependent on CourseId, and CourseId is dependent on the StudentId (the primary key of the relation.) This relation is in the second normal form, but not in the third normal form. To convert the relation in Figure 6.5 into third normal form, just break the relation into two based on the determinant of StudentId and CourseId as shown below.

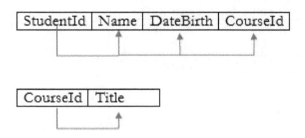

Figure 6.6 Relation in Figure 6.5 now in third normal form.

Here's another example of a relation that is in the 2nd NF, but not in the 3rd NF.

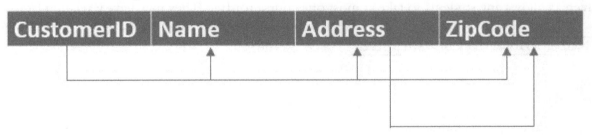

The three relations in Figure 6.3 contain no transitive dependency and thus are all in 3rd normal form.

The normalization process can go on to higher levels of normalization form. This book only covers up to the third normal form for most practical projects. The higher the normal form the less duplication of the data. However, there's a side effect in this process we will uncover in the next section.

Review Question 6.24
A relation is a two-dimensional table with unique rows. In other words, any table with a _____ is a relation.

a. primary key

b. foreign key

c. numeric column

d. two-dimensional data

Review Question 6.25

The following table is in _____ normal form (pick the highest level).

StudentId	Name	DateBirth	CourseId	Title	Grade	Semester	Location
111	Alice	1/4/2001	CS101, CS211	Intro CS, Java	A, A	Fall 2017	Lincoln311, 312
112	Tom	2/6/2000	CS201, CS211	Algorithm, Java	B, B	Fall 2017	Lincoln311, 312

a. first

b. second

c. third

d. not in any normal form

Review Question 6.26

The following table is in _____ normal form (pick the highest level).

StudentId	Name	DateBirth	CourseId	Title	Grade	semester	Location
111	Alice	1/4/2001	CS101	Intro CS	A	Fall 2017	Lincoln311
112	Tom	2/6/2000	CS201	Algorithm	B	Fall 2017	Lincoln311
111	Alice	1/4/2001	CS211	Java	A	Fall 2017	Lincoln312
112	Tom	2/6/2000	CS211	Java	B	Fall 2017	Lincoln312

a. first

b. second

c. third

d. not in any normal form

Review Question 6.27

The following relation is in _____ normal form (pick the highest level).

Suppose a university allows any students to take at most one course for free. They may have a relation like this below:

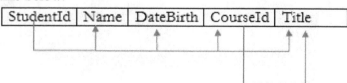

a. first

b. second

c. third

d. not in any normal form

Review Question 6.28

The following relation is in _____ normal form (pick the highest level).

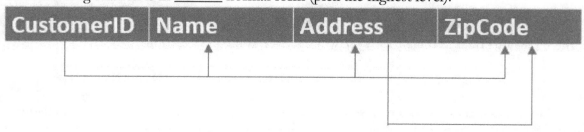

a. first
b. second
c. third
d. not in any normal form

Review Question 6.29
A relation that contains only _____ values in each cell is said in the first normal form.
a. numeric
b. text
c. useful
d. atomic

Review Question 6.30
The process of reducing data redundancy in a relation is called _____.
a. normalization
b. redundancy minimization
c. redundancy removal
d. redundancy reduction

Review Question 6.31
The normalization process is based on the functional dependency of the attributes. A relation is broken into smaller relations based on its _____.
a. size
b. determinant
c. structure
d. normal form

Review Question 6.32
A relation is in second normal form if _____.
a. it is in first normal form
b. all its values are atomic
c. every non-primary key attribute is functionally dependent on the whole primary key
d. it is in first normal form and every non-primary key attribute is functionally dependent on the whole PK

Review Question 6.33
A relation is in the third normal form if _____.
a. it is in the second normal form
b. every non-primary key attribute is functionally dependent on the whole primary key
c. it contains no transitive dependency
d. it is in the second normal form an it contains no transitive dependency

Review Question 6.34
According to the author, for most business problems, a _____ normal form is good enough for a relation.
a. first
b. second
c. third
d. fourth

6.6 Denormalization

In normalization, the higher the normal form, the less duplication in the data. Logically, you would want to go as high as you can. However, when the normal form goes up, the number of relations increases as determinants break them up. When using the data, you will have more tables and thus more joined tables. The process of joining tables is time consuming. This will affect the performance.

As a result, you need to balance the benefit of less data duplication and faster performance. After following the rules to normalize the relations, you may want to do some denormalization. The process of denormalization involves combining relations to avoid joining tables for data retrieval.

There's only one rule for denormalization: data used together should stay together (in other words, they should remain in the same relation.) For example, students and advisors are usually two separate relations. However, if the database always finds the advisor through the student or finds the student through the advisor, then you would want to combine the two relations in one.

In short, the denormalization process is not required, although you may want to use it if performance is a major concern. Remember to balance the benefits between normalization and denormalization.

Review Question 6.35
In normalization, the higher the normal form, the less duplication in the data. Logically, you would want to go _____.
a. to the second normal form
b. to the third normal form
c. to the fourth normal form
d. as high as you can

Review Question 6.36
In normalization, when the normal form goes up, the _____ increases as determinants break them up.
a. number of relations
b. primary key of relations
c. foreign key of relations
d. number of keys

Review Question 6.37
In normalization, when using the data in a higher level of normal form, you will have more tables and thus more joined tables. The process of joining tables is _____. This will affect the _____.
a. fast, data
b. fast, performance
c. time consuming, data

d. time consuming, performance

Review Question 6.38
In normalization, you need to balance the benefit of _____ and _____.
a. quick normalization, faster performance
b. quick normalization, cheaper storage
c. less data duplication, faster performance
d. less data duplication, cheaper storage

Review Question 6.39
Denormalization is the opposite process of normalization. Denormalization combines relations while normalization breaks up relations.
a. True
b. False

Review Question 6.40
Denormalization is a must for all database design.
a. True
b. False

Review Question 6.41
A rule for denormalization is to _____.
a. always keep relations in at least third normal form
b. always keep relations in at least second normal form
c. make sure data used together stay together
d. make sure at least one denormalization occurs for each database

6.7 Entity Integrity and Referential Integrity

Each entity should have a primary key so that each row (tuple to be more accurate) can be uniquely identified by the DBMS. Such a requirement is also called entity integrity. The primary key of an entity is kept as the primary key in the relations after mapping.

The relationships between entities in ERD are usually reflected by the use of foreign keys in relations. Adding a foreign key achieves referential integrity. The foreign key actually checks the column value with the primary key of the related relation. The foreign keys are added during the mapping.

For example, as shown in Figure 6.7, a student relation has AdvisorId as a foreign key. The data in the student relation are not valid because Bob has an advisor (advisor 3) that does not exist. As can be seen, the foreign key helps the data quality of the database. Referential integrity keeps data valid.

StudentId	StudentName	AdvisorId
111	Alice	1
222	Bob	3
333	Tom	2

AdvisorId	AdvisorName
1	Dr. Xavier
2	Dr. Young

Figure 6.7 Referential integrity violation example.

Review Question 6.42
All entities should have a primary key so that each row (tuple to be more accurate) can be uniquely identified by the DBMS. This requirement is called _____.
a. entity requirement
b. entity integrity
c. entity quality
d. referential integrity

Review Question 6.43
The relationships between entities in ERD are usually reflected by the use of foreign keys in relations. Adding a foreign key achieves _____.
a. entity requirement
b. entity integrity
c. entity quality
d. referential integrity

6.8 SQL INNER JOIN

SQL Example 5.16 from Chapter 5 is repeated below:

Display customers whose orders contain product ID 1. Show customer ID.

You learned how to use subquery to retrieve all the necessary data from more than one table. You cannot use a simple SELECT... FROM on a table because the customer ID and product ID do not appear in the same table.

Often, you will want to retrieve data from multiple tables. You can use INNER JOIN (often shortened to JOIN) to combine the tables and then use SELECT for the data you need. Inner join puts two tables side by side, but only those rows with matching values will appear in the joined table.

For example, if you want to know the total value of each order, you can use the OrderDetails table:

	OrderId	ProductId	Price	quantity
1	1	1	1499.99	1
2	1	3	149.99	2
3	2	1	1499.99	1
4	2	2	1599.99	1
5	2	4	99.99	6
6	2	6	189.99	5
7	3	3	159.99	2
8	3	6	199.99	1
9	3	7	109.99	2
10	3	8	69.99	2
11	3	9	1449.99	1
12	4	4	99.99	2
13	4	8	69.99	1
14	5	3	149.99	6
15	5	6	199.99	3
16	6	1	1499.99	1
17	7	2	999.99	1
18	8	7	79.99	1
19	8	8	59.99	2

However, if you also want to know the order date for each order, you have to use the Order table:

OrderId	CustomerId	EmployeeId	OrderDate
1	1	5	2017-01-03
2	1	3	2017-03-05
3	2	5	2017-02-23
4	4	5	2017-04-13
5	1	4	2017-05-03
6	3	6	2017-05-08
7	5	7	2016-11-08
8	7	2	2016-12-23

How can you have order total and order date for each order in one single SELECT statement? The answer is to join the tables. You can join the OrderDetails and Orders table according to Order ID -- that is, you put the two tables side by side with the matching values in the OrderId. For example, since OrderId = 1 has two rows in the OrderDetails table and one row in the Orders table, you will have two rows in the new joined table like this:

	OrderId	ProductId	Price	quantity	OrderId	CustomerId	EmployeeId	OrderDate
1	1	1	1499.99	1	1	1	5	2017-01-03
2	1	3	149.99	2	1	1	5	2017-01-03

Here's the result of the two tables joined. Spend a few minutes to see how the two tables are used to form this new table.

	OrderId	ProductId	Price	quantity	OrderId	CustomerId	EmployeeId	OrderDate
1	1	1	1499.99	1	1	1	5	2017-01-03
2	1	3	149.99	2	1	1	5	2017-01-03
3	2	1	1499.99	1	2	1	3	2017-03-05
4	2	2	1599.99	1	2	1	3	2017-03-05
5	2	4	99.99	6	2	1	3	2017-03-05
6	2	6	189.99	5	2	1	3	2017-03-05
7	3	3	159.99	2	3	2	5	2017-02-23
8	3	6	199.99	1	3	2	5	2017-02-23
9	3	7	109.99	2	3	2	5	2017-02-23
10	3	8	69.99	2	3	2	5	2017-02-23
11	3	9	1449.99	1	3	2	5	2017-02-23
12	4	4	99.99	2	4	4	5	2017-04-13
13	4	8	69.99	1	4	4	5	2017-04-13
14	5	3	149.99	6	5	1	4	2017-05-03
15	5	6	199.99	3	5	1	4	2017-05-03
16	6	1	1499.99	1	6	3	6	2017-05-08
17	7	2	999.99	1	7	5	7	2016-11-08
18	8	7	79.99	1	8	7	2	2016-12-23
19	8	8	59.99	2	8	7	2	2016-12-23

Let's see another example. Suppose there's a Students table like this (Dan does not have an advisor assigned yet):

StudentId	StudentName	AdvisorId
1	Alice	111
2	Bob	111
3	Chuck	222
4	Dan	Null

Table 6.11 Data for the student table

The advisor table looks like this:

AdvisorId	AdvisorName
111	Xavier
222	Young
333	Zach

Table 6.12 Data for the advisor table

From the data above, you can see that advisor 111 has two students, advisor 222 has one student, and advisor 333 has no students yet. What is the result if you INNER JOIN these two tables based on AdvisorId?

StudentId	StudentName	AdvisorId	AdivsorId	AdvisorName
1	Alice	111	111	Xavier
2	Alice	111	111	Xavier
3	Chuck	222	222	Young

Table 6.13 Data for the inner join of the student and advisor tables

We will use INNER JOIN and JOIN interchangeably. The syntax for joining two tables is:

SELECT *

FROM Table1Name JOIN Table2Name

ON Table1Name.CommonColumn = Table2Name.CommonColumn

The CommonColumn is the column that appears in both tables. In the above example, it is AdvisorId. The equal sign "=" in the ON clause can have other conditions, such as the "<" sign.

If you have more than two tables to join, you join two tables first. Then join the result of the first two tables with the third table and so on.

SQL Example 6.1

Display order details for each order. Show order ID, order date, product ID in the order, quantity, and price of that product.

SQL Example 6.1 Analysis

Because the order ID, order date, product ID, quantity, and price of the products are from two different tables, Orders and OrderDetails tables, you will need to join the two tables. The common column for the two tables is OrderId. Refer to Appendix B for which data are in which table and which field is common between the two tables.

Also, because there are two OrderId columns in the joined table, you should add the table name to qualify the column as shown in the SELECT statement below.

Note that in the SQL Example 6.1 statement below, we show two solutions. The first one shows the minimum qualifier used to avoid ambiguity. The second one shows all SELECT columns with the format of TableName.ColumnName for easy reading.

SQL Example 6.1 statement

```
SELECT Orders.OrderId, OrderDate, ProductId, Quantity, Price
FROM Sales.Orders JOIN Sales.OrderDetails
ON Orders.OrderId = OrderDetails.OrderId;
```

Or

```
SELECT Orders.OrderId, Orders.OrderDate, OrderDetails.ProductId,
OrderDetails.Quantity, OrderDetails.Price
FROM Sales.Orders JOIN Sales.OrderDetails
ON Orders.OrderId = OrderDetails.OrderId;
```

SQL Example 6.1 Output

	OrderId	OrderDate	ProductId	Quantity	Price
1	1	2017-01-03	1	1	1499.99
2	1	2017-01-03	3	2	149.99
3	2	2017-03-05	1	1	1499.99
4	2	2017-03-05	2	1	1599.99
5	2	2017-03-05	4	6	99.99
6	2	2017-03-05	6	5	189.99
7	3	2017-02-23	3	2	159.99
8	3	2017-02-23	6	1	199.99
9	3	2017-02-23	7	2	109.99
10	3	2017-02-23	8	2	69.99
11	3	2017-02-23	9	1	1449.99
12	4	2017-04-13	4	2	99.99
13	4	2017-04-13	8	1	69.99
14	5	2017-05-03	3	6	149.99
15	5	2017-05-03	6	3	199.99
16	6	2017-05-08	1	1	1499.99
17	7	2016-11-08	2	1	999.99
18	8	2016-12-23	7	1	79.99
19	8	2016-12-23	8	2	59.99

SQL Example 6.2

Display order total for each order. Show order ID and order total for each order.

SQL Example 6.2 Analysis

The necessary data are from two tables, so you need to join the two tables as shown in SQL Example 6.1.

Take a look at the output of SQL Example 6.1. Can you display the order total with the knowledge you

learned from Chapter 5? You will need a SUM() function for the total and GROUP BY clause to combine rows in each order. For example, Order ID 1 has two rows and you should combine them to find the order total.

SQL Example 6.2 statement

```
SELECT Orders.OrderId, SUM(Quantity * Price) AS "Order total"
FROM Sales.Orders JOIN Sales.OrderDetails
ON Orders.OrderId = OrderDetails.OrderId
GROUP BY Orders.OrderId;
```

SQL Example 6.2 Output

	OrderId	Order total
1	1	1799.97
2	2	4649.87
3	3	2329.92
4	4	269.97
5	5	1499.91
6	6	1499.99
7	7	999.99
8	8	199.97

SQL Example 6.3

Display suppliers and their products. Show supplier name and corresponding product names.

SQL Example 6.3 Analysis

The supplier names are in the suppliers table and the product names are in the products table. You need to join the suppliers and the products table to retrieve all data.

SQL Example 6.3 statement

```
SELECT SupplierName, ProductName
FROM Purchasing.Suppliers JOIN Purchasing.Products
ON Suppliers.SupplierId = Products.supplierid;
```

Example 6.3 Output

	SupplierName	ProductName
1	Samsong	65-Inch 4K Ultra HD Smart TV
2	Samsong	60-Inch 4K Ultra HD Smart LED TV
3	Lonovo	3200 Lumens LED Home Theater Projector
4	Canan	Wireless Color Photo Printer
5	IMB	6Wireless Compact Laser Printer
6	IMB	Color Laser Printer
7	Samsong	10" 16GB Android Tablet
8	IMB	GPS Android Tablet PC
9	Canan	20.2 MP Digital Camera

SQL Example 6.4

Display suppliers, their products, and delivery details. Show supplier name and corresponding product names, each delivery quantity, price, and date.

SQL Example 6.4 Analysis

The supplier names are in the suppliers table and the product names are in the products table. Delivery details are from the Deliveries table. You need to join the suppliers, the products, and the deliveries tables to retrieve all data. You can only join two tables at a time. The result of two joined tables is a table that can be used to join another table. The two joined tables must have a common field.

SQL Example 6.4 statement

```
SELECT SupplierName, ProductName, Quantity, Price, DeliveryDate
FROM Purchasing.Suppliers JOIN Purchasing.Products
ON Suppliers.SupplierId = Products.supplierid
JOIN Purchasing.Deliveries
ON Products.ProductId = Deliveries.ProductId;
```

Example 6.4 Output

	SupplierName	ProductName	Quantity	Price	DeliveryDate
1	Samsong	65-Inch 4K Ultra HD Smart TV	2	1099.99	2016-10-01 09:30:00.0000000
2	Samsong	65-Inch 4K Ultra HD Smart TV	5	1199.99	2016-11-01 10:20:00.0000000
3	Samsong	60-Inch 4K Ultra HD Smart LED TV	10	1199.99	2016-10-02 11:10:00.0000000
4	Lonovo	3200 Lumens LED Home Theater Projector	10	129.99	2016-10-05 09:15:00.0000000
5	Canan	Wireless Color Photo Printer	20	79.99	2016-10-07 14:00:00.0000000
6	IMB	6Wireless Compact Laser Printer	15	139.99	2016-10-07 15:30:00.0000000
7	IMB	Color Laser Printer	25	169.99	2016-10-10 10:30:00.0000000
8	Samsong	10" 16GB Android Tablet	12	79.99	2016-10-11 11:10:00.0000000
9	Samsong	10" 16GB Android Tablet	18	69.99	2016-10-12 09:50:00.0000000

SQL Example 6.5

Display suppliers, their products, and total quantity delivered. Show supplier name and corresponding product names and total quantity of that product delivered.

SQL Example 6.5 Analysis

Examine the output table from SQL Example 6.4. All necessary data is in that table. You need to join the three tables to get all the data. You also need to use an aggregate function to determine the total quantity of each product delivered. For example, the Samsong 65-inch 4K Ultra HD Smart TV is delivered twice and the total is 7 (2+5). When you use the aggregate function, you should GROUP BY the non-aggregate columns in the SELECT.

SQL Example 6.5 statement

```
SELECT SupplierName, ProductName, SUM(Quantity) AS "Total delivered"
FROM Purchasing.Suppliers JOIN Purchasing.Products
ON Suppliers.SupplierId = Products.supplierid
JOIN Purchasing.Deliveries
ON Products.ProductId = Deliveries.ProductId
GROUP BY SupplierName, ProductName;
```

Example 6.5 Output

	SupplierName	ProductName	Total delivered
1	Samsong	10" 16GB Android Tablet	30
2	Lonovo	3200 Lumens LED Home Theater Projector	10
3	Samsong	60-Inch 4K Ultra HD Smart LED TV	10
4	Samsong	65-Inch 4K Ultra HD Smart TV	7
5	IMB	6Wireless Compact Laser Printer	15
6	IMB	Color Laser Printer	25
7	Canan	Wireless Color Photo Printer	20

SQL Example 6.6

Display suppliers, their products, and the most recent delivery date of the product. Show supplier name and corresponding product names and the date of the most recent delivery.

SQL Example 6.6 Analysis

Examine the output table from SQL Example 6.4 again. All necessary data is in that table. You need to join the three tables to get all the data. You also need to use an aggregate function, MAX(), to determine the most recent date in the delivery date column. For example, the Samsong 65-inch 4K Ultra HD Smart TV is delivered twice with the delivery dates of Oct 1, 2016 and Nov. 1, 2016. When you use the aggregate function, you should GROUP BY the non-aggregate columns in the SELECT.

SQL Example 6.6 statement

```
SELECT SupplierName, ProductName, MAX(DeliveryDate) AS "Most recent
delivery"
FROM Purchasing.Suppliers JOIN Purchasing.Products
ON Suppliers.SupplierId = Products.supplierid
JOIN Purchasing.Deliveries
ON Products.ProductId = Deliveries.ProductId
GROUP BY SupplierName, ProductName;
```

Example 6.6 Output

	SupplierName	ProductName	Most recent delivery
1	Samsong	10" 16GB Android Tablet	2016-10-12 09:50:00.0000000
2	Lonovo	3200 Lumens LED Home Theater Projector	2016-10-05 09:15:00.0000000
3	Samsong	60-Inch 4K Ultra HD Smart LED TV	2016-10-02 11:10:00.0000000
4	Samsong	65-Inch 4K Ultra HD Smart TV	2016-11-01 10:20:00.0000000
5	IMB	6Wireless Compact Laser Printer	2016-10-07 15:30:00.0000000
6	IMB	Color Laser Printer	2016-10-10 10:30:00.0000000
7	Canan	Wireless Color Photo Printer	2016-10-07 14:00:00.0000000

SQL Example 6.7

Display all suppliers, their products, the most recent delivery date of the product and the quantity of the delivery. Show supplier name and corresponding product names, most recent delivery date and the quantity of that delivery.

SQL Example 6.7 Analysis

Again, all necessary data are in the output table from SQL Example 6.4. Since the only difference from SQL Example 6.6 is the quantity of that delivery, why can't we just add the quantity column to the SELECT statement of Example 6.6? Unfortunately, it will not run because the Quantity column is a non-aggregate column, so you should also add Quantity in the GROUP BY clause as shown below:

```
SELECT SupplierName, ProductName, MAX(DeliveryDate) AS "Most recent delivery", Quantity
FROM Purchasing.Suppliers JOIN Purchasing.Products
ON Suppliers.SupplierId = Products.supplierid
JOIN Purchasing.Deliveries
ON Products.ProductId = Deliveries.ProductId
```

```
GROUP BY SupplierName, ProductName, Quantity;
```

And the output will look like this:

	SupplierName	ProductName	Most recent delivery	Quantity
1	Canan	Wireless Color Photo Printer	2016-10-07 14:00:00.0000000	20
2	IMB	6Wireless Compact Laser Printer	2016-10-07 15:30:00.0000000	15
3	IMB	Color Laser Printer	2016-10-10 10:30:00.0000000	25
4	Lonovo	3200 Lumens LED Home Theater Projector	2016-10-05 09:15:00.0000000	10
5	Samsong	10" 16GB Android Tablet	2016-10-11 11:10:00.0000000	12
6	Samsong	10" 16GB Android Tablet	2016-10-12 09:50:00.0000000	18
7	Samsong	60-Inch 4K Ultra HD Smart LED TV	2016-10-02 11:10:00.0000000	10
8	Samsong	65-Inch 4K Ultra HD Smart TV	2016-10-01 09:30:00.0000000	2
9	Samsong	65-Inch 4K Ultra HD Smart TV	2016-11-01 10:20:00.0000000	5

Are the results correct? No, there are only seven products, but the results give nine most recent delivery dates. This problem is caused by the Quantity in the GROUP BY clause.

To solve this problem, move the "Most recent delivery" to a WHERE clause. Then there is no need for Quantity in the GROUP BY clause.

SQL Example 6.7 statement

```
SELECT SupplierName, ProductName, DeliveryDate, Quantity
FROM Purchasing.Suppliers JOIN Purchasing.Products
ON Suppliers.SupplierId = Products.Supplierid
JOIN Purchasing.Deliveries
ON Products.ProductId = Deliveries.ProductId
WHERE DeliveryDate = (SELECT MAX(DeliveryDate) FROM Purchasing.Deliveries
WHERE ProductId = Products.ProductId);
```

Example 6.7 Output

	SupplierName	ProductName	DeliveryDate	Quantity
1	Samsong	10" 16GB Android Tablet	2016-10-12 09:50:00.0000000	18
2	IMB	Color Laser Printer	2016-10-10 10:30:00.0000000	25
3	IMB	6Wireless Compact Laser Printer	2016-10-07 15:30:00.0000000	15
4	Canan	Wireless Color Photo Printer	2016-10-07 14:00:00.0000000	20
5	Lonovo	3200 Lumens LED Home Theater Projector	2016-10-05 09:15:00.0000000	10
6	Samsong	60-Inch 4K Ultra HD Smart LED TV	2016-10-02 11:10:00.0000000	10
7	Samsong	65-Inch 4K Ultra HD Smart TV	2016-11-01 10:20:00.0000000	5

Review Question 6.44
If the data needed are from more than one table, you can _____.
a. combine the tables
b. join the tables

c. use WHERE clause

d. use HAVING clause

Review Question 6.45

Inner join puts two tables side by side, _____.

a. but only those rows with matching values will appear in the joined table.

b. all the rows from both tables will be in the joined table.

c. but the two tables must have the same number of rows.

d. but the two tables must have the same number of columns.

Review Question 6.46

Given the following two tables, the student table and advisor table:

StudentId	StudentName	AdvisorId
1	Alice	111
2	Bob	111
3	Chuck	222
4	Dan	Null

AdvisorId	AdvisorName
111	Xavier
222	Young
333	Zach

Which of the following tables shows the result of the INNER JOIN?

a.

StudentId	StudentName	AdvisorId	AdivsorId	AdvisorName
1	Alice	111	111	Xavier
2	Alice	111	111	Xavier
3	Chuck	222	222	Young

b.

StudentId	StudentName	AdvisorId	AdivsorId	AdvisorName
1	Alice	111	111	Xavier
2	Alice	111	111	Xavier
3	Chuck	222	222	Young
4	Dan	Null	Null	Null

c.

StudentId	StudentName	AdvisorId	AdivsorId	AdvisorName
1	Alice	111	111	Xavier
2	Alice	111	111	Xavier
3	Chuck	222	222	Young
Null	Null	Null	333	Zach

d.

StudentId	StudentName	AdvisorId	AdivsorId	AdvisorName
1	Alice	111	111	Xavier
2	Alice	111	111	Xavier
3	Chuck	222	222	Young
4	Dan	Null	Null	Null
Null	Null	Null	333	Zach

6.9 SQL OUTER JOIN

Outer join is similar to the inner join you learned in the last section. It combines two tables side by side into a larger table. The difference is the treatment of rows with no match. In the case of inner join, when there is no match, the rows won't appear in the joined table. However, in case of outer join, when there is no match, some rows will still appear in the joined table depending on the type of outer join. There are three types of outer join: left, right, and full.

LEFT OUTER JOIN puts the left table first in the joined table and then finds any matching rows from the right table. Rows with no match on the left table side should still appear in the joined table. LEFT OUTER JOIN is often shortened as LEFT JOIN.

Let's see an example. Use the data from Table 6.11 Student Table and Table 6.12 Advisor Table. Assume the Student Table is the left table (FROM Student LEFT JOIN Advisor). The joined table is this:

StudentId	StudentName	AdvisorId	AdivsorId	AdvisorName
1	Alice	111	111	Xavier
2	Alice	111	111	Xavier
3	Chuck	222	222	Young
4	Dan	Null	Null	Null

Table 6.14 Data for the student left join the advisor

Compare Table 6.14 Left Join with Table 6.13 Inner Join and note the differences. All rows from the left are kept even if there is no match from the right table.

The SQL statement for the left outer join with the above example is:

SELECT *

FROM Student LEFT JOIN Advisor

ON Student.AdvisorId = Advisor.AdvisorId;

The RIGHT OUTER JOIN is just the opposite of LEFT OUTER JOIN. RIGHT OUTER JOIN puts the right table first in the joined table then finds any matching rows from the left table. Any rows from the right table that have no match should still appear in the joined table. RIGHT OUTER JOIN is often shortened as RIGHT JOIN.

Let's use the same tables of Student and Advisor and see how the right outer join works. Assume the left table is still the Student table and the right table is the Advisor table.

StudentId	StudentName	AdvisorId	AdivsorId	AdvisorName
1	Alice	111	111	Xavier
2	Alice	111	111	Xavier
3	Chuck	222	222	Young
Null	Null	Null	333	Zach

Table 6.15 Data for the Student right join the Advisor

Compare the Table 6.15 RIGHT OUTER JOIN with Table 6.14 LEFT JOIN for differences.

The SQL statement for the RIGHT OUTER JOIN of the above example is:

```
SELECT *
FROM Student RIGHT JOIN Advisor
ON Student.AdvisorId = Advisor.AdvisorId;
```

You may have a question at this point: if you switch the two tables and change RIGHT JOIN to LEFT JOIN in SQL statement, what is the difference in the result? The answer is that you will get the same table. In the example used in this chapter, the following two SQL statements result in the same joined table:

```
SELECT *
FROM Student LEFT JOIN Advisor
ON Student.AdvisorId = Advisor.AdvisorId;
```

And

```
SELECT *
FROM Advisor RIGHT JOIN Student
ON Student.AdvisorId = Advisor.AdvisorId;
```

As a result, we will rarely use RIGHT JOIN in this book because it can be replaced with LEFT JOIN.

The third type of outer join is the FULL OUTER JOIN, often shortened to FULL JOIN. The full outer join is the combination of LEFT OUTER JOIN and RIGHT OUTER JOIN. The data from both tables are kept in the joined table. If a match is found, use the matching data. If no match is found, use NULL. Let's see an example of the Student and Advisor tables and see how the full join works.

StudentId	StudentName	AdvisorId	AdivsorId	AdvisorName
1	Alice	111	111	Xavier
2	Alice	111	111	Xavier
3	Chuck	222	222	Young
4	Dan	Null	Null	Null
Null	Null	Null	333	Zach

Table 6.16 Data for the Student full join the Advisor

SQL Example 6.8

Display all suppliers. If a supplier has products on the products table, also display the product names. Otherwise, display null as the product name. Show supplier names and corresponding product names.

SQL Example 6.8 Analysis

The supplier names are in the suppliers table and the product names are in the products table. You need to join the two tables. The inner join will only display the rows with matching supplier ID. The inner join may not display all suppliers if some suppliers do not provide their products yet.

Use LEFT JOIN with the suppliers table as the left table, thus guaranteeing that all suppliers will be displayed.

SQL Example 6.8 statement

```
SELECT SupplierName, ProductName
FROM Purchasing.Suppliers LEFT JOIN Purchasing.Products
ON Suppliers.SupplierId = Products.SupplierId;
```

Example 6.8 Output

	SupplierName	ProductName
1	Pine Apple	NULL
2	IMB	6Wireless Compact Laser Printer
3	IMB	Color Laser Printer
4	IMB	GPS Android Tablet PC
5	Lonovo	3200 Lumens LED Home Theater Projector
6	Samsong	65-Inch 4K Ultra HD Smart TV
7	Samsong	60-Inch 4K Ultra HD Smart LED TV
8	Samsong	10" 16GB Android Tablet
9	Canan	Wireless Color Photo Printer
10	Canan	20.2 MP Digital Camera

SQL Example 6.9

Display all suppliers. If a supplier has delivered any product, also display the most recent delivery date of the supplier. Otherwise, display null. Show supplier name and the corresponding most recent delivery date.

SQL Example 6.9 Analysis

The supplier names are in the suppliers table and the delivery date is in the deliveries table. You need to join the two tables. However, the two tables have no common column. You need a third table that has common columns with each of the two tables. This is the products table. The products table has a common column (SupplierId) with the Suppliers table. The products table also has a common column (ProductId) with the Deliveries table. As a result, you will join three tables even though the data you need are from two tables.

Use LEFT JOIN with the supplier table as the left table, thus guaranteeing that all suppliers will be displayed. However, you cannot simply first LEFT JOIN the Suppliers table with Products table and then JOIN the Deliveries table, because the second INNER JOIN will remove any non-matched rows. The correct way to join is to first join the INNER JOIN of Products table and the Deliveries table, then RIGHT OUTER JOIN with the Suppliers table.

Because Max() is an aggregate function, you need to GROUP BY SupplierName.

SQL Example 6.9 statement

```
SELECT SupplierName, Max(DeliveryDate) AS "Most recent delivery date"
FROM Purchasing.Products JOIN Purchasing.Deliveries
ON Products.ProductId = Deliveries.ProductId
RIGHT JOIN Purchasing.Suppliers
ON Products.supplierid = Suppliers.SupplierId
GROUP BY SupplierName;
```

Example 6.9 Output

	SupplierName	Most recent delivery date
1	Canan	2016-10-07 14:00:00.0000000
2	IMB	2016-10-10 10:30:00.0000000
3	Lonovo	2016-10-05 09:15:00.0000000
4	Pine Apple	NULL
5	Samsong	2016-11-01 10:20:00.0000000

Review Question 6.47
What's the difference between outer join and inner join?
a. INNER JOIN will ignore the non-matching rows while OUTER JOIN will keep non-matching rows.
b. INNER JOIN will keep the non-matching rows while OUTER JOIN will ignore the non-matching rows.
c. Both INNER JOIN and OUTER JOIN will keep the non-matching rows. However, the OUTER JOIN result will depend on the join type.
d. Neither INNER JOIN nor OUTER JOIN will keep the non-matching rows. But, INNER JOIN may keep the non-matching rows depending on the join type.

Review Question 6.48

Given the following two tables, the student table and advisor table:

StudentId	StudentName	AdvisorId
1	Alice	111
2	Bob	111
3	Chuck	222
4	Dan	Null

AdvisorId	AdvisorName
111	Xavier
222	Young
333	Zach

Which of the following tables shows the result of the LEFT JOIN?

a.

StudentId	StudentName	AdvisorId	AdivsorId	AdvisorName
1	Alice	111	111	Xavier
2	Alice	111	111	Xavier
3	Chuck	222	222	Young

b.

StudentId	StudentName	AdvisorId	AdivsorId	AdvisorName
1	Alice	111	111	Xavier
2	Alice	111	111	Xavier
3	Chuck	222	222	Young
4	Dan	Null	Null	Null

c.

StudentId	StudentName	AdvisorId	AdivsorId	AdvisorName
1	Alice	111	111	Xavier
2	Alice	111	111	Xavier
3	Chuck	222	222	Young
Null	Null	Null	333	Zach

d.

StudentId	StudentName	AdvisorId	AdivsorId	AdvisorName
1	Alice	111	111	Xavier
2	Alice	111	111	Xavier
3	Chuck	222	222	Young
4	Dan	Null	Null	Null
Null	Null	Null	333	Zach

Review Question 6.49

Given the following two tables, the student table and advisor table:

StudentId	StudentName	AdvisorId
1	Alice	111
2	Bob	111
3	Chuck	222
4	Dan	Null

AdvisorId	AdvisorName
111	Xavier
222	Young
333	Zach

Which of the following tables shows the result of the RIGHT JOIN?

a.

StudentId	StudentName	AdvisorId	AdivsorId	AdvisorName
1	Alice	111	111	Xavier
2	Alice	111	111	Xavier
3	Chuck	222	222	Young

b.

StudentId	StudentName	AdvisorId	AdivsorId	AdvisorName
1	Alice	111	111	Xavier
2	Alice	111	111	Xavier
3	Chuck	222	222	Young
4	Dan	Null	Null	Null

c.

StudentId	StudentName	AdvisorId	AdivsorId	AdvisorName
1	Alice	111	111	Xavier
2	Alice	111	111	Xavier
3	Chuck	222	222	Young
Null	Null	Null	333	Zach

d.

StudentId	StudentName	AdvisorId	AdivsorId	AdvisorName
1	Alice	111	111	Xavier
2	Alice	111	111	Xavier
3	Chuck	222	222	Young
4	Dan	Null	Null	Null
Null	Null	Null	333	Zach

Review Question 6.50

Given the following two tables, the student table and advisor table:

StudentId	StudentName	AdvisorId
1	Alice	111
2	Bob	111
3	Chuck	222
4	Dan	Null

AdvisorId	AdvisorName
111	Xavier
222	Young
333	Zach

Which of the following tables shows the result of the OUTER JOIN?

a.

StudentId	StudentName	AdvisorId	AdivsorId	AdvisorName
1	Alice	111	111	Xavier
2	Alice	111	111	Xavier
3	Chuck	222	222	Young

b.

StudentId	StudentName	AdvisorId	AdivsorId	AdvisorName
1	Alice	111	111	Xavier
2	Alice	111	111	Xavier
3	Chuck	222	222	Young
4	Dan	Null	Null	Null

c.

StudentId	StudentName	AdvisorId	AdivsorId	AdvisorName
1	Alice	111	111	Xavier
2	Alice	111	111	Xavier
3	Chuck	222	222	Young
Null	Null	Null	333	Zach

d.

StudentId	StudentName	AdvisorId	AdivsorId	AdvisorName
1	Alice	111	111	Xavier
2	Alice	111	111	Xavier
3	Chuck	222	222	Young
4	Dan	Null	Null	Null
Null	Null	Null	333	Zach

6.10 SQL SELF JOIN

When you need data from two tables, you join the two tables. When you need data from the same table more than once, you use self-join. Self-join is not a new type of join. It is joining the same table with inner or outer join.

The self-join can be used in two situations. One use is when you want to compare two rows of the same table. With the self-join, you can compare the values from two different columns. Two rows of the same table can now be treated as two rows of different tables. Another use of self-join is for a unary relationship.

SQL Example 6.10

Display all customers with the same name. Show customer name and email address.

SQL Example 6.10 Analysis

For your convenience, we reproduced the partial table of the customers here:

CustomerId	CustomerName	Email
1	Just Electronics	jwhite@je.com
2	Beyond Electronics	green@beil.com
3	Beyond Electronics	black1@be.com
4	E Fun	bgold@efun.com
5	Overstock E	dy@os.com
6	E Fun	green@ef.com
7	Electronics4U	smith@e4u.com
8	Cheap Electronics	NULL

All the data you need are from the same table: the customers table. However, SQL cannot compare rows within the same column. Thus, you must duplicate the table and put the tables side by side. Then, by manually checking the table, you can easily find that they are Customer ID 2 and 3, then 4 and 6. The self-joined result looks like:

CustomerId	CustomerName	Email	CustomerId	CustomerName	Email
1	Just Electronics	jwhite@je.com	1	Just Electronics	jwhite@je.com
2	Beyond Electronics	green@beil.com	2	Beyond Electronics	green@beil.com
3	Beyond Electronics	black1@be.com	3	Beyond Electronics	black1@be.com
4	E Fun	bgold@efun.com	4	E Fun	bgold@efun.com
5	Overstock E	dy@os.com	5	Overstock E	dy@os.com
6	E Fun	green@ef.com	6	E Fun	green@ef.com
7	Electronics4U	smith@e4u.com	7	Electronics4U	smith@e4u.com
8	Cheap Electronics	NULL	8	Cheap Electronics	NULL

Every row has the same customer name in this joined table. However, we are only looking for duplicate customer names. Therefore, look for matching customer names with different customer IDs.

You should use the same customer name but different customer IDs for the join condition. Because there is only one table called Customers, there is no way to differentiate the two duplicate tables. Thus, we use aliases. In the SQL statement below, we use C1 to represent the first table and C2 to represent the second table.

SQL Example 6.10 statement

```
SELECT DISTINCT C1.CustomerId, C1.CustomerName, C1.Email
FROM Sales.Customers AS C1 JOIN Sales.Customers AS C2
ON (C1.CustomerId != C2.CustomerId)
AND (C1.CustomerName = C2.CustomerName);
```

Example 6.10 Output

	CustomerId	CustomerName	Email
1	2	Beyond Electronics	green@beil.com
2	3	Beyond Electronics	black1@be.com
3	4	E Fun	bgold@efun.com
4	6	E Fun	green@ef.com

SQL Example 6.11

Display employees with their manager. Show employee name and their corresponding manager's name.

SQL Example 6.11 Analysis

Both the employee's name and the manager's name are in the same table. Duplicate the employees table, one for the employee name and one for the manager's name. Then you just pick the employee name from the employee table and the manager name from the manager table. The join condition is the manager ID from the employee table equals the employee ID from the manager table.

Recall that the employees entity has a unary relationship with itself.

Because the employees table does not have an employee name column, you can use the first name to concatenate with the last name.

SQL Example 6.11 statement

```
SELECT Employee.FirstName + ' ' + Employee.LastName AS "Employee name",
Manager.FirstName + ' ' + Manager.LastName AS "Manager name"
FROM HR.Employees AS Employee JOIN HR.Employees AS Manager
ON Employee.ManagerId = Manager.EmployeeId;
```

Example 6.11 Output

	Employee name	Manager name
1	Dianne Hart	Alex Hall
2	Maria Law	Alex Hall
3	Alice Law	Alex Hall
4	Black Hart	Dianne Hart
5	Christina Robinson	Dianne Hart
6	Nicholas Pinkston	Maria Law

Review Question 6.51
In SQL statements, JOIN usually means _____.
a. INNER JOIN
b. LEFT JOIN
c. OUTER JOIN
d. SELF JOIN

6.11 SQL UNION

While JOIN puts the two tables side by side, UNION puts the two tables top and bottom. Because the two tables are top and bottom, corresponding columns must be similar. For example, suppose you are going to unionize two tables, and each table has two columns. The first table has name and age columns. The second table has a name and a date of birth column. You won't be able to unionize these two tables because the age and the date of birth columns won't match. They have different data types. Two tables must have the same data type in order to unionize. This requirement is called union compatibility.

All corresponding columns of two union tables must be union compatible. Union compatiblility means one data type can be converted to the other data type. For example, VARCHAR data type can be converted to CHAR data type so they are union compatible. Another example, NUMERIC and DATE cannot be converted to each other, so the two types are said to be not union compatible.

UNION will automatically remove any duplicates. If you want to keep the duplicated rows, use UNION ALL instead.

SQL Example 6.12
Display a mail list for all customers and suppliers. Show company name, street, city, state, country, and postal code.

SQL Example 6.12 Analysis
Examine the corresponding column of the customers table and suppliers table. You will notice that all columns are union compatible.

SQL Example 6.12 statement

```
SELECT CustomerName, StreetAddress, City, State, PostalCode, Country
```

```
FROM Sales.Customers
UNION
SELECT SupplierName, StreetAddress, City, State, PostalCode, Country
FROM Purchasing.Suppliers;
```

Example 6.12 Output

	CustomerName	StreetAddress	City	State	PostalCode	Country
1	Beyond Electronics	45 Cherry Street	Chicago	IL	32302	USA
2	Beyond Electronics	6767 GameOver Blvd	Atlanta	GA	43347	USA
3	Canan	12 Camera St	Ota	Tokyo	100-0121	Japan
4	Cheap Electronics	1010 Easy St	Ottawa	Ontario	K1A 0B1	Canada
5	E Fun	888 Main Ave.	Seattle	WA	69356	USA
6	E Fun	915 Market st.	London	England	EC1A 1BB	UK
7	Electronics4U	27 Colmore Row	Birmingham	England	B3 2EW	UK
8	IMB	123 International Blvd	Los Angeles	CA	89202	USA
9	Just Electronics	123 Broad way	New York	NY	12012	USA
10	Lonovo	33 Beijin Square	Beijing	Beijing	100201	China
11	Overstock E	39 Garden Place	Los Angeles	CA	32302	USA
12	Pine Apple	1 Pine Apple St.	Idanha	CA	87201	USA
13	Samsong	1 Electronics Road	Yeongtong	Suwon	30174	South Korea

Review Question 6.52
While JOIN puts the two tables side by side, _____ puts the two tables top and bottom.
a. LEFT JOIN
b. RIGHT JOIN
c. FULL JOIN
d. UNION

6.12 Chapter Summary

In this chapter, you learned how to minimize data redundancy by applying normalization to relations. Normalization begins with the first normal form. Then, you must examine the functional dependency among the attributes and break up a relation if necessary. Once a relation is in the first normal form, you can check if it is in the second normal form. If not, examine the functional dependency and break up a relation if necessary. Once a relation is in the second normal form, you can check if it is in the third normal form, and so on. This book suggests that all relations should be in third normal form for most practical business problems.

In SQL, you learned unionizing and different types of joins, which allow you to have data from more than one table. You can treat the joined tables as one larger table and apply all the knowledge you learned from previous chapters to that table.

6.13 Discussion Questions

Discussion 6.1

For beginners, developing a database is about building one or more tables/relations. It is important that your relations are solid. Discuss the characteristics of a good relation.

Discussion 6.2

In this chapter, you learned that duplicating data may cause anomalies. In your own words, explain what anomalies are. Use examples if necessary.

Discussion 6.3

In this chapter, we talked a lot about minimizing data redundancy. Why not simply eliminate all redundancy? In other words, can we completely remove the redundancy in a database? Why or why not?

Discussion 6.4

Normalization is a process that can reduce data redundancy. This book explains up to the third normal form and hints that there are higher normal forms. What do you think might be the reasons that you don't need to learn higher normal forms?

6.14 Database Design Exercises

Exercise One:

The following table is in which normal form (1st, 2nd, or 3rd normal form)? If it is not in the third normal form, normalize it to the third normal form. Show the normalization process.

EmployeeId	FirstName	LastName	DateHired	JobID	JobTitle	FromDate	ToDate
111123	Alice	Smith	7/15/2019	999 888	Developer, Scrum master	7/2019 6/2020	6/2020 Current
112123	Tom	Scott	2/14/2015	888 111 100	Scrum master, CTO, COO	2/2015 10.2018 3/2020	9/2018 2/2020 Current

Exercise Two

The following table is in which normal form (1st, 2nd, or 3rd normal form)? If it is not in the third normal form, normalize it to the third normal form. For simplicity, let's assume the Name field is atomic.

StudentNum	Name	Course1	Grade1	Course2	Grade2	Course3	Grade3
111	Eliza King	Intro CS	A	Java	B	SQL	A
222	John Floyd	Intro CS	B	C++	A	Java	B
113	Cory Peck	C++	B	Algorithm	C	Java	B
123	Ryan Tran	SQL	B	Java	A	Algorithm	C

6.15 SQL Exercises

Exercise 6.1

Display delivery details for each product. Show Product name, delivery ID, quantity, price, and delivery date (without the time part).

	ProductName	DeliveryId	Quantity	Price	Delivery date
1	65-Inch 4K Ultra HD Smart TV	1	2	1099.99	2016-10-01
2	65-Inch 4K Ultra HD Smart TV	2	5	1199.99	2016-11-01
3	60-Inch 4K Ultra HD Smart LED TV	3	10	1199.99	2016-10-02
4	3200 Lumens LED Home Theater Projector	4	10	129.99	2016-10-05
5	Wireless Color Photo Printer	5	20	79.99	2016-10-07
6	6Wireless Compact Laser Printer	6	15	139.99	2016-10-07
7	Color Laser Printer	7	25	169.99	2016-10-10
8	10" 16GB Android Tablet	8	12	79.99	2016-10-11
9	10" 16GB Android Tablet	9	18	69.99	2016-10-12

Exercise 6.2

Display product name and total quantity delivered for each product. Show Product ID, Product name, and total quantity delivered for that product.

	ProductId	ProductName	Delivery total unit
1	1	65-Inch 4K Ultra HD Smart TV	7
2	2	60-Inch 4K Ultra HD Smart LED TV	10
3	3	3200 Lumens LED Home Theater Projector	10
4	4	Wireless Color Photo Printer	20
5	5	6Wireless Compact Laser Printer	15
6	6	Color Laser Printer	25
7	7	10" 16GB Android Tablet	30

Exercise 6.3

Display customers and their orders. Show customer ID, customer name and corresponding order ID and order date.

	CustomerId	CustomerName	OrderId	OrderDate
1	1	Just Electronics	1	2017-01-03
2	1	Just Electronics	2	2017-03-05
3	2	Beyond Electronics	3	2017-02-23
4	4	E Fun	4	2017-04-13
5	1	Just Electronics	5	2017-05-03
6	3	Beyond Electronics	6	2017-05-08
7	5	Overstock E	7	2016-11-08
8	7	Electronics4U	8	2016-12-23

Exercise 6.4

Display customers, their orders, and order details in each order. Show customer ID, customer name, and corresponding order ID, order date, product ID, price, and quantity in the order. Sort by customer ID, Order ID, and product ID.

	CustomerId	CustomerName	OrderId	OrderDate	ProductId	Price	Quantity
1	1	Just Electronics	1	2017-01-03	1	1499.99	1
2	1	Just Electronics	1	2017-01-03	3	149.99	2
3	1	Just Electronics	2	2017-03-05	1	1499.99	1
4	1	Just Electronics	2	2017-03-05	2	1599.99	1
5	1	Just Electronics	2	2017-03-05	4	99.99	6
6	1	Just Electronics	2	2017-03-05	6	189.99	5
7	1	Just Electronics	5	2017-05-03	3	149.99	6
8	1	Just Electronics	5	2017-05-03	6	199.99	3
9	2	Beyond Electronics	3	2017-02-23	3	159.99	2
10	2	Beyond Electronics	3	2017-02-23	6	199.99	1
11	2	Beyond Electronics	3	2017-02-23	7	109.99	2
12	2	Beyond Electronics	3	2017-02-23	8	69.99	2
13	2	Beyond Electronics	3	2017-02-23	9	1449.99	1
14	3	Beyond Electronics	6	2017-05-08	1	1499.99	1
15	4	E Fun	4	2017-04-13	4	99.99	2
16	4	E Fun	4	2017-04-13	8	69.99	1
17	5	Overstock E	7	2016-11-08	2	999.99	1
18	7	Electronics4U	8	2016-12-23	7	79.99	1
19	7	Electronics4U	8	2016-12-23	8	59.99	2

Exercise 6.5

Display customers, their orders, and total value in each order. Show customer ID, customer name, and corresponding order ID, order date, and total value in each order (price * quantity).

	CustomerId	CustomerName	OrderId	OrderDate	Order total
1	1	Just Electronics	1	2017-01-03	1799.97
2	1	Just Electronics	2	2017-03-05	4649.87
3	1	Just Electronics	5	2017-05-03	1499.91
4	2	Beyond Electronics	3	2017-02-23	2329.92
5	3	Beyond Electronics	6	2017-05-08	1499.99
6	4	E Fun	4	2017-04-13	269.97
7	5	Overstock E	7	2016-11-08	999.99
8	7	Electronics4U	8	2016-12-23	199.97

Exercise 6.6

Display customers, their orders, and the most expensive unit price in the order. Show customer ID, customer name, order ID, order date, and unit price for the most expensive item in the order.

	CustomerId	CustomerName	OrderId	OrderDate	Highest unit price in order
1	1	Just Electronics	1	2017-01-03	1499.99
2	1	Just Electronics	2	2017-03-05	1599.99
3	1	Just Electronics	5	2017-05-03	199.99
4	2	Beyond Electronics	3	2017-02-23	1449.99
5	3	Beyond Electronics	6	2017-05-08	1499.99
6	4	E Fun	4	2017-04-13	99.99
7	5	Overstock E	7	2016-11-08	999.99
8	7	Electronics4U	8	2016-12-23	79.99

Exercise 6.7

Display customers, their orders, and the most expensive unit price in the order. Show customer ID, customer name, order ID, order date, unit price for the most expensive item in the order, and how many units ordered with that price in that order.

	CustomerId	CustomerName	OrderId	OrderDate	Highest unit price in order	Quantity
1	1	Just Electronics	1	2017-01-03	1499.99	1
2	1	Just Electronics	2	2017-03-05	1599.99	1
3	1	Just Electronics	5	2017-05-03	199.99	3
4	2	Beyond Electronics	3	2017-02-23	1449.99	1
5	3	Beyond Electronics	6	2017-05-08	1499.99	1
6	4	E Fun	4	2017-04-13	99.99	2
7	5	Overstock E	7	2016-11-08	999.99	1
8	7	Electronics4U	8	2016-12-23	79.99	1

Exercise 6.8

Display all customers. If a customer has placed one or more orders, include those orders. Otherwise, include null. Show customer ID, customer name, and corresponding order ID and order date.

	CustomerId	CustomerName	OrderId	OrderDate
1	1	Just Electronics	1	2017-01-03
2	1	Just Electronics	2	2017-03-05
3	1	Just Electronics	5	2017-05-03
4	2	Beyond Electronics	3	2017-02-23
5	3	Beyond Electronics	6	2017-05-08
6	4	E Fun	4	2017-04-13
7	5	Overstock E	7	2016-11-08
8	6	E Fun	NULL	NULL
9	7	Electronics4U	8	2016-12-23
10	8	Cheap Electronics	NULL	NULL

Exercise 6.9

Display all customers. If a customer has placed any orders, also display the highest unit price in any order of that customer. Otherwise, display null. We want to know each customer's highest price item ever ordered. Show customer ID, customer name, and the highest unit price in any order of that customer.

	CustomerId	CustomerName	Highest unit price
1	1	Just Electronics	1599.99
2	2	Beyond Electronics	1449.99
3	3	Beyond Electronics	1499.99
4	4	E Fun	99.99
5	5	Overstock E	999.99
6	6	E Fun	NULL
7	7	Electronics4U	79.99
8	8	Cheap Electronics	NULL

Exercise 6.10

Display all employees with the same last name. Show their full name and date of birth.

	Employee name	BirthDate
1	Dianne Hart	1978-12-03
2	Black Hart	1982-11-09
3	Maria Law	1988-07-13
4	Alice Law	1988-12-13

Exercise 6.11

Display all employees. If an employee is a manager, include the supervisees' name. otherwise, display null. Show manager and supervisee full name.

	Manager	Supervisee
1	Alex Hall	Dianne Hart
2	Alex Hall	Maria Law
3	Alex Hall	Alice Law
4	Dianne Hart	Black Hart
5	Dianne Hart	Christina Robinson
6	Maria Law	Nicholas Pinkston
7	Alice Law	NULL
8	Black Hart	NULL
9	Christina Robinson	NULL
10	Nicholas Pinkston	NULL

Exercise 6.12

Display all states the LifeStyle has a business (customer or supplier). Show state and country.

	State	Country
1	Beijing	China
2	CA	USA
3	England	UK
4	GA	USA
5	IL	USA
6	NY	USA
7	Ontario	Canada
8	Suwon	South Korea
9	Tokyo	Japan
10	WA	USA

6.16 Solutions to Review Questions

6.1 C; 6.2 B; 6.3 C; 6.4 B; 6.5 D; 6.6 D; 6.7 D; 6.8 C; 6.9 A; 6.10 D; 6.11 D; 6.12 D; 6.13 C; 6.14 A; 6.15 C;

6.16 B; 6.17 C; 6.18 A; 6.19 C; 6.20 A; 6.21 A; 6.22 B; 6.23 B; 6.24 A; 6.25 D; 6.26 A; 6.27 B; 6.28 B; 6.29 D;

6.30 A; 6.31 B; 6.32 D; 6.33 D; 6.34 C; 6.35 D; 6.36 A; 6.37 D; 6.38 C; 6.39 A; 6.40 B; 6.41 C; 6.42 B; 6.43

D; 6.44 B; 6.45 A; 6.46 A; 6.47 A; 6.48 B; 6.49 C; 6.50 D; 6.51 A; 6.52 D;

CHAPTER 7: RELATIONAL ALGEBRA AND SQL DATA MANIPULATION

Chapter Learning Objectives

7.1 Explain relational algebra.

7.2 Infer the need for relational algebra.

7.3 Exemplify the complete set operations.

7.4 Implement data retrieval in both SQL and relational algebra.

7.5 Explain why INTERSECTION and JOIN operations are not part of the complete set.

7.6 Use SQL INSERT statement to add data to a table.

7.7 Use SQL DELETE statement to remove data from a table.

7.8 Use SQL UPDATE statement to modify data in a table.

7.1 What Is Relational Algebra?

"Relational" is the adjective form of relations or tables. Algebra means using letters and symbols to represent numbers in mathematical expressions and equations. For example, instead of writing 2+3, you can use algebra to write a + b. The "+" is called an operator. Relational algebra is using letters and symbols to represent relations and operations. The operations are either unary or binary. The unary operation works on just one relation, such as SELECT operation. The binary operation works on two relations, such as JOIN.

In this chapter, you will learn the following unary operations:

SELECT

PROJECT

RENAME

You will also learn the following binary operations:

UNION

INTERSECTION

SET DIFFERENCE

CARTESIAN PRODUCT

JOIN

Review Question 7.1
The _____ uses letters and symbols to represent relations and operations.
a. arithmetic
b. relational algebra
c. relational symbol
d. relational operation

Review Question 7.2
Which of the following is a unary relational operation?
a. PROJECT
b. UNION
c. INTERSECTION
d. SET DIFFERENCE

Review Question 7.3
Which of the following is a unary relational operation?
a. JOIN
b. UNION
c. SELECT
d. SET DIFFERENCE

Review Question 7.4
Which of the following is a binary relational operation?
a. SELECT
b. PROJECT
c. RENAME
d. SET DIFFERENCE

Review Question 7.5
Which of the following is a binary relational operation?
a. SELECT
b. PROJECT

c. RENAME
d. UNION

7.2 Why Should You Learn Relational Algebra?

In the previous chapters, you learned how to write SQL statements to retrieve the data you need. You don't necessarily need to know relational algebra, the mathematics behind SQL, in order to use SQL. However, understanding relational algebra can help you write queries more efficiently and effectively. This is like you know all the arithmetic operations. Do you really need algebra? Let's see an example and let you answer the question yourself.

What is 264*264 + 2*264*736 + 736*736?

Without algebra, you would calculate the answer to be 1000000.

With algebra, you would do this instead: 264*264 +2*264*736+ 736*736 = (264+736)(264+736)=1000*1000=1000000. You get the same answer, but which way takes less time?

In algebra, there is a formula: a*a + 2*a*b + b*b = (a+b)(a+b).

A database administrator told me he wanted to learn relational algebra because one of his colleagues improved his SQL statements significantly by working with relational algebra.

A relation is a set. According to the set theory, element sequence in a set does not make any difference. For example, the following two sets, R and S, are the same:
R = {1, 3, 6}; S = {6, 1, 3};
Additionally, a set won't allow duplicate elements. For example, you cannot have a set like this:
T = {1, 3, 3};
Instead, the T set should be T= {1, 3};

Relational algebra is the theory behind all SQL statements. You learned how to write SQL statements in the previous chapters. This is a good time to summarize what you learned in the previous chapters.

Review Question 7.6
Understanding relational algebra can help you write _____ more efficiently and effectively.
a. SQL queries
b. formulas
c. expressions
d. algebras

Review Question 7.7
A relation in a relational database is NOT a(n) _____.
a. algebra operator
b. set
c. table
d. a set of tuples

Review Question 7.8
According to the set theory, element sequence in a set _____.
a. should be from large to small
b. should be from small to large
c. makes two sets different
d. does not make any differences

Review Question 7.9
Which of the following is NOT a set?
a. {1, 2, 3}
b. {1, 2, c}
c. {1, 2, 1}
d. all examples are set.

Review Question 7.10
The _____ is the theory behind all SQL statements.
a. relational algebra
b. SQL concept
c. SQL theory
d. SQL foundation

7.3 The SELECT Operation

The SELECT operation is used to retrieve rows of data (also called tuples in relational language) that meet certain conditions from a relation. The expression is:

$\sigma_{\texttt{<selection condition>}}(\mathsf{R})$

where the σ (sigma) symbol is used to denote the SELECT operator and the selection condition is a Boolean expression specified for the attributes of relation R. For example:

Using the practice database in the book (Appendix B has the data,) retrieve all the products of supplier number 5 in relational algebra. The relational expression is:

σ_{\<supplierId = 5\>}Products

The following figure shows the Products table and the result of the SELECT operation on the table (a result set or result table):

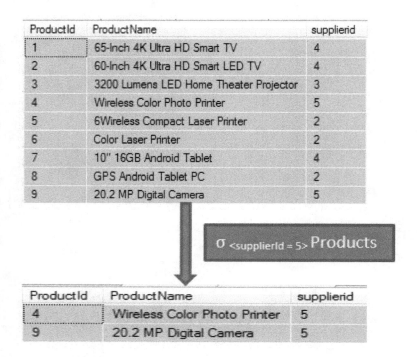

Figure 7.1 A relation and the result of SELECT operation.

For another example, retrieve all deliveries with product quantities of 10 or more units. You will get the following relational expression:

σ <quantity >= 10> Deliveries

As another example, retrieve all deliveries with product quantity of 10 or more units and unit price of $1000 or more. You will get the following relational expression.

σ <quantity >= 10 AND price >= 1000> `Deliveries`

Let's see the SQL statements from the above three relational expressions:

```
SELECT * FROM Products WHERE SupplierId = 5;
SELECT * FROM Deliveries WHERE Quantity >= 10;
SELECT * FROM Deliveries WHERE Quantity >= 10 AND Price >= 1000;
```

Even though SELECT appears in both relational expressions and SQL statements, they have very different meanings. In the expression, the SELECT operator determines which rows to appear in the result set while the SELECT clause in SQL statements determines which columns to pick. The SELECT of relational expressions is similar to the WHERE clause in SQL statements.

Review Question 7.11
The SELECT of relational expressions is similar to the _____ clause in SQL statements.
a. SELECT
b. FROM
c. ORDER BY
d. WHERE

Review Question 7.12
The _____ operation is used to retrieve rows of data that meet certain conditions from a relation.
a. SELECT
b. PROJECT
c. RENAME
d. UNION

Review Question 7.13
Which SQL statement is equivalent to the following relational algebra expression?
σ <supplierId = 3> Products
a. SELECT * FROM SupplierId = 3;
b. SELECT * FROM Products WHERE SupplierId = 3;
c. SELECT SupplierId FROM Products WHERE SupplierId = 3;
d. SELECT SupplierId, 3 FROM Products;

7.4 The PROJECT Operation

The PROJECT operation is used to retrieve columns of data from a relation. The expression is:

$$\pi_{<attribute\ list>}(R)$$

where the π (pi) symbol represents the PROJECT operator and the columns selected from relation R are in the attribute list.

Let's see an example from the same database used throughout the book. Write the expression to retrieve all product names from the product table

$$\pi_{<ProductName>}\ Products$$

The following figure shows the Products table and the result table after the above PROJECT operation:

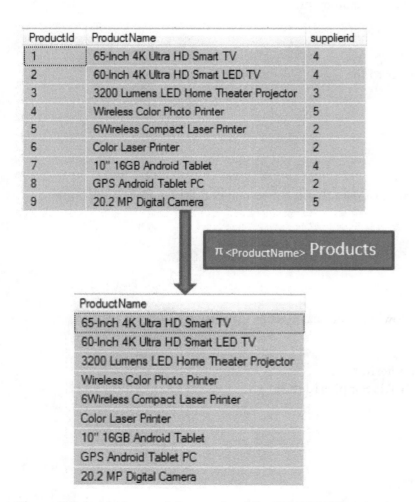

Figure 7.2 A relation and the result of the PROJECT operation.

What happens if there are two products with the same name? If the ProductName is the only attribute retrieved, the duplication product names will be removed. Remember that a set only has unique members (and therefore no duplications.)

Let's see another example. Write the expression to display all products delivered with product ID and delivery date.

π <ProductId, DeliveryDate> `Deliveries`

How about combining both SELECT and PROJECT operators? Write the expression to retrieve all product names from supplier ID 3.

π <ProductName> σ <supplierId = 3> `Products`

The expression can become difficult to read, especially when the problem is more complex. We suggest that you use the RENAME operation that will be discussed in the next section.

The corresponding SQL statements for the expressions in this section is:

```
SELECT DISTINCT ProductName FROM Products;
SELECT DISTINCT ProductId, DeliveryDate FROM Deliveries;
SELECT DISTINCT ProductName FROM Deliveries WHERE SupplierId = 3;
```

Review Question 7.14
The PROJECT of relational expressions is similar to the _____ clause in SQL statements.
a. SELECT
b. FROM
c. ORDER BY
d. WHERE

Review Question 7.15
The _____ operation is used to retrieve columns of data from a relation.
a. SELECT
b. PROJECT
c. RENAME
d. UNION

Review Question 7.16

Which SQL statement is equivalent to the following relational algebra expression?

π <ProductId, DeliveryDate> Deliveries

a. SELECT ProductId, DeliveryDate FROM Deliveries;

b. SELECT * FROM Deliveries;

c. SELECT ProductId FROM Deliveries WHERE DeliveryDate = GETDATE();

d. SELECT * FROM Deliveries WHERE ProductId = @ProductId;

7.5 The RENAME Operation

The result of a relational expression is also a relation, but it does not have a name. The RENAME operator is often used to assign a name to that relation.

Let's rewrite the expression to retrieve all product names from supplier ID 3 from last section here with the RENAME operator:

Supplier3Product <-- σ <supplierId = 3> Products

Supplier3ProductName <-- π <ProductName> Supplier3Product

In the above example, you first RENAME the result of all products from supplier ID 3 as Supplier3Product. The <-- symbol points to the newly assigned name. Next, you use PROJECT on the new relation (Supplier3Product) to keep only the product name and use RENAME to rename the new result as Supplier3ProductName.

Let's see another example.

Retrieve all deliveries with product quantity of 10 or more units. Show ProductId and DeliveryDate.

Delivery10OrMore <-- σ <quantity >= 10> Deliveries

Result <-- π <ProductId, DeliveryDate> Deliveriy10OrMore

Here's another example:

Write the relational expression to retrieve all deliveries with product quantity of 10 or more units and unit price of 1000 or more. Show DeliveryId, ProductId, and DeliveryDate.

Delivery10Unit1000Price <-- σ <quantity >= 10 AND price >= 1000> Deliveries

Result <-- π <DeliveryId, ProductId, DeliveryDate> Delivery10Unit1000Price

Keep in mind that these operations may be used in different orders to suit different circumstances.

These are the corresponding SQL statements for the examples in this section:

```
SELECT DISTINCT ProductName FROM Deliveries WHERE SupplierId = 3;
SELECT DISTINCT ProductId, DeliveryDate FROM Deliveries WHERE Quantity >= 10;
SELECT DISTINCT DeliveryId, ProductId, DeliveryDate FROM Deliveries WHERE Quantity
>= 10 AND Price >= 1000;
```

The above examples used RENAME for relations. However, RENAME can also be used for columns. For example:

```
R(DeliveryId, Units_Delivered, Wholesale_Price) <-- π <DeliveryId, Quantity, Price>
Deliveries
```

In the above expression, the columns were renamed Quantity as Units_Delivered and Price as Wholesale_Price in a new relation called R with the same tuples from the Deliveries.

Review Question 7.17
The result of a relational expression is _____.
a. a special relation
b. a nameless relation
c. a special tuple
d. a nameless tuple

Review Question 7.18
What is the following symbol in relational algebra?
<--
a. SELECT
b. PROJECT
c. RENAME
d. UNION

Review Question 7.19
The RENAME operation can only be used to rename relations/tables.
a. True.
b. False.

Review Question 7.20
What is the following symbol in relational algebra?
π
a. SELECT
b. PROJECT
c. RENAME

d. UNION

7.6 The UNION operation

The UNION operation includes all rows from both relations with duplications removed. The expression is

`R1 U R2`

Where R1 is a relation and R2 is another relation. UNION will include all rows from R1 and R2 with duplicates removed. Similar to the SQL statement, UNION compatibility is also required.

For example, write a relational expression to display all orders handled by Employee 5 or placed after April 1, 2017.

`OrderByEmployee5 <-- σ <EmployeeId = 5> Orders`

`OrderAfter04012017 <-- σ <OrderDate > '20170401'> Orders`

`Result <-- OrderByEmployee5 U OrderAfter04012017;`

The following figure shows the UNION operation. Note a duplicated row is removed.

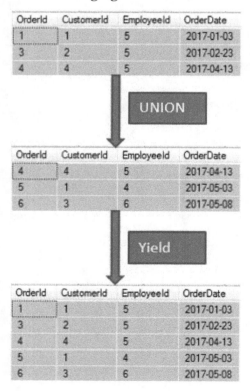

Figure 7.3 Two relations and the result relation after the UNION operation.

The corresponding SQL statement is

```
SELECT * FROM Orders WHERE EmployId = 5

UNION

SELECT * FROM Orders WHERE OrderDate > '20170401';
```

Review Question 7.21
In the following expression: **R1 U R2**. The two relations R1 and R2 must _____
a. have the same number of attributes
b. have the same number of rows
c. be union compatible
d. be from the same relation

Review Question 7.22
The _____ operation includes all rows from both relations with duplicates removed.
a. SELECT
b. PROJECT
c. RENAME
d. UNION

Review Question 7.23
Which SQL statement is equivalent to the following relational algebra expression?
```
OrderByEmployee5 <-- σ <EmployeeId = 5> Orders
OrderAfter04012017 <-- σ <OrderDate > '20170401'> Orders
Result <-- OrderByEmployee5 U OrderAfter04012017;
```
a. SELECT * FROM Orders
b. SELECT OrderId FROM Orders UNION SELECT OrderDate FROM Orders;
c. SELECT * FROM Orders WHERE EmployId = 5 UNION SELECT * FROM Orders WHERE OrderDate > '20170401';
d. there's no equivalent in SQL.

7.7 The INTERSECTION Operation

The INTERSECTION operation keeps only the common rows between two relations. The expression is

```
R1 ∩ R2
```

Where R1 is a relation and R2 is another relation. The INTERSECTION will include all rows that appear in both R1 and R2. Similar to the SQL statement, UNION compatibility is also required.

For example, write relational expressions to display all orders handled by Employee 5 and placed after April 1, 2017.

```
OrderByEmployee5 <-- σ <EmployeeId = 5> Orders

OrderAfter04012017 <-- σ <OrderDate > '20170401'> Orders

Result <-- OrderByEmployee5 ∩ OrderAfter04012017;
```

The following figure shows the two relations and the result of the INTERSECTION operation.

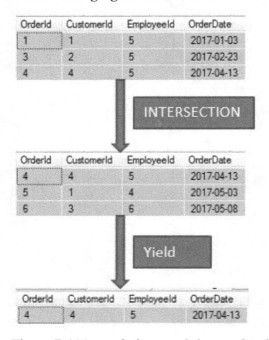

Figure 7.4 Two relations and the result relation after the INTERSECTION operation.

The corresponding SQL statement (note that instead of INTERSECTION, use INTERSECT in T-SQL) is:

```
SELECT * FROM Orders WHERE EmployId = 5

INTERSECT

SELECT * FROM Orders WHERE OrderDate > '20170401';
```

Review Question 7.24

In the following expression: R1 ∩ R2. The two relations R1 and R2 must _____
a. have the same number of attributes
b. have the same number of rows
c. be union compatible
d. be from the same relation

Review Question 7.25

The _____ operation keeps only the common rows between two relations.
a. UNION
b. INTERSECTION
c. SET DIFFERENCE

d. CARTESIAN PRODUCT

7.8 The SET DIFFERENCE Operation

The SET DIFFERENCE operation keeps only the rows that appear in the first relation and not in the second relation. The expression is

R1 - R2

where R1 is a relation and R2 is another relation. The SET DIFFERENCE will include all rows that appear in R1 but not in R2. Similar to the SQL statement, UNION compatibility is required.

For example, write relational expressions to display all orders handled by Employee 5 but not placed after April 1, 2017.

OrderByEmployee5 <-- σ <EmployeeId = 5> Orders

OrderAfter04012017 <-- σ <OrderDate > '20170401'> Orders

Result <-- OrderByEmployee5 - OrderAfter04012017;

The following figure shows the two relations and the result relation after the SET DIFFERENCE operation.

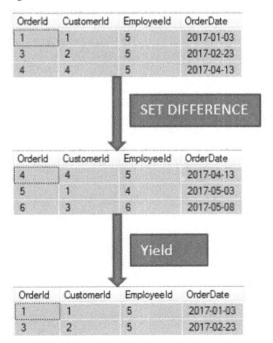

Figure 7.5 Two relations and the result relation after the SET DIFFERENCE operation.

The corresponding SQL statement (note that instead of SET DIFFERENCE, use EXCEPT in T-SQL) is:

```
SELECT * FROM Orders WHERE EmployId = 5
EXCEPT
SELECT * FROM Orders WHERE OrderDate > '20170401';
```

Note that INTERSECTION can be expressed in terms of union and set difference as follows, assuming R and S are two relations:

```
R∩S=((R∪S)-(R-S))-(S-R)
```

Review Question 7.26
Which relational algebra operator does NOT require union compatibility?
a. UNION
b. CARTESIAN PRODUCT
c. INTERSECTION
d. SET DIFFERENCE

Review Question 7.27
The corresponding T-SQL clause for SET DIFFERENCE is _____.
a. SELECT
b. UNION
c. DIFFERENCE
d. EXCEPT

Review Question 7.28
The _____ operation keeps only the rows that appear in the first relation and not in the second relation.
a. UNION
b. INTERSECTION
c. SET DIFFERENCE
d. CARTESIAN PRODUCT

Review Question 7.29
Which of the following relational algebra equations is true?
a. R∩S=((R∪S)−(R-S))+(S−R)
b. R∩S=((R∪S)+(R-S))−(S−R)
c. R∩S=((R∪S)−(R-S))−(S−R)
d. R∩S=((R∪S)−(R+S))−(S−R)

7.9 The CARTESIAN PRODUCT Operation

Suppose the relation R1 has a1 number of attributes and r1 number of rows and another relation, R2, has a2 attributes and r2 rows. The result of using CARTESIAN PRODUCT on R1 and R2 is a new relation that has a1+ a2 number of attributes and r1×r2 number of rows. Each row from R1 should be combined with each row from R2 for a result of r1×r2 number of rows. The expression is

```
R1 × R2
```

Let's see an example. Write the relational expression to list all possible combinations of suppliers and products.

```
Result <-- Suppliers × Products
```

Refer to Appendix B. The Supplier table has 7 columns and 5 rows and the Products table has 3 columns and 9 rows. So, the Result table will have 10 columns and 45 rows.

The following figure shows the Suppliers and the Products tables and the result of the CARTESIAN PRODUCT (due to the width of this book, the supplier address was omitted for display purposes):

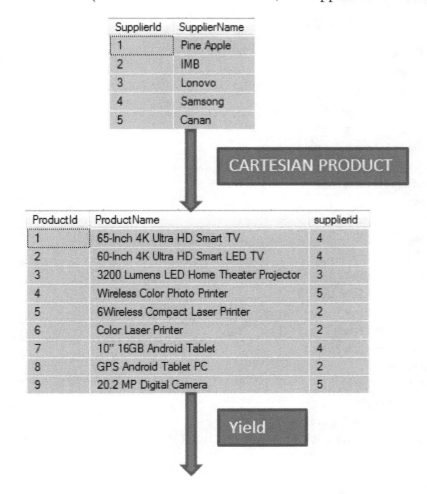

SupplierId	SupplierName	ProductId	ProductName	SupplierId
1	Pine Apple	1	65-Inch 4K Ultra HD Smart TV	4
1	Pine Apple	2	60-Inch 4K Ultra HD Smart LED TV	4
1	Pine Apple	3	3200 Lumens LED Home Theater Projector	3
1	Pine Apple	4	Wireless Color Photo Printer	5
1	Pine Apple	5	6Wireless Compact Laser Printer	2
1	Pine Apple	6	Color Laser Printer	2
1	Pine Apple	7	10" 16GB Android Tablet	4
1	Pine Apple	8	GPS Android Tablet PC	2
1	Pine Apple	9	20.2 MP Digital Camera	5
2	IMB	1	65-Inch 4K Ultra HD Smart TV	4
2	IMB	2	60-Inch 4K Ultra HD Smart LED TV	4
2	IMB	3	3200 Lumens LED Home Theater Projector	3
2	IMB	4	Wireless Color Photo Printer	5
2	IMB	5	6Wireless Compact Laser Printer	2
2	IMB	6	Color Laser Printer	2
2	IMB	7	10" 16GB Android Tablet	4
2	IMB	8	GPS Android Tablet PC	2
2	IMB	9	20.2 MP Digital Camera	5
3	Lonovo	1	65-Inch 4K Ultra HD Smart TV	4
3	Lonovo	2	60-Inch 4K Ultra HD Smart LED TV	4
3	Lonovo	3	3200 Lumens LED Home Theater Projector	3
3	Lonovo	4	Wireless Color Photo Printer	5
3	Lonovo	5	6Wireless Compact Laser Printer	2
3	Lonovo	6	Color Laser Printer	2
3	Lonovo	7	10" 16GB Android Tablet	4
3	Lonovo	8	GPS Android Tablet PC	2
3	Lonovo	9	20.2 MP Digital Camera	5
4	Samsong	1	65-Inch 4K Ultra HD Smart TV	4
4	Samsong	2	60-Inch 4K Ultra HD Smart LED TV	4
4	Samsong	3	3200 Lumens LED Home Theater Projector	3
4	Samsong	4	Wireless Color Photo Printer	5
4	Samsong	5	6Wireless Compact Laser Printer	2
4	Samsong	6	Color Laser Printer	2
4	Samsong	7	10" 16GB Android Tablet	4
4	Samsong	8	GPS Android Tablet PC	2
4	Samsong	9	20.2 MP Digital Camera	5
5	Canan	1	65-Inch 4K Ultra HD Smart TV	4
5	Canan	2	60-Inch 4K Ultra HD Smart LED TV	4
5	Canan	3	3200 Lumens LED Home Theater Projector	3
5	Canan	4	Wireless Color Photo Printer	5
5	Canan	5	6Wireless Compact Laser Printer	2
5	Canan	6	Color Laser Printer	2
5	Canan	7	10" 16GB Android Tablet	4
5	Canan	8	GPS Android Tablet PC	2
5	Canan	9	20.2 MP Digital Camera	5

Figure 7.6 Two relations and the result relation after the CARTESIAN PRODUCT operation.

You may notice that there are not many cases in which the CARTESIAN PRODUCT operation will be used. However, it is a basic operation for the JOIN operation introduced next.

Review Question 7.30
There are not many cases in which the CARTESIAN PRODUCT operation will be used. However, it is a basic operation for the _____ operation.
a. UNION
b. INTERSECTION
c. SET DIFFERENCE
d. JOIN

Review Question 7.31
Suppose relation R1 has a1 attributes and r1 rows and another relation, R2, has a2 attributes and r2 rows. The result of using CARTESIAN PRODUCT on R1 and R2 is a new relation that has _____ number of attributes.
a. a1 + a2
b. a1 − a2
c. a1 * a2
d. a1 / a2

Review Question 7.32
Suppose relation R1 has a1 attributes and r1 rows and another relation, R2, has a2 attributes and r2 rows. The result of using CARTESIAN PRODUCT on R1 and R2 is a new relation that has _____ number of rows.
a. r1 + r2
b. r1 − r2
c. r1 * r2
d. r1 /r2

Review Question 7.33
Suppose relation R1 has a1 attributes and r1 rows and another relation, R2, has a2 attributes and r2 rows. The result of using _____ on R1 and R2 is a new relation that has a1+a2 number of attributes and r1×r2 number of rows. Each row from R1 should be combined with each row from R2 for a result of r1×r2 number of rows.
a. UNION
b. INTERSECTION
c. SET DIFFERENCE
d. CARTESIAN PRODUCT

7.10 The JOIN Operation

So far, you learned seven relational operations. They are SELECT, PROJECT, RENAME, UNION, INTERSECTION, SET DIFFERENCE, and CARTESIAN PRODUCT. We usually consider the operations SELECT, PROJECT, RENAME, UNION, SET DIFFERENCE, and CARTESIAN

PRODUCT to be part of a complete set. INTERSECTION is left out. Why is that? It is due to the fact that INTERSECTION can be expressed as UNION and SET DIFFERENCE as shown in Section 7.8.

Similarly, JOIN is not a part of the complete set because it can be expressed as the CARTESIAN PRODUCT followed by the SELECT operation. The expression for JOIN is

R1 $\bowtie$<join condition> R2

For example, write a relational expression to display all suppliers and their products. Do not show the suppliers without any products (Join condition is shown as subscript).

CurrentSupplierProduct <-- Suppliers $\bowtie$supplierId Products

The same result can be achieved by the following two steps:

SupplierProduct <-- Suppliers × Products;
CurrentSupplierProduct <-- σ <supplierId = supplierId> SupplierProduct;

Refer to Figure 7.6 for the CARTESIAN PRODUCT and the following figure shows the second step (SELECT) of JOIN:

SupplierId	SupplierName	ProductId	ProductName	SupplierId
4	Samsong	1	65-Inch 4K Ultra HD Smart TV	4
4	Samsong	2	60-Inch 4K Ultra HD Smart LED TV	4
3	Lonovo	3	3200 Lumens LED Home Theater Projector	3
5	Canan	4	Wireless Color Photo Printer	5
2	IMB	5	6Wireless Compact Laser Printer	2
2	IMB	6	Color Laser Printer	2
4	Samsong	7	10" 16GB Android Tablet	4
2	IMB	8	GPS Android Tablet PC	2
5	Canan	9	20.2 MP Digital Camera	5

Figure 7.7 The result relation after SELECT from the CARTESIAN PRODUCT relation.

Review Question 7.34
The INTERSECTION operation is not part of the complete set of six operations because _____.
a. it can be expressed in terms of UNION and SET DIFFERENCE
b. it is rarely used
c. it is too late to be introduced
d. the complete set of six is a good number

Review Question 7.35
The _____ operation can be expressed as CARTESIAN PRODUCT followed by the SELECT operations.
a. UNION
b. INTERSECTION
c. SET DIFFERENCE
d. JOIN

Review Question 7.36
Select the relational expression that is the same as the following:
```
SupplierProduct <-- Suppliers X Products;
CurrentSupplierProduct <-- σ <supplierId=supplierId> SupplierProduct;
```
a. CurrentSupplierProduct <-- Suppliers U Products;
b. CurrentSupplierProduct <-- Suppliers ∩ Products;
c. CurrentSupplierProduct <-- Suppliers ⋈ Products
d. CurrentSupplierProduct <-- Suppliers - Products;

7.11 The SQL INSERT Statement

The data stored in a database changes all the time. When LifeStyle LLC hires a new employee, a new row for the employee has to be inserted. When a supplier delivers a product, a new row in the deliveries table is inserted. If the delivered product is new, a new row in the products table should also be inserted before the new row in the deliveries table can be inserted. In this section, you will learn ways to insert data.

The syntax for inserting a single row into a table is:

```
INSERT INTO TableName (Column1, Column2, ...) VALUES (Value1, Value2, ...).
```

Not all columns of a table have to be in the INSERT statement unless they are required (NOT NULL) columns. Also, the sequence in the SQL INSERT statement does not have to be the same as that in the table. However, each value in the SQL statement must have a matching data type for the one in the table. Finally, the column and value in the SQL statement must be paired.

The following is the syntax for inserting multiple rows into a table:

```
INSERT INTO TableName(Column1, Column2, ...) VALUES (Row1Value1, Row2Value2, ...),
                                  (Row2Value1, Row2Value2, ...)
```

Note the comma between rows of values. It is a common typo of omitting that comma.

You can also insert data from another table. The syntax is:

```
INSERT INTO Table1Name(Column1, Column2, ...)
    SELECT ColumnOne, ColumnTwo, ...
    FROM Table2Name;
```

SQL Example 7.1

LifeStyle LLC just hired a new employee. Write an SQL statement to add the employee to the database. The new employee data is shown below:

FirstName	LastName	BirthDate	HireDate	HomeAddress	City	State	PostalCode	Phone	ManagerId
Ryan	Price	1991-10-15	2015-09-22	123 Broadway Blvd	New Canton	VA	23123	(434) 290-1223	3

SQL Example 7.1 Analysis

You can apply the syntax straightaway to this example. The table name is HR.Employees. All the column names and corresponding values are given.

Note in the SQL statement below, there's the letter N in front of the string value. This is to convert the data type from VARCHAR to NVARCHAR. The default string data type is VARCHAR and the database uses NVARCHAR. The difference between VARCHAR and NVARCHAR is that the latter can hold characters of international language (N stand for National), such as Korean, Japanese, and Chinese).

The INSERT statement is easy to understand. However, typos are also frequent. The column name must be the same as it appears in the table and the column value must be the same data type as in the table.

You should not provide an employee ID because it is an IDENTITY field which means a unique value will be automatically provided by the SQL Server.

SQL Example 7.1 statement

```
INSERT INTO HR.Employees (FirstName, LastName, BirthDate, HireDate,
HomeAddress, City, State, PostalCode, Phone, ManagerId)
    VALUES(N'Ryan', N'Price', '19911015', '20150922', N'123 Broadway Blvd',
N'New Canton', N'VA', 23123, N'(434) 290-1223', 3);
```

SQL Example 7.1 Output

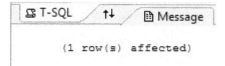

```
(1 row(s) affected)
```

SQL Example 7.2

LifeStyle LLC just hired a new employee. But this time, you only know the new employee's first name, last name, birth date, and hire date. Write an SQL statement to add the employee to the database. The new employee data is shown below:

FirstName	LastName	BirthDate	HireDate
James	Anderson	1990-03-12	2015-11-11

SQL Example 7.2 Analysis

The INSERT syntax only requires that you provide the data for those columns that do not allow NULL value. In other words, you don't have to provide all values for a row. However, the column names and their corresponding values still must be matched.

SQL Example 7.2 statement

```
INSERT INTO HR.Employees (LastName, FirstName, BirthDate, HireDate) VALUES
(N'Anderson', N'James', '19900312', '20151111');
```

SQL Example 7.2 Output

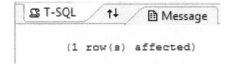

```
(1 row(s) affected)
```

SQL Example 7.3

LifeStyle LLC just hired two new employees. Write an SQL statement to add both employees to the database. The new employee data is shown below:

FirstName	LastName	BirthDate	HireDate
Adam	Smith	1989-02-01	2016-09-19
Kyle	Johnson	1988-12-23	2016-09-19

SQL Example 7.3 Analysis

This is a straightforward application of the syntax for inserting multiple rows.

SQL Example 7.3 statement

```
INSERT INTO HR.Employees (FirstName, LastName, HireDate, BirthDate) VALUES
    (N'Adam', N'Smith', '20160919', '19890201'),
    (N'Kyle', N'Johnson', '20160919', '19881223');
```

SQL Example 7.3 Output

```
(2 row(s) affected)
```

SQL Example 7.4

Supplier ID 2 becomes a new customer of LifeStyle LLC. To avoid typos, write an SQL statement to copy the data of supplier 2 from the suppliers table into the customers table.

SQL Example 7.4 Analysis

This is also an example where you can apply the syntax directly.

SQL Example 7.4 statement

```
INSERT INTO Sales.Customers (CustomerName, StreetAddress, City, State,
PostalCode, Country)
    SELECT SupplierName, StreetAddress, City, State, PostalCode, Country
    FROM Purchasing.Suppliers
    WHERE SupplierId = 2;
```

SQL Example 7.4 Output

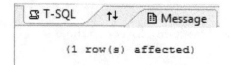

```
(1 row(s) affected)
```

SQL Example 7.5

Twelve units of product ID 1 were just delivered. Write an SQL statement to add the record in the deliveries table.

SQL Example 7.5 Analysis

The purpose of this example is to learn how the default value works. When developers create a new table, they can set certain default values for certain columns. For example, the deliverydate of the deliveries table has a default value of the system's date and time. If you also won't provide a delivery date when inserting a new row of delivery, the SQL Server will insert the timestamp of the moment you inserted the row. Similarly, when you do not provide a price, the default value is $0.

SQL Example 7.5 statement

```
INSERT INTO Purchasing.Deliveries (ProductId, Quantity)
    VALUES (1, 12);
```

SQL Example 7.5 Output

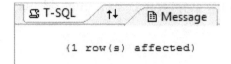

```
(1 row(s) affected)
```

Review Question 7.37
Which of the following is the T-SQL syntax for inserting a single row into a table (data are not from different tables?)
a. INSERT INTO TableName (Column1, Column2, ...) VALUES (Value1, Value2, ...).
b. INSERT INTO TableName(Column1, Column2, ...) VALUES (Row1Value1, Row2Value2, ...),
          (Row2Value1, Row2Value2, ...)
c. INSERT INTO Table1Name(Column1, Column2, ...)
   SELECT ColumnOne, ColumnTwo, ...
   FROM Table2Name;
d. INSERT INTO TableName (Value1, Value2, ...) FOR (Column1, Column2, ...);

Review Question 7.38
Which of the following is the T-SQL syntax for inserting multiple rows into a table (data are not from different tables?)
a. INSERT INTO TableName (Column1, Column2, ...) VALUES (Value1, Value2, ...).
b. INSERT INTO TableName(Column1, Column2, ...) VALUES (Row1Value1, Row1Value2, ...),
          (Row2Value1, Row2Value2, ...)
c. INSERT INTO Table1Name(Column1, Column2, ...)
   SELECT ColumnOne, ColumnTwo, ...
   FROM Table2Name;
d. INSERT INTO TableName (Value1, Value2, ...) FOR (Column1, Column2, ...);

Review Question 7.39

Which of the following is the T-SQL syntax for inserting rows of data into a table with data from a different table?

a. INSERT INTO TableName (Column1, Column2, ...) VALUES (Value1, Value2, ...).

b. INSERT INTO TableName(Column1, Column2, ...) VALUES (Row1Value1, Row2Value2, ...),
          (Row2Value1, Row2Value2, ...)

c. INSERT INTO Table1Name(Column1, Column2, ...)
   SELECT ColumnOne, ColumnTwo, ...
   FROM Table2Name;

d. INSERT INTO TableName (Value1, Value2, ...) FOR (Column1, Column2, ...);

7.12 The SQL UPDATE Statement

Users will need to edit a row in a table from time to time. For example, when a new employee is hired, he or she may not have a home address yet. You can still enter the employee basic data (e.g. first name, last name, date of birth, and hire date) into the employees table. In a few days, when the employee has a home address, you can update the row with the new data.

The syntax for UPDATE is:

```
UPDATE TableName
SET Column1Name = NewValue1,
     Column2Name = NewValue2,
     ....
   ColumnxName = NewValuex
WHERE Condition;
```

If you omit the WHERE clause, the whole table is updated with the new value for the columns, which is typically not the desired result. So, do not forget the WHERE clause. With the WHERE clause, only those rows that meet the condition will be updated.

SQL Example 7.6

LifeStyle LLC just received the price for the product delivered in SQL Example 7.5. The new price is $1449.99. Write the SQL statement to update the record.

SQL Example 7.6 Analysis

This is an example in which you can apply the syntax directly. Just use the SELECT statement to check the deliveryId before applying the following statement. In the example, we use the ID of 10. Yours may be different.

SQL Example 7.6 statement

```
UPDATE Purchasing.Deliveries
SET Price = 1449.99
WHERE DeliveryId = 10;
```

SQL Example 7.6 Output

```
(1 row(s) affected)
```

SQL Example 7.7

One of the newly hired employee, James Anderson, just submitted the new address below:

HomeAddress	City	State	PostalCode	Phone
201 Jefferson St.	Buckingham	VA	23123	(434) 290-5456

Write a SQL statement to update his record in the database.

SQL Example 7.7 Analysis

This is also an example where you can apply the syntax directly. In the following statement, we use the EmployeeId of 9 for James Anderson. The ID for James Anderson may be different in your database because the column has the identity constraint (which means automatically generated). You can use the SELECT statement to find the EmployeeId for James Anderson in your database.

You may notice that the ManagerId column is still Null for James Anderson. That's ok. You can update it again when you know the manager ID later on.

SQL Example 7.7 statement

```
UPDATE HR.Employees
SET HomeAddress = '201 Jefferson St.',
    City = 'Buckingham',
    State = 'VA',
    PostalCode = '23123',
```

```
    Phone = '(434) 290-5456'
WHERE EmployeeId = 9;
```

SQL Example 7.7 Output

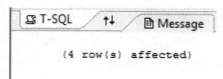

SQL Example 7.8

Write an SQL statement to add the ManagerId of 3 to all newly hired employees (all new employees you inserted in this chapter).

SQL Example 7.8 Analysis

This example practices how to update multiple rows in one statement. All you need is the WHERE clause. Originally, there are seven employees (See Appendix B). All new employees inserted in this chapter have an employee ID greater than seven. You can use WHERE EmployeeId > 7.

SQL Example 7.8 statement

```
UPDATE HR.Employees
SET ManagerId = 3
WHERE EmployeeId > 7;
```

SQL Example 7.8 Output

SQL Example 7.9

You just realized it is too early to assign the manager ID for those new employees. Write an SQL statement to delete the manager ID for those employees.

SQL Example 7.9 Analysis

You cannot use the DELETE statement (explained in the next section) to delete a partial row. The correct way to delete a partial row is by using the UPDATE statement. Basically, you set those values to NULL.

SQL Example 7.9 statement

```
UPDATE HR.Employees
SET ManagerId = Null
WHERE EmployeeId > 7;
```

SQL Example 7.9 Output

```
(4 row(s) affected)
```

Review Question 7.40
Write an SQL statement to change the price of an OrderDetails table from $2.00 to $2.10 for all quantities under 10.
a. UPDATE OrderDetails SET Price FROM 2.0 TO 2.1 WHERE Quantity < 10;
b. UPDATE OrderDetails SET Price = 2.1 WHERE Quantity < 10;
c. UPDATE OrderDetails CHANGE Price FROM 2.0 TO 2.1 WHERE Quantity < 10;
d. UPDATE OrderDetails SET Price = 2.1 WHERE Price = 2.0 AND Quantity < 10;

7.13 The SQL DELETE Statement

When an employee leaves the company or an order is cancelled, you may want to delete the corresponding rows to keep the data updated. The syntax for delete is:

```
DELETE FROM TableName
WHERE condition;
```

The DELETE statement removes complete rows from the table that meet the condition. If you omit the WHERE clause, all data will be removed. The table is still there, but with no data.

SQL Example 7.10

The shipment of twelve units of product ID 1 in Example 7.5 was a mistake by the supplier. It was supposed to ship to a different wholesaler. Write the SQL statement to remove that row.

SQL Example 7.10 Analysis

This example practices how to delete a row. You can use the SELECT statement to find the ID of that delivery:

```
SELECT * FROM Purchasing.Deliveries;
```

In our case, the deliveryID is 10. You can now issue the DELETE statement with the WHERE clause:

```
WHERE DeliveryId = 10;
```

SQL Example 7.10 statement

```
DELETE FROM
Purchasing.Deliveries
WHERE DeliveryId = 10;
```

SQL Example 7.10 Output

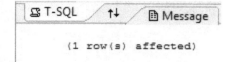

```
(1 row(s) affected)
```

SQL Example 7.11

Delete all new employees you inserted in this chapter.

SQL Example 7.11 Analysis

The difference between deleting a single row and multiple rows is the WHERE clause. You should be very careful when deleting multiple rows.

SQL Example 7.11 statement

```
DELETE FROM
HR.Employees
WHERE EmployeeId > 7;
```

SQL Example 7.11 Output

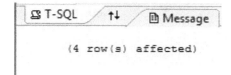

```
(4 row(s) affected)
```

Review Question 7.41
Which of the following is the SQL syntax for deleting rows of data with matching conditions?
a. DELETE FROM TableName WHERE condition;
b. DELETE ROWS FROM TableName WHERE condition;
c. DELETE FROM TableName;
d. DELETE ROWS FROM TableName;

7.14 Chapter Summary

In this chapter, you learned what relational algebra is and why you should learn it. Eight relational

operations were introduced. By now, you should be able to write most relational data retrievals through

both SQL statements and relational algebra expressions.

In SQL statements, you learned how to insert new rows into the table, update existing rows in the table, and

delete all rows of the table that meet certain conditions.

This chapter completes the journey of how to develop a database with tables and retrieve and manipulate

data in the tables. In the next chapter, you will apply the knowledge learned to a real- world project.

7.15. Discussion

Discussion 7.1

You don't have to know relational algebra in order to retrieve data from the database. Throughout the book,

you learned that SQL SELECT statements accomplish exactly the same thing. Do you agree with the author

that you should learn relational algebra? Why or Why not.

Discussion 7.2

Compare the following two statements. One statement is from the section about UNION. The other is from the section about INTERSECTION. Why does INTERSECTION not remove duplicates? Explain. The UNION operation includes all rows from both relations R1 and R2 with duplicates removed The INTERSECTION will include all rows that appear in both R1 and R2.

Discussion 7.3

This chapter introduces eight relational operations, but only six of them are part of the complete set. Why are the other two excluded from the complete set?

7.16 Relational Algebra Exercise

Write relational expressions to accomplish these tasks. Use the same database from Appendix B.

a. Retrieve the company name, contact, and email of all domestic (USA) customers.

b. Retrieve the company name, contact, and email of all customers who have ever placed an order.

c. Retrieve the company name, contact, email, order date, quantity, and price for all customers with all orders.

7. 17 SQL Exercises

Exercise 7.1

LifeStyle LLC has a new customer who provides the following data. Write an SQL statement to add the customer to the database. The new customer data is shown below:

CustomerName	StreetAddress	City	State	PostalCode	Country	Contact	Email
E Store	11 Pine Pl	Seattle	WA	69301	USA	Eric Wade	wade@estore.com

Exercise 7.2

LifeStyle LLC has another new customer. But, this time, you only know the new customer's name. Write an SQL statement to add the customer to the database. The new customer's data is shown below:

CustomerName
Magic E

Exercise 7.3

LifeStyle LLC gains two more customers. Write an SQL statement to add both customers to the database. The new customer data is shown below:

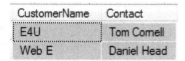

Exercise 7.4

Customer ID 5 becomes a new supplier of LifeStyle LLC. To avoid typos, write an SQL statement to copy the data of customer 5 from the customers table into the suppliers table (because the suppliers do not have contact and email columns, do not copy these two columns from the customers table).

Exercise 7.5

Order ID 8 has a missing product ID 1 because the customer is still negotiating the price. The manager wants to include the data in the OrderDetails table with the default values for the price and quantity. Write an SQL statement to add product ID 1 to the order details table for Order ID 8.

Exercise 7.6

The order details for Order ID 8 of product ID 1 you inserted in Exercise 7.5 now has a known quantity of 10 units. Write an SQL statement to update the record.

Exercise 7.7

One of the newly added customers, Magic E, just submitted the new address below. Write an SQL statement to update the customer's record.

StreetAddress	City	State	PostalCode	Country
168 Pine Apple Ln	San Francisco	CA	10101	USA

Exercise 7.8

Write an SQL statement to add the email customers@lifestyle.com to all newly added customers (all customers you inserted in this chapter exercises).

Exercise 7.9

You just realized it is a mistake to assign all newly added customers an email of customers@lifestyle.com. Write an SQL statement to delete the emails for those customers.

Exercise 7.10

The customer and the manager cannot reach an agreement on Order ID 8 of Product ID 1. You inserted a row in the OrderDetails table in Exercise 7.5. Now write an SQL statement to delete that row in order details.

Exercise 7.11

Write an SQL statement to delete all new customers you added in this chapter's exercises.

7.18 Solutions to Review Questions

7.1 B; 7.2 A; 7.3 C; 7.4 D; 7.5 D; 7.6 A; 7.7 A; 7.8 D; 7.9 C; 7.10 A; 7.11 D; 7.12 A; 7.13 B; 7.14 A; 7.15 B; 7.16 A; 7.17 B; 7.18 C; 7.19 B; 7.20 B; 7.21 C; 7.22 D; 7.23 C; 7.24 C; 7.25 B; 7.26 B; 7.27 D; 7.28 C; 7.29 C; 7.30 D; 7.31 A; 7.32 C; 7.33 D; 7.34 A; 7.35 D; 7.36 C; 7.37 A; 7.38 B; 7.39 C; 7.40 D; 7.41 A;

CHAPTER 8: A PROJECT AND SQL CREATE STATEMENTS

Chapter Learning Objectives

8.1 Develop a relational database with the given business description.

8.2 Summarize the processes of database development.

8.3 Implement physical design with an appropriate Transact-SQL data type.

8.4 Write Transact-SQL statements to create databases and tables with the given physical ERD.

8.5 Write SQL statements to work with a database you created.

8.1 The Panda Language School (PLS) Business Description

The Panda Language School, founded in 1994, is a non-profit organization. The primary mission of PLS is to provide an avenue for students of all ages and ethnic backgrounds to learn the Chinese language, arts, and culture. Most students are children aged 5 to 15.

PLS is operated in its 50,000 square feet facility and its financial support is mainly from tuition and donations from individuals, private businesses, and institutions. Its activities are also supported by volunteers. Each year, it offers 50+ Chinese Language classes for Chinese-speaking and non-Chinese-speaking children and adults. PLS also provides over 100 Chinese Arts/Culture, sports, math and college preparation, and specialty training courses, as well as a variety of club activities.

The school opens from 10:00am to 7:00pm on weekends and most holidays as well as selected evenings from 5:00pm to 7:00pm on weekdays. PLS is the largest Chinese school in the tri-state area. PLS strives to continue serving as the best place for students to learn the Chinese language, arts, and culture.

The following describes how the business is run related to the database they want.

A new family needs to fill out a form like the following (bottom part is cut off due to the size limit)

The Panda Language School (PLS),
NEW FAMILY REGISTRATION FORM

FAMILY INFORMATION

Last name in Chinese		Date in this address	
Phone		☐ Chinese American	
Cell		☐ Other	
E-mail			
Home address City, State ZIP Code			

GUARDIAN INFORMATION

Guardian 1 name		Guardian 2 name	
Guardian 1 address		Guardian 2 address	
Guardian 1 Phone		Guardian 2 Phone	
Guardian 1 Cell		Guardian 2 Cell	
Guardian 1 E-mail		Guardian 2 E-mail	

STUDENT INFORMATION

First name		Phone	
Last name		Date of birth	
Gender		E-mail	
Relationship to Guardian		Additional Information	
First name		Phone	
Last name		Date of birth	
Gender		E-mail	
Relationship to Guardian		Additional Information	
First name		Phone	
Last name		Date of birth	
Gender		E-mail	
Relationship to Guardian		Additional Information	

AGREEMENT

1. By submitting this application, you authorize The Panda Language School (PLS), to contact you for any PLS related activities and events.
2. PLS may share your information with other organizations for educational related purposes.

SIGNATURES			
Signature		Signature	
Name		Name	
Date		Date	

Table 8.1 A family registration form for PLS new families.

The application is free. Once accepted, students can fill out the following form for course registration every semester. The registration form will be kept in the cabinet and inside each family folder. The tuition is required at the time of registration but will be handled in a separate software system. Students can fill out multiple forms stapled together if they want to take more than one course. The data on the form will be entered into a spreadsheet by a secretary to share with the school administrators and the instructors.

The Panda Language School (PLS),
COURSE REGISTRATION FORM

STUDENT INFORMATION			
Guardian name		Phone	
Student name		Date of birth	
Gender		E-mail	
Relationship to Guardian		Additional Information	
COURSE INFORMATION			
Course Number		Start Date	
Course Title		Finish Date	
Meet day			
Meet Time			
Instructor Name			
SCHOOL USE			
Approval		School Note:	
Tuition Paid			
Scholarship Amount			
Registered			

Table 9.2 A course registration form for PLS students.

The school also keeps the instructor data on a 3 by 5 index card. Basic information includes name, address, phone, email, emergency contact, date hired, and type (paid or volunteer).

For courses offered, there's no official prerequisite. On the registration form, the school will inform the students what class they can or cannot take. The prerequisite is often self explanatory from the course title.

For example, Chinese Language 1 is the prerequisite for Chinese Language 2. Parents can always call the school or arrange a free test to see which level the child may best fit in.

All courses are on a list in a spreadsheet. In addition to the information listed in the registration form, each course has a maximum capacity. Seat availability is updated by the secretary who also manages registration. One of the most often asked questions from the administrators is how many students can register for a certain course.

Students receive grades of A, B, C, D, F, P, W for each course, as submitted by the instructor.

PLS wants you to develop the database so they can remove all paperwork to save both employee time and conserve the environment. Specifically, they want to:

1. Be able to manipulate family, instructor, course information.

2. Allow students to register for courses, check registration and grade.

3. Allow instructors to post course grade.

Feel free to contact PLS if you have any questions.

8.2 PLS Business Rules

The following is a list of business rules extracted from the business description in Section 8.1 (The business has agreed not to store any payment data in this database):

Each family can have up to 2 parents/guardians. Each guardian is related to exactly one family.

Each family can have one or more children/students. Each child is from exactly one family.

Each student can register for any number of courses. Each course can have several students.

Each course is taught by one instructor. An instructor can teach many courses.

A family has an id, last name, phone, cellphone, email, home address, city, state, and zip code.

A student has an id, first name, last name, gender, relationship, phone, email, birth date, and note.

A course has a number, title, meet day, meet time, start date, end date, and seat capacity.

A guardian has an id, name, address, phone, cell, and email.

An instructor has an id, name, address, phone, email, hire date, and type.

The relationship between the student and course has a grade.

8.3 Entity Relationship Diagram

Based on the business rules above, develop a simple conceptual ERD. Then, with the business description, add all attributes to their corresponding entities and relationships. A conceptual ERD is displayed in Figure 8.1. A logical ERD is displayed in Figure 8.2.

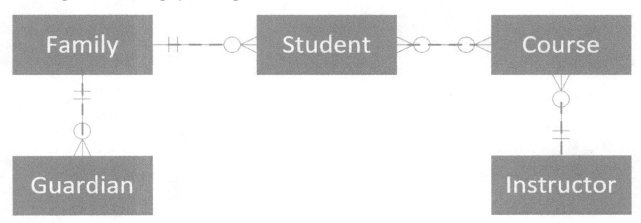

Figure 8.1 Conceptual ERD of PLS database.

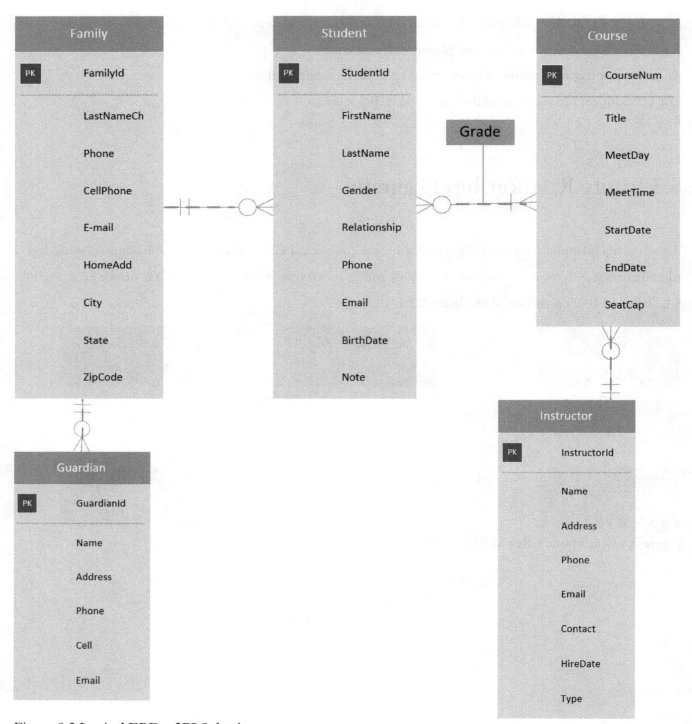

Figure 8.2 Logical ERD of PLS database.

8.4 Mapping ERD to Relations

Next, follow ERD to the relations mapping rules outlined in Chapter 5. Figure 8.3 shows the mapping result.

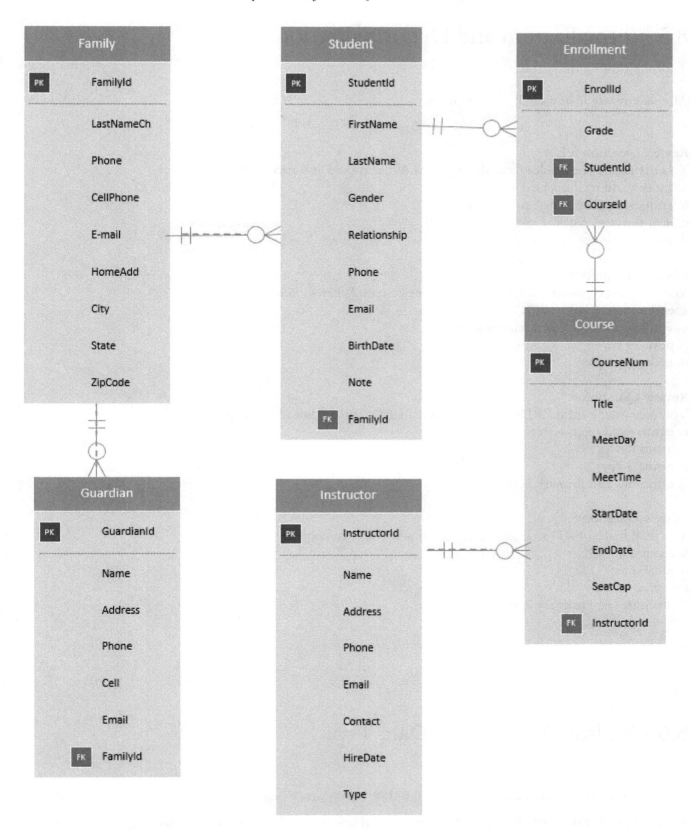

Figure 8.3 Relations that map the logical ERD of PLS database.

8.5 Normalization and Denormalization

All relations are in at least 3rd normal form.

Review Question 8.1
You extract business rules from descriptions. What should you focus on?
a. entities and relationships
b. entities, relationships, and attributes
c. how business work
d. make it simple

Review Question 8.2
You construct conceptual ERDs from business rules. What should you focus on?
a. entities and relationships
b. entities, attributes, and relationships
c. primary keys
d. make it simple

Review Question 8.3
You construct logical ERDs from conceptual ERDs. What should you focus on?
a. entities and relationship
b. attributes
c. primary keys
d. attributes and primary keys

Review Question 8.4
You map logical ERD to relations. What should you focus on?
a. foreign keys
b. attributes
c. primary keys
d. attributes and primary keys

8.6 Physical Design with Data Type

The design process so far can apply to any DBMSs. In physical design, the PLS decides to go with SQL Server. Next, the data type for each attribute of the relations should be added. Transact-SQL (T-SQL for short) has the following data type available:

Character strings / Unicode character strings

The character strings data type is used to store alphanumeric characters, such as student name and street address among others. The popular character string data types are char and varchar.

Use char if all data in an attribute is the same size. For example, US Zip code is always five digits, so you can set the data type as CHAR(5).

Use varchar if the data of the attribute has variable length, such as first name and last name. You set the maximum length of the attribute. For example, the data type for the first name attribute can be VARCHAR(120), assuming a person's first name will not go over 120 characters.

In either char or varchar, the largest number you can put in the parentheses is 8000. In case the attribute value may be more than 8000 characters, use varchar(max) as the data type, which can hold a value up to 2GB.

If the attribute values include foreign languages such as Arabic, Japanese, or Korean, instead of using char or varchar, you should use nchar or nvarchar. Adding an "n" in front of char or varchar indicates it is Unicode and can hold foreign languages that take two bytes in each character. The "n" stands for national. In this book, we use the Unicode version so it can hold both English and foreign languages.

Exact numeric

The exact numeric data type is used to store numbers with exact value, such as bank account balance, product price, or number of credit hours a student has taken. The more popular exact numeric types include bit, int, money, and numeric.

Use bit if the attribute values are all Boolean with 1 for TRUE and 0 for FALSE.

Use int if the attribute values are whole numbers between approximately -2 million to +2 million.

Use money if the attribute values are currency of any state.

Use numeric if the attribute value is stored with fixed precision and scale. The format is numeric (p, s) where the p stands for precision (which is the total number of digits allowed) and s stands for scale (which is total digits to the right of the decimal place.) The largest number for p is 38 with a default value of 18 and s is any digit between 0 and p with a default value of 0. The value for s cannot be specified if the value for p is not specified, so NUMERIC (, 3) won't work.

Let's see some examples of how numeric(p, s) works.

NUMERIC (3, 1) will hold a number up to 99.9. The total number of digits is 3, with only one of the three digits allowed to be after the decimal.

NUMERIC (5,3) will hold a number up to 99.999. The total number of digits is 5, with only three of the five digits allowed to be after the decimal.

Date and Time

The date and time data type are used to store date and time values. The more popular types are date and datetime2.

Use date data type if the attribute value is a date. The default string literal format is 'YYYY-MM-DD' (such as '2022-12-15'.)

Use datetime2 data type if the attribute value contains both the date and the time of day. It also allows fractional seconds for higher precision. The default string literal format is 'YYYY-MM-DD hh:mm:ss[.fractional seconds]'. The square bracket [] indicates the optional part. An example can be '2012-12-21 07:34:00.1523423'

Binary Strings

The binary strings data type is used to store binary data, such as image files. The more popular types are binary and varbinary.

Use binary(n) if the attribute value is a fixed-length binary data of n bytes. The maximum value for n is 8000.

Use varbinary(n) if the attribute value is variable-length binary data of up to n bytes. The maximum value for n is 8000.

Use varbinary(max) if the attribute value is variable-length binary data that exceeds 8000 bytes.

Review Question 8.5
In which step of the relational database design process should you pick a DBMS?
a. conceptual
b. logical
c. physical
d. as early as possible

Review Question 8.6
NCHAR is a data type in SQL Server. What does n in NCHAR stand for?
a. normalization
b. normal
c. national
d. NoSQL

Review Question 8.7
In T-SQL, which of the following is a Unicode character string data type?
a. NVARCHAR
b. CHAR
c. TEXT
d. VARCHAR

Review Question 8.8
In T-SQL, varchar(n) can be used to hold a character string. The digit n is for the largest number of bytes the attribute may have. What is the largest value for n according to the book?
a. 1000
b. 2000
c. 4000
d. 8000

Review Question 8.9
In T-SQL, what's the difference between the VARCHAR and NVARCHAR data type?
a. VARCHAR is used for foreign languages.
b. NVARCHAR is used for foreign languages only.
c. VARCHAR can be used for both English and foreign languages.
d. NVARCHAR can be used for both English and foreign languages.

Review Question 8.10
In T-SQL, which data type is used to store values of True or False?
a. Boolean
b. Logic
c. T/F
d. bit

Review Question 8.11
In T-SQL, what precision and scale are needed for a number like 22.345?
a. numeric(2, 3)
b. numeric(2, 5)
c. numeric(5, 3)
d. numeric(3, 2)

Review Question 8.12
In T-SQL, if you need both date and time of the day with fractional seconds, which data type is recommended?
a. date
b. datetime
c. datetime2
d. any of the options

Review Question 8.13
In T-SQL, varbinary data type is often used to store _____.
a. images
b. variables
c. numbers
d. digits

Review Question 8.14
In T-SQL, which of the following data type can be used to store a name called "Alice"?
a. CHAR(5)
b. CHAR(6)
c. VARCHAR(6)
d. Any of the three options

Review Question 8.15
In T-SQL, which of the following is NOT a data type for numbers?
a. bit
b. binary
c. money
d. numeric

Review Question 8.16
If you insert '2023-02-05' for the value of a datetime2 data type, what is the actual value stored?
a. 2023-02-05
b. 2023-02-06
c. 2023-02-05 00:00:00 0000000
d. It will cause an error because of a mismatched data type.

Review Question 8.17
The default string literal format for datetime2 is _____.
a. YYYY-MM-DD
b. YYYY-MM-DD hh:mm:ss
c. MM-DD-YYYY
d. MM-DD-YYYY hh:mm:ss

Review Question 8.18
Use _____ data type if the attribute values are whole numbers between approximately -2 million to +2 million.
a. smallint
b. mediumint
c. int
d. largeint

8.7 Transact-SQL Codes to Create Database and Tables

To run SQL code in Visual Studio, the first thing you need is to connect to a database. The statement for connecting is:

```
USE databaseName;
```

Before you create your first database, you should connect to a default database called *master*.

When scripting for a new database, you are unlikely to run all code successfully in just one attempt. When you try the second attempt to run the code, there will be some tables already created in the first attempt that will cause trouble. We suggest adding a deletion line before you create a database so that you can run the script as many times as you need. Every run of the script will first delete the database and then create a fresh one. Do not use the statement for a database in production.

The statement to delete/drop a database is

```
DROP DATABASE databaseName;
```

Add an IF statement to avoid deleting the database the first time you run it, as shown below:

```
DROP DATABASE IF EXISTS databaseName;
```

Now, you are ready to create a database. The statement for creating database is:

```
CREATE DATABASE databaseName;
```

Some statements should be in their own batch. This is like how some products cannot ship with other products, they have to ship in their own container. For T-SQL, some statements require to be in their own batch. One such statement is CREATE DATABASE. Just add the keyword GO to cut the code from the remaining code into different batches.

Next, create schemas for the database objects. You can think of schemas as containers that can be used for better organization of the database objects. In this case, schemas are used for organizing the tables and other objects. A schema should have an authorization setting, like how a container has a lock. The default user account is dbo (the default schema in SQL Server). The schema can allow better security with different authorization settings for different schemas.

The syntax for creating a schema is:

```
CREATE SCHEMA schemaName AUTHORIZATION dbo;
```

Finally, it is time for creating tables. The Create Table syntax is:

```
CREATE TABLE SchemaName.TableName
(
    fieldName dataType Null or NOT Null,
    ......
    CONSTRAINT
);
```

You can add IDENTITY to a field to indicate that the value for the field will be automatically generated by the SQL Server. The IDENTITY is often used together with the primary key field. However, SQL Server only promises the uniqueness of the values, no guarantee of the sequence. This may cause problems for foreign keys. As a result, we sometimes turn it off as shown in the examples of the next section.

There are three types of constraints introduced in this chapter. One is the primary key constraint with the following syntax:

```
CONSTRAINT PK_TableName PRIMARY KEY (primary_key_field);
```

Where, PK_TableName is the name of the primary key and can be any legal name. But, it is conventional to use PK and underscore followed by the table name.

A foreign key constraint has the following syntax:

```
CONSTRAINT FK_TableName_ReferenceTableName FOREIGN KEY (foreign_key_field)
REFERENCES ReferenceTableName (primary_key_of_referenced_table);
```

Recall that a foreign key is a field in the current table which is also a primary key in a referenced table. A FOREIGN KEY CONSTRAINT must reference a table that is created before the current one. As a result, tables in the script cannot be created in any order you like.

The check constraint can ensure certain conditions in fields are met. For example, you can use CHECK to make sure a course start date is before the end date.

The rest of the section lists the complete code for creating the database for PLS.

```sql
-- Connect to SQL Server master database
USE master;

-- Drop database just in case you need to start all over
DROP DATABASE IF EXISTS PLS;

-- Create database
CREATE DATABASE PLS;
GO

-- Connect to PLS
USE PLS;
GO

-- Create schemas
CREATE SCHEMA Customer AUTHORIZATION dbo;
GO
CREATE SCHEMA School AUTHORIZATION dbo;
GO

-- Create tables
CREATE TABLE Customer.Families
(
    FamilyId       INT             NOT NULL    IDENTITY,
    LastNameCh     NVARCHAR(20)    NOT NULL,
    Phone          NVARCHAR(15)    NOT NULL,
    CellPhone      NVARCHAR(15)    NULL,
    Email          NVARCHAR(50)    NOT NULL,
    HomeAddress    NVARCHAR(50)    NULL,
    City           NVARCHAR(20)    NULL,
    [State]        NVARCHAR(20)    NULL,
    Zipcode        NVARCHAR(10)    NULL,
    CONSTRAINT PK_Families PRIMARY KEY (FamilyId)
);

CREATE TABLE Customer.Guardians
(
    GuardianId     INT             NOT NULL    IDENTITY,
    [Name]         NVARCHAR(20)    NOT NULL,
    [Address]      NVARCHAR(50)    NULL,
    Phone          NVARCHAR(15)    NOT NULL,
    Cell           NVARCHAR(15)    NULL,
```

```
    Email           NVARCHAR(50)    NOT NULL,
    FamilyId        INT             NOT NULL,
    CONSTRAINT PK_Guardians PRIMARY KEY (GuardianId),
    CONSTRAINT FK_Guardians_Families FOREIGN KEY (FamilyId) REFERENCES Customer.Families
(FamilyId)
);

CREATE TABLE Customer.Students
(
    StudentId       INT             NOT NULL    IDENTITY,
    FirstName       NVARCHAR(20)    NOT NULL,
    LastName        NVARCHAR(20)    NOT NULL,
    Gender          NVARCHAR(10)    NULL,
    Relation        NVARCHAR(10)    NOT NULL,
    Phone           NVARCHAR(15)    NULL,
    Email           NVARCHAR(50)    NULL,
    BirthDate       DATE            NOT NULL,
    Note            NVARCHAR(1000)  NULL,
    FamilyId        INT             NOT NULL,
    CONSTRAINT PK_Students PRIMARY KEY (StudentId),
    CONSTRAINT FK_Students_Families FOREIGN KEY (FamilyId) REFERENCES Customer.Families
(FamilyId)
);

CREATE TABLE School.Instructors
(
    InstructorId    INT             NOT NULL    IDENTITY,
    [Name]          NVARCHAR(20)    NOT NULL,
    [Address]       NVARCHAR(50)    NULL,
    Phone           NVARCHAR(15)    NOT NULL,
    Email           NVARCHAR(50)    NOT NULL,
    Contact         NVARCHAR(20)    NOT NULL,
    HireDate        DATE            NOT NULL,
    [Type]          NVARCHAR(10)    NULL,
    CONSTRAINT PK_Instructors PRIMARY KEY (InstructorId)
);

CREATE TABLE School.Courses
(
    CourseNum       INT             NOT NULL    IDENTITY,
    Title           NVARCHAR(30)    NOT NULL,
    MeetDay         NVARCHAR(30)    NULL,
    MeetTime        NVARCHAR(30)    NULL,
    StartDate       DATE            NULL,
    EndDate         DATE            NULL,
    SeatCap         INT             NULL,
    InstructorId    INT             NULL,
    CONSTRAINT PK_Courses PRIMARY KEY (CourseNum),
    CONSTRAINT FK_Courses_Instructors FOREIGN KEY (InstructorId) REFERENCES School.Instructors
(InstructorId),
    CONSTRAINT CHK_StartEndDate CHECK (StartDate < EndDate)
);

CREATE TABLE Customer.Enrollments
(
    EnrollId        INT             NOT NULL IDENTITY,
    Grade           NCHAR(1)        NULL,
    StudentId       INT             NOT NULL,
    CourseNum       INT             NOT NULL,
    CONSTRAINT PK_Enrollments PRIMARY KEY (EnrollId),
```

```
    CONSTRAINT FK_Enrollments_Students FOREIGN KEY (StudentId) REFERENCES Customer.Students
(StudentId),
    CONSTRAINT FK_Enrollments_Courses FOREIGN KEY (CourseNum) REFERENCES School.Courses
(CourseNum)
);
```

Review Question 8.19
The schema can allow better security in relational database with _____.
a. two-factor passwords
b. less passwords to memorize
c. different authorization settings for different schema
d. the up to date technologies

Review Question 8.20
We often use IDENTITY in SQL Server for primary keys. However, there is no guarantee that the value provided will be _____.
a. unique
b. in sequence
c. accurate
d. useful

Review Question 8.21
To run SQL code in Visual Studio, the first thing you need is to connect to a database. The statement for connecting is: _____.
a. CONNECT databaseName;
b. CONNECT TO databaseName;
c. CONNECT TO DATABASE databaseName;
d. USE databaseName;

Review Question 8.22
When scripting for a new database, you are unlikely to run all code successfully in just one attempt. When you try the second attempt to run the code, there will be some tables already created in the first attempt that will cause trouble. We suggest adding a _____ line before you create a database so that you can run the script as many times as you need.
a. new database
b. update database
c. insertion
d. deletion

Review Question 8.23
Some statements should be in their own batch. This is like how some products cannot ship with other products, they have to ship in their own container. Add the keyword _____ to cut the code from the remaining code into different batches.
a. BATCH
b. NEW BATCH
c. GO
d. CUT

Review Question 8.24

A schema should have an authorization setting, like how a container has a lock. The default user account is _____ (the default schema in SQL Server).
a. dbo
b. dba
c. dbms
d. schema

Review Question 8.25
When creating a table, you can add _____ to a field to indicate that the value for the field will be automatically generated by the SQL Server.
a. AUTO_INCREMENT
b. ID
c. AUTO_GENERATE
d. IDENTITY

Review Question 8.26
When creating a table, the _____ field is often used together with the primary key field.
a. FIRST
b. IDENTITY
c. DEFAULT
d. LAST

Review Question 8.27
When creating a table, which of the following is NOT a CONSTRAINT type?
a. PRIMARY KEY
b. FOREIGN KEY
c. RELATION
d. CHECK

Review Question 8.28
In T-SQL localhost, the first step for creating a database is _____.
a. issuing "CREATE DATABASE" statement
b. connecting to DATABASE
c. connecting to SQL Server master database
d. setting permission for the new database

Review Question 8.29
In T-SQL, a _____ is a container that includes one or more tables of a database.
a. SELECT statement
b. database
c. schema
d. table

Review Question 8.30
At the physical level of database design, a table has one or more fields. Most fields have three parts, _____, _____, and _____.
a. field name, field nickname, and data type
b. field name, data type, and nullable
c. field name, field nickname, and nullable
d. database name, table name, and field name

Review Question 8.31
In addition to fields, a table can have constraints. What are the three constraints we covered in this chapter?
a. Primary Key, check, and Foreign Key
b. Primary Key, check, and Non-primary Key
c. Foreign Key, check, and Non-foreign Key
d. Key, check, and non-key

Review Question 8.32
Suppose a table has the following constraint:

```
    CONSTRAINT FK_Students_Families FOREIGN KEY (FamilyId) REFERENCES Customer.Families
(FamilyId)
```

Which table(s) can you find a field called "FamilyId"?
a. Family table only
b. The table with the constraint only
c. both Family table and the table with the constraint
d. neither Family table nor the table with the constraint

8.8 Sample SQL Statements for Working with the Database

In this section you will write SQL statements to answer the following questions:

1. Insert one family with one guardian and two children.

2. Insert one instructor and two courses taught by that instructor.

3. Enroll students to classes.

4. Display all students who enrolled in a specific course.

5. Assign grades to students who enrolled in a course.

6. Display total number of students enrolled in a specific course.

The rest of the section contains all statements to accomplish the above tasks. Every time you run this code, you must re-execute the script in Section 8.7 to make sure you have a fresh database. It is a good idea to put the two scripts in one file so that you will always have a fresh database to work with.

```
-- Q1. Insert a family with one guardian and two children
SET IDENTITY_INSERT Customer.Families ON;
INSERT INTO Customer.Families (FamilyId, LastNameCh, Phone, CellPhone, Email, HomeAddress,
City, [State], ZipCode)
    VALUES (1, 'Chen', '2021112233', '2021112234', 'chen1234@gmail.com', '101 Chinaberry
St', 'Peking', 'OH', '50505');
SET IDENTITY_INSERT Customer.Families OFF;
```

```
INSERT INTO Customer.Guardians ([Name], Phone, Email, FamilyId)
    VALUES ('Li', '2021212134', 'li1234@gmail.com', 1);
SET IDENTITY_INSERT Customer.Students ON;
INSERT INTO Customer.Students (StudentId, FirstName, LastName, Relation, BirthDate,
FamilyId) VALUES
    (1, 'Alice', 'Chen', 'Daughter', '20101010', 1),
    (2, 'Tom', 'Chen', 'Son', '20120922', 1);
SET IDENTITY_INSERT Customer.Students OFF;

-- Q2. Insert one instructor and two courses taught by that instructor
SET IDENTITY_INSERT School.Instructors ON;
INSERT INTO School.Instructors(InstructorId, [Name], Phone, Email, Contact, HireDate)
    VALUES (1, 'Bruce Lee', '2021231234', 'brucelee123@gmail.com', 'Anna Lee',
'20170104');
SET IDENTITY_INSERT School.Instructors OFF;
SET IDENTITY_INSERT School.Courses ON;
INSERT INTO School.Courses(CourseNum, Title, MeetDay, MeetTime, StartDate, EndDate,
SeatCap, InstructorId) VALUES
    (1, 'KongFu Step 1', 'Saturdays', '5:00-5:30PM', '20170701', '20170801', 10, 1),
    (2, 'Chinese Classic Music 1', 'Sundays', '5:30-6:00PM', '20170701', '20170801', 15,
1);
SET IDENTITY_INSERT School.Courses OFF;
-- Q3. Enrol Alice to Bruce Lee's Kongfu Step 1 (coursenum is 1) and Chinese Classic Music
-- (courseNum is 2)
-- Enroll Tom to Bruce Lee's Chinese Classic Music 1 (coursenum is 2)
INSERT INTO Customer.Enrollments (StudentId, CourseNum) VALUES
    (1, 1),
    (1, 2),
    (2, 2);

-- Q4. Display all students from Chinese Classic Music 1 (courseNum is 2);
SELECT Students.StudentId, Students.FirstName + ' ' + Students.LastName AS "Student Name",
Courses.Title
    FROM Customer.Students JOIN Customer.Enrollments
    ON Students.StudentId = Enrollments.StudentId
    JOIN School.Courses
    ON Enrollments.CourseNum = Courses.CourseNum
    WHERE Courses.CourseNum = 2;

-- Q5. Assign grades to students in Chinese Classic Music
-- Alice (Student ID 1) A, Tom (Student ID 2) C
UPDATE Customer.Enrollments
    SET Grade = 'A'
    WHERE StudentId = 1 AND CourseNum = 2;
UPDATE Customer.Enrollments
    SET Grade = 'C'
    WHERE StudentId =2 AND CourseNum = 2;

-- Q6. Display number of students registered for Chinese Classic Music (CourseNum 2)
SELECT COUNT(*) AS "Number of students in Chinese Classic Music"
FROM Customer.Enrollments
WHERE CourseNum = 2;
```

8.9 Chapter Summary

In this chapter, you experienced the process of applying database development knowledge to a real-world database project. The chapter starts with a business description of the mini-world, which includes the requirements from the customer. Next, business rules are extracted from the description. With good business rules, it is easy to construct the conceptual and logical ERD. Next, mapping the ERD to relations, normalize and denormalize the relations. In physical ERD, add data type to the attributes of the relations. Finally, write SQL statements and run the statements to create the database with all necessary tables.

8.10 Discussion

Discussion 8.1

This book introduces the following major activities for developing relational databases: mini-world business descriptions, business rules, conceptual ERD, logical ERD, map ERD to relations, normalize/denormalize relations, physical design with data type, and generating SQL statements to create databases and tables. In your opinion, how important is the above sequence? Can any activity be executed before another not following that sequence?

Discussion 8.2

The majority of statements in Section 8.7 create tables. Can these tables be created in any order/sequence? Why or why not?

Discussion 8.3

Database development is both an art and science. There is more than one database that can meet the business requirements. For example, in the PLS database, you can denormalize the relations by combining Family and Guardian relations into one relation, which results in a different database. Can you think of another database from the one provided in this chapter for the PLS database?

8.11 Project Exercise One

The Tiger State University (TSU) has a tutoring office that would like to replace its current paper-based system with an online application. They would like you to develop the database for them.

The tutoring office has a list of tutors with tutor ID, first name, last name, highest education, course number and course title for which the tutor can help, and their available date and time. Usually a tutor would set up available dates and times 5 to 7 days ahead. The available time slot is automatically set to 30 minutes intervals. So, for example, a tutor's available date and time can be Tuesday, February 16, 2021, 9am, 9:30am, 5pm, 5:30pm, and 6pm.

Tutor Form

TutorID	First Name	Last Name	Education Level	Course No.	Available Time
1	Justin	Calson	Senior	CHEM101	M, 2/15/2021, 9:30am, 2pm, T, 2/16/2021, 10am, 4:30pm
2	Nate	Scott	master	COMP101, COMP102	T, 2/16/2021, 9am, 1:30am, 5pm, 5:30pm, 6pm
3	Jeremy	Hayes	bachelor	CHEM 101, COMP101	W, 2/17/2021, 9:30am, 10am

Any student at TSU can sign up for tutoring. A student would have to provide student ID, first name and last name, course number, and the title and instructor name and email for the course he or she needs help with. Then, the student picks an available time slot from the tutor form by checking the available date and time on the tutor form and filling out the date and time in the sign-up form.

Sign up form

Student ID	First Name	Last Name	Course No.	Course Title	Instructor Name	Instructor Email	Check-in
231654	Tanner	Dawson	CHEMP101	Intro to Chemistry	Grace Church	Church2 @tsu.edu	T, 2/16/2021, 4:30pm
231654	Tanner	Dawson	COMP101	Intro to CS	John Meyer	Meyer22 @tsu.edu	T, 2/16/2021, 5pm

Both walk-in and scheduled appointments use the same sign up form. In other words, walk in students should also fill out the tutor form and signup form.

For simplicity, the tutoring office's database won't share any data with the university's database.

Your task:

1. Write out all possible business rules.

2. Develop a conceptual ERD.

3. Develop a logical ERD.

4. Map the ERD to relations.

5. Implement any necessary normalization/denormalization.

6. Write SQL statements to create the database and the tables.

7. Write SQL statements to answer the following questions (always use make-up data if not provided).

    a. Add data provided in the tutor form.

    b. Update one tutor's available date and time to a different date and time.

    c. Add data about your database course. Make up a new tutor for the course.

    d. Display all available tutoring time slots for COMP101. Show the slot time and tutor names.

    e. Add data provided in the signup form.

    f. Insert your data for the signup form. You need a tutor for COMP101.

    g. Display how many time slots are filled for tutoring COMP101.

8.12 Project Exercise Two

The Tiger State University's (TSU) athletic department wants to keep track of their student athletes' academic performances. They need your help to develop a database to replace their current spreadsheet-based practice.

An athletic student has a student ID, first name, last name, sports played and the corresponding coach's name, office address and phone. The majority of students play only one sport, but occasionally, a student may play two sports or more. There are about 25 sports at TSU. A coach can coach one or more teams.

An athletic student is also required to take between 4 to 6 courses per semester to meet the scholarship requirements. A course has course number, title, credit (an integer between 1 and 5) current semester (fall, spring, and summer) and year, instructor name, instructor office address, phone, and email. The class schedule is also recorded.

The instructors are required to report two grades, one in the middle of the semester and one final grade. For those students who receive a grade of D or below, the department will inform the coach and create a plan for the student to catch up. A plan is just a short paragraph with a date created. When a plan's objectives are achieved, the plan is marked as accomplished.

Your task:

1. Write out all possible business rules.

2. Develop a conceptual ERD.

3. Develop a logical ERD.

4. Map the ERD to relations.

5. Implement any normalization/denormalization.

6. Write SQL statements to create the database and the tables.

7. Write SQL statements to answer the following questions (use made-up data when they are not given).

   a. Add three students who play three different sports. One of the students plays two sports.

   b. Add between 4 to 6 courses to each student. Some of these courses are taken by more than one student.

   c. Assign midterm grades to each course for each student. One student received two Ds and another student received one D. All other grades are C or better.

   d. Display students with grades below C. Show student ID, name, sport(s) played, coach name, the course(s) that have a grade lower than C, and the instructor information.

   e. Display total credit hours for each student for the current semester.

8.13 Project Exercise Three

The Vacation Inn is a small family-owned hotel located in the Great Lake Resort area. The owners would like to have a housekeeping tracking software that would allow them to track when a room is cleaned or under cleaning and by whom. They also want the application to calculate the total wages for each contracted janitor by the end of each week. A janitor is paid by the number of rooms he or she cleaned and the type of the room.

A janitor has a first name, last name, street address, city, state, zip code, and phone number. A janitor can clean any type of room in the Vacation Inn.

There are three types of rooms in Vacation Inn. They are suites, one King-size bed, and two Queen-size beds. The wages for each type of room are $7, $5, and $6 accordingly. However, these types and pay rates are changing. For example, just a few years ago, smoking rooms were deleted. Now, the whole hotel is smoke free.

The room numbers for the suites are 201, 202, 203, 204, and 205. The room numbers for the King-size bedrooms are 101, 103, 105, 107, 109, 111, 113, 115, and 117. The room numbers for the two Queen-size bedrooms are 102, 104, 106, 108, 110, 112, 114, 116, and 118. A guest room that needs cleaning should be indicated in the database so that the janitors know which rooms to clean.

Each janitor will have a tablet with all room numbers that need cleaning on the screen. When the janitor touches a room, the clock begins recording. When the job is done, the janitor touches a button on their screen to stop recording. Even though janitors are not paid by the hour. It is required by law to make sure they paid above the state minimum wage.

Your task:

1. Write out all possible business rules.

2. Develop a conceptual ERD

3. Develop a logical ERD.

4. Map the ERD to relations.

5. Implement any normalization/denormalization.

6. Write SQL statements to create the database and the tables.

7. Write SQL statements to answer the following questions (use made-up data when they are not given).

    a. Add all three types of rooms with all room numbers in the database

    b. Add three contracted janitors.

    c. Update the room list so that 2 suites, 7 double rooms, and 8 single rooms need cleaning.

    d. List all room numbers for rooms that need cleaning.

    e. Pick any three rooms from C, and assign three janitors to the rooms. Show that two janitors have finished.

    f. Display all rooms that are in the process of cleaning, including the clock in time and the janitor's name.

8.14 Solutions to Review Questions

8.1 B; 8.2 A; 8.3 D; 8.4 A; 8.5 C; 8.6 C; 8.7 A; 8.8 D; 8.9 D; 8.10 D; 8.11 C; 8.12 C; 8.13 A; 8.14 D; 8.15 B; 8.16 C; 8.17 B; 8.18 C; 8.19 C; 8.20 B; 8.21 D; 8.22 D; 8.23 C; 8.24 A; 8.25 D; 8.26 B; 8.27 C; 8.28 C; 8.29 C; 8.30 B; 8.31 A; 8.32 C;

APPENDIX A: SQL SCRIPT FOR GENERATING LIFESTYLE DATABASE

```sql
USE master;

IF DB_ID(N'LifeStyleDB') IS NOT NULL DROP DATABASE LifeStyleDB;

CREATE DATABASE LifeStyleDB;
GO

USE LifeStyleDB;
GO

CREATE SCHEMA HR AUTHORIZATION dbo;
GO
CREATE SCHEMA Sales AUTHORIZATION dbo;
GO
CREATE SCHEMA Purchasing AUTHORIZATION dbo;
GO

CREATE TABLE Sales.Customers
(
  CustomerId      INT       NOT NULL IDENTITY,
  CustomerName    NVARCHAR(50) NOT NULL,
  StreetAddress   NVARCHAR(50) NULL,
  City            NVARCHAR(20) NULL,
  [State]         NVARCHAR(20) NULL,
  PostalCode      NVARCHAR(10) NULL,
  Country         NVARCHAR(20) NULL,
  Contact         NVARCHAR(50) NULL,
  Email           NVARCHAR(50) NULL,
  CONSTRAINT PK_Customers PRIMARY KEY(CustomerId)
);

CREATE TABLE HR.Employees
(
  EmployeeId  INT       NOT NULL IDENTITY,
```

```sql
FirstName        NVARCHAR(50) NOT NULL,
LastName         NVARCHAR(50) NOT NULL,
BirthDate        DATE      NOT NULL,
HireDate         DATE      NOT NULL,
HomeAddress      NVARCHAR(50) NULL,
City             NVARCHAR(20) NULL,
[State]          NVARCHAR(20) NULL,
PostalCode       NVARCHAR(10) NULL,
Phone            NVARCHAR(20) NULL,
ManagerId        INT          NULL,
CONSTRAINT PK_Employees PRIMARY KEY(EmployeeId),
CONSTRAINT FK_Employees_Employees FOREIGN KEY(ManagerId)
  REFERENCES HR.Employees(EmployeeId),
CONSTRAINT CHK_BirthDate CHECK(BirthDate <= CAST(SYSDATETIME() AS DATE)),
CONSTRAINT CHK_HireDate CHECK(BirthDate < HireDate)
);

CREATE TABLE Purchasing.Suppliers
(
SupplierId       INT      NOT NULL IDENTITY,
SupplierName     NVARCHAR(50) NOT NULL,
StreetAddress    NVARCHAR(50) NULL,
City             NVARCHAR(20) NULL,
[State]          NVARCHAR(20) NULL,
PostalCode       NVARCHAR(10) NULL,
Country          NVARCHAR(20) NULL,
CONSTRAINT PK_Supplier PRIMARY KEY(SupplierId)
);

CREATE TABLE Purchasing.Products
(
ProductId        INT      NOT NULL IDENTITY,
ProductName      NVARCHAR(40) NOT NULL,
supplierid       INT      NOT NULL,
CONSTRAINT PK_Products PRIMARY KEY(ProductId),
CONSTRAINT FK_Products_Suppliers FOREIGN KEY(SupplierId)
  REFERENCES Purchasing.Suppliers(SupplierId)
);

CREATE TABLE Purchasing.Deliveries
(
    DeliveryId       INT          NOT NULL IDENTITY,
    ProductId        INT          NOT NULL,
    Quantity         INT          NOT NULL,
    Price            MONEY        NOT NULL
        CONSTRAINT DF_Deliveries_price DEFAULT(0),
    DeliveryDate DateTime2    NOT NULL
        CONSTRAINT DF_Deliveries_DeliveryDate DEFAULT(SYSDATETIME()),
    CONSTRAINT PK_Deliveries PRIMARY KEY (DeliveryId),
    CONSTRAINT FK_Deliveries_Products FOREIGN KEY(ProductId)
```

```
        REFERENCES Purchasing.Products(ProductId),
      CONSTRAINT CHK_Deliveries_Price CHECK (Price >= 0)
);

CREATE TABLE Sales.Orders
(
 OrderId        INT       NOT NULL IDENTITY,
 CustomerId     INT       NOT NULL,
 EmployeeId     INT       NOT NULL,
 OrderDate      DATE      NOT NULL,
 CONSTRAINT PK_Orders PRIMARY KEY(OrderId),
 CONSTRAINT FK_Orders_Customers FOREIGN KEY(CustomerId)
  REFERENCES Sales.Customers(CustomerId),
 CONSTRAINT FK_Orders_Employees FOREIGN KEY(EmployeeId)
  REFERENCES HR.Employees(EmployeeId)
);

CREATE TABLE Sales.OrderDetails
(
 OrderId        INT          NOT NULL,
 ProductId      INT          NOT NULL,
 Price          MONEY        NOT NULL
  CONSTRAINT DF_OrderDetails_price DEFAULT(0),
 quantity  SMALLINT          NOT NULL
  CONSTRAINT DF_OrderDetails_qty DEFAULT(1),
 CONSTRAINT PK_OrderDetails PRIMARY KEY(Orderid, Productid),
 CONSTRAINT FK_OrderDetails_Orders FOREIGN KEY(OrderId)
  REFERENCES Sales.Orders(OrderId),
 CONSTRAINT FK_OrderDetails_Products FOREIGN KEY(ProductId)
  REFERENCES Purchasing.Products(ProductId),
 CONSTRAINT CHK_quantity  CHECK (quantity > 0),
 CONSTRAINT CHK_price CHECK (price >= 0)
);

SET IDENTITY_INSERT Sales.Customers ON;
INSERT INTO Sales.Customers(CustomerId, CustomerName, StreetAddress, City, [State], PostalCode, Country,
Contact, Email)
     VALUES(1, 'Just Electronics', '123 Broad way', 'New York', 'NY', '12012', 'USA', 'John White',
'jwhite@je.com');
INSERT INTO Sales.Customers(CustomerId, CustomerName, StreetAddress, City, [State], PostalCode, Country,
Contact, Email)
     VALUES(2, 'Beyond Electronics', '45 Cherry Street', 'Chicago', 'IL', '32302', 'USA', 'Scott Green',
'green@beil.com');
INSERT INTO Sales.Customers(CustomerId, CustomerName, StreetAddress, City, [State], PostalCode, Country,
Contact, Email)
     VALUES(3, 'Beyond Electronics', '6767 GameOver Blvd', 'Atlanta', 'GA', '43347', 'USA', 'Alice Black',
'black1@be.com');
INSERT INTO Sales.Customers(CustomerId, CustomerName, StreetAddress, City, [State], PostalCode, Country,
Contact, Email)
     VALUES(4, 'E Fun', '888  Main Ave.', 'Seattle', 'WA', '69356', 'USA', 'Ben Gold', 'bgold@efun.com');
```

```
INSERT INTO Sales.Customers(CustomerId, CustomerName, StreetAddress, City, [State], PostalCode, Country,
Contact, Email)
     VALUES(5, 'Overstock E', '39 Garden Place', 'Los Angeles', 'CA', '32302', 'USA', 'Daniel Yellow', 'dy@os.com');
INSERT INTO Sales.Customers(CustomerId, CustomerName, StreetAddress, City, [State], PostalCode, Country,
Contact, Email)
     VALUES(6, 'E Fun', '915 Market st.', 'London', 'England', 'EC1A 1BB', 'UK', 'Frank Green', 'green@ef.com');
INSERT INTO Sales.Customers(CustomerId, CustomerName, StreetAddress, City, [State], PostalCode, Country,
Contact, Email)
     VALUES(7, 'Electronics4U', '27 Colmore Row', 'Birmingham', 'England', 'B3 2EW', 'UK', 'Grace Smith',
'smith@e4u.com');
INSERT INTO Sales.Customers(CustomerId, CustomerName, StreetAddress, City, [State], PostalCode, Country)
     VALUES(8, 'Cheap Electronics', '1010 Easy St', 'Ottawa', 'Ontario', 'K1A 0B1', 'Canada');
SET IDENTITY_INSERT Sales.Customers OFF;

SET IDENTITY_INSERT HR.Employees ON;
INSERT INTO HR.Employees(EmployeeId, FirstName, LastName, BirthDate, HireDate, HomeAddress, City, [State],
PostalCode, Phone, ManagerId)
     VALUES(1, 'Alex', 'Hall', '19900203', '20150809', '85 Main Ln', 'New Canton', 'VA', '23123', '(434) 290-3322',
NULL);
INSERT INTO HR.Employees(EmployeeId, FirstName, LastName, BirthDate, HireDate, HomeAddress, City, [State],
PostalCode, Phone, ManagerId)
     VALUES(2, 'Dianne', 'Hart', '19781203', '20100801', '209 Social Hall Blvd', 'New Canton', 'VA', '23123', '(434)
290-1122', 1);
INSERT INTO HR.Employees(EmployeeId, FirstName, LastName, BirthDate, HireDate, HomeAddress, City, [State],
PostalCode, Phone, ManagerId)
     VALUES(3, 'Maria', 'Law', '19880713', '20120821', '258 Blinkys St', 'New Canton', 'VA', '23123', '(434) 531-
5673', 1);
INSERT INTO HR.Employees(EmployeeId, FirstName, LastName, BirthDate, HireDate, HomeAddress, City, [State],
PostalCode, Phone, ManagerId)
     VALUES(4, 'Alice', 'Law', '19881213', '20120422', '300 Vista Valley Blvd', 'Buckingham', 'VA', '23123', '(434)
531-1010', 1);
INSERT INTO HR.Employees(EmployeeId, FirstName, LastName, BirthDate, HireDate, HomeAddress, City, [State],
PostalCode, Phone, ManagerId)
     VALUES(5, 'Black', 'Hart', '19821109', '20150412', '1 Old Fifteen St', 'Buckingham', 'VA', '23123', '(434) 531-
1034', 2);
INSERT INTO HR.Employees(EmployeeId, FirstName, LastName, BirthDate, HireDate, HomeAddress, City, [State],
PostalCode, ManagerId)
     VALUES(6, 'Christina', 'Robinson', '19780713', '20140615', '217 Chapel St', 'New Canton', 'VA', '23123', 2);
INSERT INTO HR.Employees(EmployeeId, FirstName, LastName, BirthDate, HireDate, HomeAddress, City, [State],
PostalCode, ManagerId)
     VALUES(7, 'Nicholas', 'Pinkston', '19771005', '20130522', '26 N James Madison Rd', 'Buckingham', 'VA',
'23123', 3);
SET IDENTITY_INSERT HR.Employees OFF;

SET IDENTITY_INSERT Purchasing.Suppliers ON;
INSERT INTO Purchasing.Suppliers(SupplierId, SupplierName, StreetAddress, City, [State], PostalCode, Country)
     VALUES(1, 'Pine Apple', '1 Pine Apple St.', 'Idanha', 'CA', '87201', 'USA');
INSERT INTO Purchasing.Suppliers(SupplierId, SupplierName, StreetAddress, City, [State], PostalCode, Country)
     VALUES(2, 'IMB', '123 International Blvd', 'Los Angeles', 'CA', '89202', 'USA');
INSERT INTO Purchasing.Suppliers(SupplierId, SupplierName, StreetAddress, City, [State], PostalCode, Country)
```

```
        VALUES(3, 'Lonovo', '33 Beijin Square', 'Beijing', 'Beijing', '100201', 'China');
INSERT INTO Purchasing.Suppliers(SupplierId, SupplierName, StreetAddress, City, [State], PostalCode, Country)
        VALUES(4, 'Samsong', '1 Electronics Road', 'Yeongtong', 'Suwon', '30174', 'South Korea');
INSERT INTO Purchasing.Suppliers(SupplierId, SupplierName, StreetAddress, City, [State], PostalCode, Country)
        VALUES(5, 'Canan', '12 Camera St', 'Ota', 'Tokyo', '100-0121', 'Japan');
SET IDENTITY_INSERT Purchasing.Suppliers OFF;


SET IDENTITY_INSERT Purchasing.Products ON;
INSERT INTO Purchasing.Products(ProductId, ProductName, supplierid)
        VALUES(1, '65-Inch 4K Ultra HD Smart TV', 4);
INSERT INTO Purchasing.Products(ProductId, ProductName, supplierid)
        VALUES(2, '60-Inch 4K Ultra HD Smart LED TV', 4);
INSERT INTO Purchasing.Products(ProductId, ProductName, supplierid)
        VALUES(3, '3200 Lumens LED Home Theater Projector', 3);
INSERT INTO Purchasing.Products(ProductId, ProductName, supplierid)
        VALUES(4, 'Wireless Color Photo Printer', 5);
INSERT INTO Purchasing.Products(ProductId, ProductName, supplierid)
        VALUES(5, '6Wireless Compact Laser Printer', 2);
INSERT INTO Purchasing.Products(ProductId, ProductName, supplierid)
        VALUES(6, 'Color Laser Printer', 2);
INSERT INTO Purchasing.Products(ProductId, ProductName, supplierid)
        VALUES(7, '10" 16GB Android Tablet', 4);
INSERT INTO Purchasing.Products(ProductId, ProductName, supplierid)
        VALUES(8, 'GPS Android Tablet PC', 2);
INSERT INTO Purchasing.Products(ProductId, ProductName, supplierid)
        VALUES(9, '20.2 MP Digital Camera', 5);
SET IDENTITY_INSERT Purchasing.Products OFF;

SET IDENTITY_INSERT Purchasing.Deliveries ON;
INSERT INTO Purchasing.Deliveries(DeliveryId, ProductId, Quantity, Price, DeliveryDate)
        VALUES(1, 1, 2, 1099.99, '20161001 9:30');
INSERT INTO Purchasing.Deliveries(DeliveryId, ProductId, Quantity, Price, DeliveryDate)
        VALUES(2, 1, 5, 1199.99, '20161101 10:20');
INSERT INTO Purchasing.Deliveries(DeliveryId, ProductId, Quantity, Price, DeliveryDate)
        VALUES(3, 2, 10, 1199.99, '20161002 11:10');
INSERT INTO Purchasing.Deliveries(DeliveryId, ProductId, Quantity, Price, DeliveryDate)
        VALUES(4, 3, 10, 129.99, '20161005 9:15');
INSERT INTO Purchasing.Deliveries(DeliveryId, ProductId, Quantity, Price, DeliveryDate)
        VALUES(5, 4, 20, 79.99, '20161007 14:00');
INSERT INTO Purchasing.Deliveries(DeliveryId, ProductId, Quantity, Price, DeliveryDate)
        VALUES(6, 5, 15, 139.99, '20161007 15:30');
INSERT INTO Purchasing.Deliveries(DeliveryId, ProductId, Quantity, Price, DeliveryDate)
        VALUES(7, 6, 25, 169.99, '20161010 10:30');
INSERT INTO Purchasing.Deliveries(DeliveryId, ProductId, Quantity, Price, DeliveryDate)
        VALUES(8, 7, 12, 79.99, '20161011 11:10');
INSERT INTO Purchasing.Deliveries(DeliveryId, ProductId, Quantity, Price, DeliveryDate)
        VALUES(9, 7, 18, 69.99, '20161012 9:50');
SET IDENTITY_INSERT Purchasing.Deliveries OFF;
```

```
SET IDENTITY_INSERT Sales.Orders ON;
INSERT INTO Sales.Orders(OrderId, CustomerId, EmployeeId, OrderDate)
    VALUES(1, 1, 5, '20170103');
INSERT INTO Sales.Orders(OrderId, CustomerId, EmployeeId, OrderDate)
    VALUES(2, 1, 3, '20170305');
INSERT INTO Sales.Orders(OrderId, CustomerId, EmployeeId, OrderDate)
    VALUES(3, 2, 5, '20170223');
INSERT INTO Sales.Orders(OrderId, CustomerId, EmployeeId, OrderDate)
    VALUES(4, 4, 5, '20170413');
INSERT INTO Sales.Orders(OrderId, CustomerId, EmployeeId, OrderDate)
    VALUES(5, 1, 4, '20170503');
INSERT INTO Sales.Orders(OrderId, CustomerId, EmployeeId, OrderDate)
    VALUES(6, 3, 6, '20170508');
INSERT INTO Sales.Orders(OrderId, CustomerId, EmployeeId, OrderDate)
    VALUES(7, 5, 7, '20161108');
INSERT INTO Sales.Orders(OrderId, CustomerId, EmployeeId, OrderDate)
    VALUES(8, 7, 2, '20161223');
SET IDENTITY_INSERT Sales.Orders OFF;


INSERT INTO Sales.OrderDetails(OrderId, ProductId, Price, quantity)
    VALUES(1, 1, 1499.99, 1);
INSERT INTO Sales.OrderDetails(OrderId, ProductId, Price, quantity)
    VALUES(1, 3, 149.99, 2);
INSERT INTO Sales.OrderDetails(OrderId, ProductId, Price, quantity)
    VALUES(2, 1, 1499.99, 1);
INSERT INTO Sales.OrderDetails(OrderId, ProductId, Price, quantity)
    VALUES(2, 4, 99.99, 6);
INSERT INTO Sales.OrderDetails(OrderId, ProductId, Price, quantity)
    VALUES(2, 6, 189.99, 5);
INSERT INTO Sales.OrderDetails(OrderId, ProductId, Price, quantity)
    VALUES(2, 2, 1599.99, 1);
INSERT INTO Sales.OrderDetails(OrderId, ProductId, Price, quantity)
    VALUES(3, 6, 199.99, 1);
INSERT INTO Sales.OrderDetails(OrderId, ProductId, Price, quantity)
    VALUES(3, 7, 109.99, 2);
INSERT INTO Sales.OrderDetails(OrderId, ProductId, Price, quantity)
    VALUES(3, 8, 69.99, 2);
INSERT INTO Sales.OrderDetails(OrderId, ProductId, Price, quantity)
    VALUES(3, 3, 159.99, 2);
INSERT INTO Sales.OrderDetails(OrderId, ProductId, Price, quantity)
    VALUES(3, 9, 1449.99, 1);
INSERT INTO Sales.OrderDetails(OrderId, ProductId, Price, quantity)
    VALUES(4, 8, 69.99, 1);
INSERT INTO Sales.OrderDetails(OrderId, ProductId, Price, quantity)
    VALUES(4, 4, 99.99, 2);
INSERT INTO Sales.OrderDetails(OrderId, ProductId, Price, quantity)
    VALUES(5, 6, 199.99, 3);
INSERT INTO Sales.OrderDetails(OrderId, ProductId, Price, quantity)
```

```
        VALUES(5, 3, 149.99, 6);
INSERT INTO Sales.OrderDetails(OrderId, ProductId, Price, quantity)
        VALUES(6, 1, 1499.99, 1);
INSERT INTO Sales.OrderDetails(OrderId, ProductId, Price, quantity)
        VALUES(7, 2, 999.99, 1);
INSERT INTO Sales.OrderDetails(OrderId, ProductId, Price, quantity)
        VALUES(8, 7, 79.99, 1);
INSERT INTO Sales.OrderDetails(OrderId, ProductId, Price, quantity)
        VALUES(8, 8, 59.99, 2);
```

APPENDIX B: LIFESTYLE DATABASE TABLES

Sales.Customers Table

CustomerId	CustomerName	StreetAddress	City	State	PostalCode	Country	Contact	Email
1	Just Electronics	123 Broad way	New York	NY	12012	USA	John White	jwhite@je.com
2	Beyond Electronics	45 Cherry Street	Chicago	IL	32302	USA	Scott Green	green@beil.com
3	Beyond Electronics	6767 GameOver Blvd	Atlanta	GA	43347	USA	Alice Black	black1@be.com
4	E Fun	888 Main Ave.	Seattle	WA	69356	USA	Ben Gold	bgold@efun.com
5	Overstock E	39 Garden Place	Los Angeles	CA	32302	USA	Daniel Yellow	dy@os.com
6	E Fun	915 Market st.	London	England	EC1A 1BB	UK	Frank Green	green@ef.com
7	Electronics4U	27 Colmore Row	Birmingham	England	B3 2EW	UK	Grace Smith	smith@e4u.com
8	Cheap Electronics	1010 Easy St	Ottawa	Ontario	K1A 0B1	Canada	NULL	NULL

HR.Employees Table

EmployeeId	FirstName	LastName	BirthDate	HireDate	HomeAddress	City	State	PostalCode	Phone	ManagerId
1	Alex	Hall	1990-02-03	2015-08-09	85 Main Ln	New Canton	VA	23123	(434) 290-3322	NULL
2	Dianne	Hart	1978-12-03	2010-08-01	209 Social Hall Blvd	New Canton	VA	23123	(434) 290-1122	1
3	Maria	Law	1988-07-13	2012-08-21	258 Blinkys St	New Canton	VA	23123	(434) 531-5673	1
4	Alice	Law	1988-12-13	2012-04-22	300 Vista Valley Blvd	Buckingham	VA	23123	(434) 531-1010	1
5	Black	Hart	1982-11-09	2015-04-12	1 Old Fifteen St	Buckingham	VA	23123	(434) 531-1034	2
6	Christina	Robinson	1978-07-13	2014-06-15	217 Chapel St	New Canton	VA	23123	NULL	2
7	Nicholas	Pinkston	1977-10-05	2013-05-22	26 N James Madis...	Buckingham	VA	23123	NULL	3

Purchasing.Suppliers Table

SupplierId	SupplierName	StreetAddress	City	State	PostalCode	Country
1	Pine Apple	1 Pine Apple St.	Idanha	CA	87201	USA
2	IMB	123 International Blvd	Los Angeles	CA	89202	USA
3	Lonovo	33 Beijin Square	Beijing	Beijing	100201	China
4	Samsong	1 Electronics Road	Yeongtong	Suwon	30174	South Korea
5	Canan	12 Camera St	Ota	Tokyo	100-0121	Japan

Purchasing.Products Table

ProductId	ProductName	supplierid
1	65-Inch 4K Ultra HD Smart TV	4
2	60-Inch 4K Ultra HD Smart LED TV	4
3	3200 Lumens LED Home Theater Projector	3
4	Wireless Color Photo Printer	5
5	6Wireless Compact Laser Printer	2
6	Color Laser Printer	2
7	10" 16GB Android Tablet	4
8	GPS Android Tablet PC	2
9	20.2 MP Digital Camera	5

Purchasing.Deliveries Table

DeliveryId	ProductId	Quantity	Price	DeliveryDate
1	1	2	1099.99	2016-10-01 09:30:00.0000000
2	1	5	1199.99	2016-11-01 10:20:00.0000000
3	2	10	1199.99	2016-10-02 11:10:00.0000000
4	3	10	129.99	2016-10-05 09:15:00.0000000
5	4	20	79.99	2016-10-07 14:00:00.0000000
6	5	15	139.99	2016-10-07 15:30:00.0000000
7	6	25	169.99	2016-10-10 10:30:00.0000000
8	7	12	79.99	2016-10-11 11:10:00.0000000
9	7	18	69.99	2016-10-12 09:50:00.0000000

Sales.Orders Table

OrderId	CustomerId	EmployeeId	OrderDate
1	1	5	2017-01-03
2	1	3	2017-03-05
3	2	5	2017-02-23
4	4	5	2017-04-13
5	1	4	2017-05-03
6	3	6	2017-05-08
7	5	7	2016-11-08
8	7	2	2016-12-23

Sales.OrderDetails Table

	OrderId	ProductId	Price	quantity
1	1	1	1499.99	1
2	1	3	149.99	2
3	2	1	1499.99	1
4	2	2	1599.99	1
5	2	4	99.99	6
6	2	6	189.99	5
7	3	3	159.99	2
8	3	6	199.99	1
9	3	7	109.99	2
10	3	8	69.99	2
11	3	9	1449.99	1
12	4	4	99.99	2
13	4	8	69.99	1
14	5	3	149.99	6
15	5	6	199.99	3
16	6	1	1499.99	1
17	7	2	999.99	1
18	8	7	79.99	1
19	8	8	59.99	2

ABOUT THE AUTHOR

Lucy Scott was born in Mason City Iowa. She currently resides in Boston Massachusetts and lives with her husband Leonard and their two Labrador retrievers, Lola and Buddy.

Printed in the USA
CPSIA information can be obtained
at www.ICGtesting.com
LVHW081158181023
761376LV00013B/231